Developments in
French Politics

Developments in French Politics

Edited by
Peter A. Hall
Jack Hayward
Howard Machin

St. Martin's Press
New York

All rights reserved. For information, write:
Scholarly and Reference Division,
St. Martin's Press, Inc., 175 Fifth Avenue,
New York, N.Y. 10010

First published in the United States of America in 1990

Printed in Hong Kong

ISBN 0–312–04751–7 cloth

ISBN 0–312–04752–5 paper

Library of Congress Cataloging-in-Publication Data

Developments in French politics/edited by Peter A. Hall, Jack
  Hayward, Howard Machin.
      p.   cm.
    Includes bibliographical references.
    ISBN 0–312–04751–7. — ISBN 0–312–04752–5 (pbk.)
    1. France—Politics and government—1981– I. Hall, Peter A.,
  1950–   . II. Hayward, Jack Ernest Shalom.   III. Machin, Howard.
  JN2594.2.D48 1990
  944.087′8—dc20   90–8199
                                                                  CIP

Contents

List of Maps and Tables

Maps

Tables

Preface

This book originated from a lunch-time discussion at the London School of Economics (LSE) between Gordon Smith, Patrick Dunleavy and Howard Machin; our first thanks go to Gordon and Patrick but also to Steven Kennedy, our publisher, all of whom gave valuable advice and encouragement throughout the project. We are also grateful to Jacques Lagroye, Vincent Wright and our two unknown readers for many helpful suggestions, most of which we followed. The editors and contributors owe a great deal to the German Marshall Fund (via Harvard's Centre for European Studies) and the Suntory-Toyota International Centre for Economics and Related Disciplines (LSE) for supporting a two-day colloquium to discuss every part of the book at a very early stage. At that meeting we appreciated comments from Alain Jeunemaître and John Keeler, then both Visitors at LSE. Peter Hall's work on France was generously supported by the Lurcy Charitable and Educational Trust, and Jonah Levy provided excellent research assistance on pressure groups. Howard Machin wishes to thank the Direction des relations culturelles, scientifiques et techniques of the French Ministry of Foreign Affairs, and the Cultural Service of the French Embassy in London for their generous support for his fieldwork. Our special thanks to two other European Research staff at LSE: June Burnham for translations of the chapters by François Platone and Françoise Dreyfus, and Marian Clark for secretarial, administrative and moral support.

Howard Machin
Jack Hayward
Peter Hall

Notes on the Contributors

Stephen E. Bornstein is Professor of Political Science at McGill University, Canada, and co-author of *The State in Capitalist Europe*.

Françoise Dreyfus teaches Public Law at the Université de Paris 1 (Panthéon-Sorbonne) and is co-author of *Les Institutions Politiques et Administratives de la France*.

Gary P. Freeman is Professor of Government at the University of Texas, Austin, and author of *Immigrant Labor and Racial Conflict in Industrial Societies*.

Alain Guyomarch is Lecturer in French Politics at the Roehampton Institute and a CNRS–ESRC Research Scholar at LSE.

Peter A. Hall is Professor of Government at Harvard University in the Centre for European Studies and author of *Governing the Economy*.

Martin Harrison is Professor of Politics at Keele University and co-author (with Philip Williams) of *De Gaulle's Republic* (1960) and *Politics and Society in de Gaulle's Republic* (1971).

Jack Hayward is Professor of Politics at Hull University and author of *Governing France: The One and Indivisible Republic*.

Jolyon Howorth is Professor of French Civilisation at the University of Bath and co-editor (with George Ross) of *Contemporary France: A Review*.

Howard Machin is Lecturer in French Politics at the LSE and author of *The Prefect in French Public Administration*.

Sonia Mazey is Lecturer in Government at Brunel University and co-editor (with Michael Newman) of *Mitterrand's France*.

François Platone, Research Fellow of the Fondation Nationale des Sciences Politiques at CEVIPOF in the Institut d'Etudes Politiques de Paris, has contributed to several collections on elections and voting behaviour.

Martin Schain is Professor of Politics at New York University and author of *French Communism and Local Power* (1985).

Vincent Wright, a former Reader in French Politics at LSE, is a Fellow of Nuffield College, Oxford. His works on French politics and history include *The Government and Politics of France*, and he co-edits (with Gordon Smith) *West European Politics*.

Abbreviations

CDS	Centre des Démocrates Sociaux
CERES	Centre d'Etudes et de Recherches Socialistes
CFDT	Confédération Française Démocratique du Travail
CGT	Confédération Générale du Travail
CNCL	National Commission for Communication and Liberty
CNPF	Conseil National du Patronat Français
CSMF	Confédération des Syndicats Médicaux Français (French Confederation of Medical Unions)
DDASS	Direction Départmentale des Affaires Sanitaires et Sociales
DDE	Direction Départementale d'Equipement
DGD	Dotation Générale de Décentralisation
DGE	Dotation Générale d'Equipement
EC	European Community
EMS	European Monetary System
ENA	Ecole Nationale d'Administration
FEN	Fédération de l'Education Nationale
FNSEA	Fédération Nationale des Syndicats d'Exploitants Agricoles
FN	Front National
FO	Force Ouvrière
ONI	Office National d'Immigration
PCF	Parti Communiste Français
PR	Parti Républicain
PS	Parti Socialiste
PUF	Presses Universitaires de France
RPF	Rassemblement du Peuple Français
RPR	Rassemblement pour la République
SNPMI	Syndicat National de la Petite et Moyenne Industrie
SOFRES	Société Française d'Enquêtes par Sondages
UDF	Union pour la Démocratie Française

MAP 1 *France: regions,* départements *and main towns*

Introduction

HOWARD MACHIN

It is not necessary to be French, or to have a vast knowledge of the history, institutions and social structure of France to read and enjoy this book. Indeed, the contributors come from Britain, Canada and the USA as well as from France, and all were chosen not only for their expertise on the topics they cover but also for their experience in explaining the intricacies of French politics to those deprived, by accident of birth, of the privilege of growing up in France. The authors also represent a variety of ideological and academic views and the themes of the book reflect this diversity of approaches.

Developments in French Politics is designed primarily for students of politics, French and European studies, to be read alongside or instead of most traditional texts. The editors hope it will appeal also to other students, schoolteachers, civil servants, politicians, business people and anyone else who wants up-to-date information and analysis in a readable form.

One recurrent theme of the book is the Europeanisation of French politics during the 1980s. This implies that most politicians and ordinary citizens now acknowledge what de Gaulle vehemently denied for so long: that France is an integral part of a supranational EC. Its economy is interdependent with those of the other eleven members, its monetary policy is tied in the EMS with the West German Bundesbank, and its economic policies in most areas (agriculture, industry, taxation, transport, public procurement and international economic relations) are now made jointly through the European mechanisms based in Brussels. Since 1986 French passports, the symbols of individual and national identity, bear the words 'European Community' *above* 'French Republic'. Furthermore, France has signed the Schengen Agreement, so in 1991 all frontier controls on the Belgian, German and Luxembourg borders will disappear. In 1988, when President Mitterrand made his New Year's Eve broadcast to the nation, he could still shock some old nationalists by his European style: he spoke from Strasbourg, seat of the European Parliament, not Paris: the twelve-starred European flag stood alongside the *tricolore* (the French flag) in the background; and he admitted 'France is our homeland, but Europe is our future'. To many, however, he was simply stating the obvious: French politics and policy-making are intrinsically and increasingly part of a greater European whole.

Europeanisation, however, also has a second meaning. Domestic politics are increasingly normal, in the sense of resembling those of France's similar-sized European neighbours, West Germany, Britain and Italy. For many years, and sometimes by deliberately nationalist policies, this was not the case. Then France was often cited as a special case. Political institutions were unstable and illegitimate, with governments usually too weak, as in the Third and Fourth Republics (1870–1940 and 1946–58). Hence there were repeated revolutions and changes of regime from 1789 until the Fourth Republic fell in 1958. Political parties were viewed as exceptionally ideological, divided and unstructured. The administration was described as unusually vast, legalistic, powerful and centralised. The economy was seen as underdeveloped before 1940, but 'miraculous' during the 'Thirty Golden Years' of 5 per cent per annum growth from 1945 to 1975. Social group structure was characterised as particularly atomistic ('a nation of non-joiners'), and traditions of individualism, Catholicism, communism and state-dependency were identified as particular problems. In the 1970s there was still a vast literature which argued that France was a special case, irrelevant for comparisons with any other state. If some of these writings reflected misperceptions by their writers about the rest of the world, they were not all completely wrong. In the 1980s, however, it is appropriate to focus on French politics as an interesting variant of a European pattern. If this collection contains no specific chapter on these two types of 'Europeanisation' it is because most chapters discuss them in some way.

Since 1981, politics have been dominated by François Mitterrand; indeed the 1980s may be described as the Mitterrand decade. If there still exists a tendency for his sympathisers to write and talk as if civilisation as we know it began in 1981 (in 1982 Socialists often referred to pre-1981 politics as the *'ancien régime'* or even the 'dark ages'), the developments described in this book do not constitute a real break with the reforms and changes of the previous two decades. Post-colonial, semi-presidential, reformist, European and market-orientated policies and politics have been evolving since the end of that great national trauma, the Algerian War.

Many of the changes of the 1980s appear to represent a trend towards less conflictual politics after the dramatic reinforcement of the Executive and presidentialisation by de Gaulle. One notable change is that there is a growing consensus amongst the major political forces about the basic parameters of politics. The minor parties – PCF, FN and Green – still present radical alternatives, but the big parties who have governed the country in the 1980s (the Socialists, RPR and UDF) advocate only modest reforms, even if they all continue to attack each other as extremists. Related to this is a second change, the retreat of the state; if part of state power is now pooled in Brussels, some too has been handed out to local governments. The old image of excessive centralisation was always somewhat exaggerated but the waves of decentralisation laws of the 1980s treat it as irrelevant, although the unitary nature of the state is untouched. Furthermore, the state is retreating not just in relation to other public authorities but also in relation to private bodies, to firms and to social groups. After carrying out a nationalisation programme in 1982, the Socialist Governments then began to deregulate the economy, and the RPR–UDF Government of 1986–8 continued deregulating and began to privatise large parts of the public sector as well. Since 1988 the Socialist Government has stopped privatisation but not deregulation, and it insists that public sector firms are run according to market logic. The *dirigiste* state may not yet have completely disappeared, but governments no longer claim to have all the answers to economic problems. So, too, the old idea that the neutral state (serving a national interest) must restrain social groups which pursue only selfish, sectoral interests, no longer holds sway. Instead pluralism is alive and respected: indeed, the Rocard Government prided itself on establishing close links with leaders of 'civil society'.

The role of women in a traditionally male-dominated political elite has also grown, although perhaps not as much as many expected. The Socialist Governments of 1981–6 included the first Minister for Women's Rights, the first female Minister of Agriculture, and the first woman to hold the top ministerial rank of *Ministre d'Etat* (Questiaux in 1981). The plan to introduce minimum quotas for female candidates on party lists for municipal elections, however, fell foul of the Constitutional Council.

Within the political system the president remains the key figure, but does not decide everything, and the government can still operate effectively if the president is marginalised by a hostile parliamentary coalition, as during *cohabitation* from 1986 to 1988. To appreciate all these most recent developments in their historic context we must briefly consider politics before 1958, the main changes made by de Gaulle and the present constitutional framework.

Between 1870, when the Emperor Napoleon III fell, and 1958, when de Gaulle took power, French institutions, parties and political leaders were almost always stigmatised by one adjective: weak. The weakness of leaders in domestic politics both caused and reflected their weakness in international and European affairs. Institutional arrangements and party organisation ensured that strong leadership was impossible in normal circumstances. After the defeat in 1877 of an attempt to provide effective presidential leadership the presidency had been largely limited to ceremonial duties. But prime ministers and governments were also weak. One reason for this weakness was their lack of constitutional powers. Another was governmental instability (there were 108 governments during the 70 years of the Third Republic and 25 in the twelve of the Fourth Republic) which, in turn, reflected the fragility of coalitions in a multi-party system and the lack of authority of party leaders over their deputies and senators. Many voters despised the inability of their politicians to provide stable and effective government.

There was, however, one important exception to the rule of the survival of the weakest. In moments of national danger and real threat – from the German invasion in 1914 or from the Vietcong in Indochina in 1954 – politicians might make a temporary truce and turn to a 'strong leader', a Clemenceau or a Mendès France. Normal politics would then be suspended, and the 'saviour figure' allowed massive personal power. Once the danger had passed, however, the leader would be thanked, discarded, and thereafter treated with considerable distrust.

As the leader of the Free French during the Second World War and President of the Provisional Government of France after 1944, de Gaulle had already once played the 'saviour figure' role, but in 1946 he had made the mistake of leaving power. His attempt to return in triumph as the leader of his own political force, the RPF, had failed. In 1958 a new crisis existed: no one in Paris seemed capable of even forming a government, whilst the army and settlers were out of control in Algeria, fighting the nationalist uprising. If de Gaulle agreed to return to power to solve the Algerian crisis, he had no intention subsequently of leaving the political system in the mess in which he found it. He became Prime Minister but his condition was that a new constitution, the Fifth Republic, would be adopted, and he would become President.

The 1958 constitution did not, however, give de Gaulle all he wanted. His compromise with the old politicians produced an inconsistent text which reinforced the role of the president and greatly strengthened the prime minister and government in relation to Parliament but still respected the idea of parliamentary government. De Gaulle became the first president, but could not even claim to represent the whole nation since his election was by an electoral college of some 80 000 *notables* (local leaders). He had only a vague constitutional responsibility to 'arbitrate' for the smooth functioning of the political system, a right to adopt full powers in a situation of national emergency (under article 16), and the precise powers to choose the prime minister and to dissolve the Assembly. Despite these drawbacks, de Gaulle was able to run the system in a semi-presidential way from the start. In 1958 he knew that, because of Algeria, the Assembly would not reject him or his chosen ministers, whatever its theoretical power of censure and the minority status of his own supporters in the 'Gaullist' party. With Prime Minister Debré always willing to defer to him, de Gaulle took over the effective leadership of government not only in Algerian affairs, but also in foreign policy, defence and any other area of interest to him.

In 1962, Algeria became independent, so de Gaulle was no longer needed. He did not depart to write more volumes of memoirs, as his many opponents had hoped, but instead set out to complete the constitutional reform begun in 1958. He proposed a referendum on a constitutional amendment to endow the presidency with the legitimacy of election by universal suffrage. In response, the old parties used their Assembly majority to censure the Government but the President did not retreat. He dissolved Parliament and asked the electorate not only to vote 'yes' at the referendum but also to give him a 'presidential majority' in the Assembly. De Gaulle won game, set and match: his amendment was approved and his coalition got an overall majority. Paradoxically for a man who purported to despise parties, he thus began a long process of presidentialisation, 'nationalisation' and of improvements in discipline and organisation in all parties and coalitions. The first step, in 1962, the creation of a disciplined presidential coalition, involved the rise of de Gaulle's 'own' party to a 'dominant' position, with four-fifths of the deputies in his parliamentary majority as well as the posts of prime minister and president. The new type of competition forced the other parties to adapt, but it took them a long time.

In 1962, for the first time since Napoleon III, the new prime minister and government could expect to remain in office for the full five years of the legislature, unless, of course, the president decided they should be changed. The presidential leadership of government which had begun in 1958 was thus given a degree of institutional and party system legitimation. The 1962 amendment, however, did not fully presidentialise the constitution; it only concerned the method of appointment, not the definition of the president's powers. The formal institutional framework set down in the October 1958 text remained untouched and, apart from some minor changes in 1974, has passed unscathed through the 1980s. It is the very ambiguity of the 1958 constitution which has allowed it to survive and adapt so well to changing circumstances.

The president's claim to power is based on his democratic legitimacy: he is elected by universal suffrage every seven years, through a two-ballot system in which only the two candidates who lead at the first ballot can stand at the second, so the winner always has over 50 per cent of the votes. Apart from this the constitution provides the president only with a duty, under article 5, to 'arbitrate' for the smooth functioning of the political system, a foreign policy responsibility under article 52 ('he negotiates and ratifies treaties'), and the power to appoint the prime minister and the ministers (but only those proposed by the prime minister, under article 8), to dissolve the National Assembly (but only once in twelve months, under article 12), to authorise the government to hold a referendum (article 11) and to take full governmental powers in an emergency (article 16). In other respects the president's constitutionally defined role is that of a traditional head of state: he is commander-in-chief of armed forces; he chairs meetings of the council of ministers; he has the right of pardon; he appoints senior civil and military officers of the state; and he signs laws and decrees. He has no powers of veto over laws and all decisions in his 'traditional' role require prime ministerial or ministerial countersignature. The president has no constitutional power to dismiss the prime minister, and he can only sack ministers if the prime minister suggests it.

The constitution makes it clear that the government, led by the prime minister and responsible to Parliament, has the role and power 'to decide and implement the policy of the nation' (article 20). Prime ministerial leadership is specifically defined: he proposes who shall be appointed ministers, he 'directs' the work of the government, he is 'responsible' for national defence, determines the areas of competence of his ministers (all under article 21) and he can choose to make a bill a 'question of confidence', thereby putting the life of his government at risk (article 49). The prime minister may choose to resign, but only the National Assembly can oblige him to do so (by voting a motion of censure).

To rule France the government is required to obtain parliamentary approval for many of its policy decisions. Explicit approval is necessary for new laws and for the annual budget, but the 1958 text was innovative in France because it limited the domain of parliamentary law-making. Article 34 provides a list of subjects on which Parliament can legislate, and on all other matters the government acts by decree. This is typical of the constitutional provisions concerning Parliament, which seem designed to limit its powers. There are two houses, the Senate and the National Assembly, but they do not have equal powers. In most circumstances, if the government agrees, the Assembly can outvote the Senate. The upper house is thus lower in power, prestige and legitimacy than the Assembly, a reflection of the fact that the 319 senators are elected only indirectly, by an electoral college (for nine-year terms with one-third coming up for re-election every three years). The Senate cannot censure a government, but neither can it be dissolved by presidential decree. These privileges are reserved for the Assembly, whose 577 deputies are directly elected by universal suffrage every five years. The electoral system for the deputies is not fixed by the constitution but by law; for most of the Fifth Republic a single-member, two-ballot system has been used (see Chapter 3), but for the 1986 election a form of proportional representation was adopted.

The constitution did, however, set many other limits on the activities of Parliament. The length of parliamentary sessions is fixed (to 80 days in autumn and 90 days in spring by article 28), the number of permanent committees is limited to six for each house and control of the time-table in the Assembly is effectively placed in the hands of the government. Even the procedure for censuring the government is made difficult since an absolute majority of the full membership of the Assembly must vote the motion for the government to fall (the halt, the lame and the dead vote for the government!). It is even possible, if the president agrees, for the government to by-pass Parliament by submitting a bill to a referendum (under article 11); this costly procedure has only been used seven times since 1958, most recently in November 1988 (see Chapter 11). Finally, the deputies and senators are not free to change the rules of procedure without the approval of the Constitutional Council.

A major innovation in 1958 was the creation of a Constitutional Council with responsibility for supervising the fairness of national elections, judging the constitutionality of laws and resolving conflicts over the meaning of the constitution, notably over article 34. The Council may only consider the constitutionality of laws referred to it before their official promulgation. Only the president, the prime minister, the speakers of the Assembly and of the Senate and, since 1974, any group of sixty deputies or senators are empowered to make such referrals. One-third of the nine members of the Council is replaced every three years, when the president and the speakers of both houses each choose one new member for nine years. If a law is ruled unconstitutional by the Council there is no appeal; the only possibility for reversing such a judgement would be by amending the constitution. This is theoretically a difficult procedure (laid down in article 89) as it requires either a three-fifths' majority of the members of both Houses of Parliament meeting jointly, or a majority in both houses and a majority in a referendum.

It was precisely this article which de Gaulle circumvented in 1962 by using article 11. He authorised the government's proposal for the referendum on the grounds that it concerned 'the organisation of public powers' (as stipulated in article 11). Whatever the constitutionality of this decision (the Constitutional Council is not empowered to judge the decisions of the president), the majority in favour of the referendum proposal and the success of the presidential coalition in the elections to the Assembly made it politically operational.

In and after 1962, however, the system remained only 'semipresidential', since it depended on the existence of coincident majorities at presidential and parliamentary elections. Throughout the 1960s and 1970s the electors maintained this coincidence, although Pompidou replaced de Gaulle as president and Giscard d'Estaing just scraped in after Pompidou's death in 1974. Giscard d'Estaing experienced a rather different situation from either of his predecessors since his 'own' party, the UDF, did not dominate his coalition, and its ally in the presidential coalition, Chirac's RPR, proved a very prickly partner. It was not until 1981, however, that a freshly elected president faced a hostile majority in the Assembly, and only in 1986 did a newly elected majority encounter a hostile incumbent president. Finally, in 1988 a newly elected president faced an Assembly in which his followers had only a 'relative majority'; this advent of minority government suggested another kind of potential fragility in French politics.

The first two parts of this book, about 'the political system' and 'the governmental system', examine the basic features of politics and government in France. Part Three consists of three case studies of public policy-making, and Part Four examines four controversial issues of current importance. No book can answer all the questions a lively-minded student could ask about French politics; here we focus only on the main changes in the last decade, and what we can learn from analysing these changes about the underlying distribution of power within the political system.

The changing terms of ideological debate are examined in Chapter 1, where Jack Hayward shows how the inheritance of the 1789 Revolution, the Left–Right split, is no longer a deep ideological divide. Marxism–Leninism has lost its intellectual hegemony on the Left, replaced by reformist, and increasingly managerial socialism. On the Centre–Right, the distinctive statist nationalism of de Gaulle and his followers has mellowed. There is no longer avowed hostility to European integration, but the flirtation with market liberalism in the 1980s has not proved as electorally rewarding as hoped. The extreme Right, however, has gained a much bigger audience for its xenophobic ideas. In short, there is much more ideological consensus between the main political forces, and piecemeal reformism is now bitterly attacked only by the FN and the remnant of the PCF. In Chapter 2, on changes in the parties and party system, Howard Machin shows how the two coalitions of Left and Centre-Right, each composed of two parties, have broken down. The internal dynamics of individual parties contributed to this fragmentation, but so too did the changes to electoral rules and the institutional distribution of power. If these changes facilitated the emergence of the FN (and later the Greens) there were also important social developments which the parties attempted to exploit. The rise of FN on the Right and the dominant position (albeit in a minority since 1986) of the Socialist Party reflect the success of both in linking with new social movements.

In Chapter 3, on changing public attitudes and electoral behaviour, François Platone argues that despite the decline of the PCF, the rise of the FN and the development of the Greens, the division of the electorate into two blocs, Left and Right, is still strong. Unemployment has remained the most important concern of voters but, since 1986, there is little faith in the ability of any party to solve it, so it no longer plays a key role in determining election results. Changes in the social base of politics are also examined by Peter Hall in Chapter 4, on pluralism and pressure group activity. If some groups (notably trade unions) have declined, associational life in general is alive and thriving and pluralism is developing, albeit with a statist bias. Although many groups and some ministries and state agencies develop close – almost incestuous – relations, with an element of clientelism, the existence of numerous divisions within the state allows interest groups to play off one part of the state against another. Faced by so many conflicting demands, the state often looks more like a battlefield than an army.

This theme of the balancing of opposing forces in relatively peaceful negotiations, rather than the clear victory of one camp or alliance, is reiterated in chapters 5–8 which examine the governmental system. First of all, Howard Machin considers the evolution of political leadership from the president-dominated days of 1980 (Giscard d'Estaing) and 1981 (Mitterrand with a Socialist majority in Parliament) to *cohabitation* when the Centre-Right Government led by Chirac took command, and President Mitterrand took a back seat. After 1988, the minority Rocard Government survived thanks to the division of its opponents and the support of the president for its moderate consensual style. If the break-up of old coalitions and rise of new parties, along with decentralisation and Europeanisation, led to a fragmentation of elites, leadership still remained highly personalised. Vincent Wright, in Chapter 6, argues that the administrative machine once had a central logic, the Napoleonic model, but over the years, as the scope of state interventionism grew, there were ever-increasing internal conflicts. Recent reforms have not reinstated the original model, but rather added new complications. These internal 'checks and balances' are perhaps inadequate, but at least they complement the official mechanisms for controlling the government and administration.

Françoise Dreyfus, in Chapter 7, argues that the many devices for controlling the rulers have remained rather inadequate, despite the growth of autonomous regulatory agencies and the interventions of such bodies as the European Court in recent years. Discussing decentralisation in Chapter 8, Sonia Mazey shows that the balance between centre and periphery has not been modified as much as some Socialists have claimed: in part because centralisation was traditionally overrated, in part because the reforms of the 1960s and 1970s had already made an impact, and in part because the full effect of the Socialist reforms has not yet been felt. With four levels of government, France has now a highly complex and fragmented system and more reforms seem likely.

In the third section, public policies and policy-making in three key areas are examined. Peter Hall (in Chapter 9) shows how in economic policy-making, France (like its neighbours) has experienced a 'retreat of the state'; if the influence of both the market and the European Commission have grown, the massive apparatus of *dirigisme* has not been entirely dismantled. In Chapter 10, Gary P. Freeman considers the difficulty for welfare policy-makers in modifying the long-term programme of expanding welfare provision to meet the new challenges of unemployment and unfavourable demographic trends. The decentralised, semi-autonomous structures of welfare institutions and high public expectations further complicated this adaptation. In his analysis of foreign and defence policies, Jolyon Howorth (Chapter 11) argues that below the continuity of discourse about national independence there has been a noticeable trend towards practices of interdependence, not only in the European domain but also in defence.

Our current controversies section starts with Alain Guyomarch's analysis (Chapter 12) of the evolution of debates about law and order, civil liberties and justice. This demonstrates how political parties have sought to discredit their rivals and promote their own electoral advantage by advocating distinctive policies, whilst creating and feeding media and public anxieties. Even here, however, the adversarial style of politics did not preclude a wide measure of consensus and continuity. The contrast between political competition and policy continuity was equally apparent in the area of media reform, examined by Martin Harrison in Chapter 13. Here the continuity was the result of rapid technical change and the increasing internationalisation of media, whilst the constant changing of broadcasting control authorities reflected the traditional governmental desire for spoils posts and its equally traditional fear of letting those in opposition gain any influence over broadcasting content. The promotion of French cultural interests, a constantly avowed goal of media policy-makers, received little support from the actual policies carried out. Unfortunately limitations of space prevented us from including a more general examination of the controversies surrounding the very generous public spending for 'arts and cultural' policies, of which successive governments have been so proud. Martin Schain's study of the debates surrounding changing policies on immigration in Chapter 14 returns to the theme of competitive party discourse masking some continuity of policy, although here there is a contrast between the attempts of some Centre–Right politicians to win back defectors to the FN by adopting the policies advocated by the extreme Right and those of the Socialists to avoid stirring up trouble except amongst their opponents. Stephen Bornstein follows with an analysis not of the gory details of the many scandals of the last decade, but of the institutional, political, social and cultural factors underlying these scandals in Chapter 15.

In the final Chapter, Jack Hayward develops some of the main themes – Europeanisation, pluralism, power-sharing, the growth of ideological and policy consensus – which run through all the chapters. It also reminds us of the complex relations between politics and those in France who analyse it, French political scientists. Echoing Françoise Dreyfus, Hayward notes that excessive legalism remains a characteristic not only of the state but also of its students. Electoral studies and opinion polls not only observe but also influence political debates, as both Guyomarch and Schain note in different areas. These features mean that political science in France has no need of the 'new institutionalism' of the Anglo-Saxons, but could perhaps benefit from more emphasis on policy and less on politics.

Throughout the book references are given in the Harvard system, with the author and date cited in the text in parenthesis. A full list of all the works cited is found at the end of the book, together with a short guide to further reading for each chapter and a full index.

PART ONE

The Political System

1

Ideological Change: The Exhaustion of the Revolutionary Impetus

JACK HAYWARD

Two hundred years after the French Revolution, that historic upheaval still remains an indispensable initial point of reference for an understanding of contemporary French politics. This is because it simultaneously symbolises both the unifying founding myth of the democratic republic and the divisive dualism between a revolutionary 'Left' and a counter-revolutionary 'Right'. Their substance has subsequently changed but their forms have stubbornly survived intact. The Revolution's long-term effect was to promote the cultural, social, political, administrative and economic integration of the country, proclaimed as realities long before they were achieved (if they can yet be said to be fully achieved). The creation of a unitary state – asserted to be 'one and indivisible' – entitled to wield legitimate power because it was based upon the sovereign popular will, was the principal instrument of unification. Administrative centralisation, military conscription and national education were intended to achieve uniformity, if not equality. Fraternity was celebrated in secular festivals, at which the nation worshipped itself and its national symbols, its flag and its anthem. Liberty was to be guaranteed to all by a constitutionally enshrined declaration of individual rights, as well as by the ability of all citizens to be represented in a National Assembly which would make laws that would apply to all.

While mass democracy may have sought to mobilise and unite the nation, it was also associated with processes of development

15

that created a pluralistic civil society. People did not conceive of themselves simply as undifferentiated citizens owing allegiance to the state, which embodied their common interests. They had their own individual and group interests, which might figure more prominently in their minds and more fervently in their affections. Even to play an active role as citizens, they would divide into supporters of rival political groupings, differentiated by their appeal to people's sectional, religious, class, regional and local, as well as ideological, loyalties. Now while such partisan appeals might lead to a proliferation of faction-ridden parties, the French Revolution was able to superimpose upon them a dualism that forced people to choose whether they were for or against. Not merely traditionalism but modernisation itself became a tradition, though the forces each represented did not always find easy expression through the party system.

The Fifth Republic's move away from Centrist coalitions towards bipolarisation readily fits into the dualist mould of a clash between the Right and the Left, so it is worth briefly considering the origin of this French Revolutionary legacy to universal political terminology. This dichotomy can be dated. It was born on 11 September 1789 at a meeting of the Estates General transmuted into a National Assembly. This feudal institution had not met for 175 years, but was on that day discussing whether the King should have a veto over the decisions of the people's representatives. The nobility were seated on the left side of the chamber, the commoners or Third Estate in the middle and the clergy on the right side. When it came to the vote on the issue of the royal veto, the commoners voted against and the clergy in favour, with the nobility split. At that point, the members of the nobility who favoured the King's veto crossed the floor to sit on the right with the clergy, while the commoners and anti-veto nobility grouped themselves on the left. In the subsequent revolutionary legislature, this Right–Left split was not perpetuated in the seating arrangements of the Constituent and National Assemblies. The 'Left' sat on the upper seats and were known as the 'Mountain', while the 'Right' sat on the lower seats. Nevertheless, the revival of Parliament in the nineteenth century resurrected the Left–Right political dichotomy and with it a continuing reference back to the legitimising myths of the 1789 Revolution. Because the 'Left' was identified with the protagonists of the Revolution and the Right with its antagonists, the parties of the Left usually enjoyed greater ideological legitimacy. To be described as of the Right carried a counter-revolutionary connotation in the nineteenth century and is a political label that has usually been shunned, along with terms such as 'conservative' (which is equated with being reactionary). Of course the Right has asserted positive as well as negative political norms: those of the family, Catholic religion, elitism and, more recently, capitalism. In the 1980s, there has even been a greater willingness to accept the designation 'Right' rather than the use of euphemisms such as 'Moderate', 'Independent', 'Republican' or 'Majority'. This may be a paradoxical sign that precisely because France has achieved a greater ideological consensus, it is now possible for the Right to re-emerge in its true colours. In that sense, the Revolution would at last be over.

Retro-Communism: The End of Marxism–Leninism's Intellectual Hegemony

The perpetuation of the French Revolution as the prime point of political reference was given a new lease of life by the Russian Revolution because the PCF presented itself as the legitimate inheritor of the nation's revolutionary legacy. Seeing Robespierre and the Jacobins through the eyes of Lenin and the Bolsheviks, the PCF's historians presented 1793–4 as the failed attempt by a dictatorial avant-garde, acting in the name of the oppressed people, to achieve a complete and comprehensive break with the past. The class conflict that followed the Revolution in 1848, particularly as seen through the eyes of Marx, demonstrated the need for a defeated leaderless proletariat to be provided with the direction it lacked. The Paris Commune of 1871 was represented as another abortive attempt to bring about something closer to a communist revolution, but it was the 1917 Bolshevik Revolution that had at last achieved the liberation of the proletariat. It was both the model and the leadership that committed revolutionaries elsewhere should follow. Thanks in part to its affinities with the Blanquist tradition within French socialism, Leninism found ready acceptance by the majority of Socialist party members who broke away to form the PCF in 1920.

There are three main components of the revolutionary tradition which survived long after any realistic prospect of an actual revolution had vanished (Furet, 1981; Judt, 1986, pp. 107–8, 177). First, there is an attempt to combine a conception of the transfer of power as a process – what Proudhon and later Trotsky called 'permanent revolution' – with a simple notion that it is a specific act, the seizure of power as envisaged by Blanqui and Lenin. Second, the model of revolutionary power is one wielded by a dictatorial group, a dedicated professional elite, acting for but exercised over the mass of the people. Last, the people are both assumed to be synonymous with the proletariat and to be united. Despite the fact that it was clear quite soon after the Bolshevik Revolution that the prospect was remote of such a revolution being repeated in an advanced industrial society (as indeed France was becoming), it remained both an expectation and an aspiration for the militant minority who were attracted to the PCF. The party modelled its organisation as well as its strategy upon that of the Soviet Communist party in the 1920s and slavishly continued to do so after the Second World War, even when it became ever more anachronistic, inappropriate and ineffective in Soviet Russia itself.

The Marxist–Leninist intellectual hegemony within France, achieved during the 30 years from the end of the Second World War to the mid-1970s, was paradoxical, given that Marxism had never been a powerful intellectual force since its first impact in the 1880s. France has never produced a really original Marxist thinker, such as Gramsci in Italy, being confined to a subordinate role by the *ouvriérisme* (obsessive 'workerism') that has been so powerful in the French labour movement. Although it attracted the support of prominent intellectuals from the 1920s until the 1960s, they were mainly utilised as propagandists and to suggest virtue by association in the periods when the PCF was seeking allies, such as in the mid-1930s period of the Popular Front. Otherwise, they were reduced to the status of cultural workmen, with the party leadership playing the role of 'collective intellectual' and expounding the day-to-day implications of 'scientific socialism'. Following the Stalinist model, the PCF managed the *tour de force* of sustaining a Soviet-style rigid surveillance of cultural orthodoxy in a country renowned for its independent-minded intellectual elites. With the assistance of prestigious but complaisant fellow-travellers, the PCF established a reign of intellectual terror, based on the premise that the patriotic party of the Resistance and of the working class could not be wrong. Alternative views were ignored or condemned out of a combination of cultural insularity and the discredit that Right-wing views suffered by association with the collaborationist and reactionary Vichy regime. While this domination by default continued in a weakened form into the 1960s, the impact of the May 1968 events – which the PCF was unable to understand or to use to further its own purposes – and the belated acknowledgement in the 1970s of the full horrors of Soviet repression condemned by Solzhenitsyn, produced a dramatic and total reversal. It was significantly not because of intellectual argument as such that Marxism 'lost its stranglehold upon the intellectual imagination in France, a grip it had exercised unbroken for a generation. In the space of less than a decade it became fashionable to be not just non-Marxist, but anti-Marxist', to the point that 'Marxism in France is now history' (Judt, 1986, pp. 170–1).

Although the legitimacy of Marxism–Leninism derived from its links with the labour movement rather than strictly intellectual argument, it was necessary to acquire a theoretically respectable foundation for the PCF's ideological monopoly. Despite Raymond Aron's 1955 exposure of this ideology as 'the opium of the intellectuals', it was possible for its exponents to argue their case by appeals to a Marxist theory of alienation or of surplus value. The last PCF intellectual – a rather marginal one at that – to acquire respectful attention outside the committed faithful was Althusser, who asserted Marx's economic 'scientificity by ontological ratiocination' and 'attributed to intellectuals a central role in the class struggle as participants in 'theoretical practice' which asked of them only that they practise theory' (Judt, 1986, pp. 182 and 192). However, it was not really this kind of esoteric Marxism but the vulgar Leninism purveyed by the party hacks that mattered and it too became irrelevant as books and articles by a flood of party dissidents exposed 'Gallocommunism' to withering criticism (Duhamel and Weber, 1979). It was a striking feature of the late 1970s debate between the PCF leadership and its dissidents – whether of the liberal-reformist kind like Jean Elleinstein or the fundamentalist-revolutionary kind like Louis Althusser – that none of them challenged the shibboleth of democratic centralism. This remains the key to the party's identity. The critics argued that it had been badly practised, a Leninist balance between the two components having been destroyed by a Stalinist subordination of democracy to bureaucratic and authoritarian centralism. This rescue operation was spurned and the PCF's ideological bankruptcy has become increasingly evident from its opportunistic switching between soft and hard lines. In the process, it has given the unmistakable impression that its leaders are concerned with holding on to as much as they can of their shrinking electoral support rather than retaining any pretence to intellectual consistency. The erstwhile revolutionary purpose still retains a residual symbolic role, but what remains is an enfeebled political organisation fighting for survival in the ineffectual defence of the sectional interests of its ageing clientele, rather than adapting to changing circumstances in more than a purely tactical fashion.

Socialist Reformism and Catch-All Compromise

The PCF's catastrophic electoral decline in the last decade has been matched by the Socialist party's spectacular rise, the reward for its willingness to make the strategic changes that its sectarian rival on the Left refused to carry out. By the 1988 National Assembly elections, when it looked as though the PCF would not be able to win more than a handful of seats, the PS considered 'presenting' it with a few, but in the end contented itself with the gesture of reducing the number of seats required to form a parliamentary group. However, at the end of the 1960s, the future of democratic socialism had seemed to be growing ever dimmer. Both under Léon Blum and Guy Mollet, the Socialists had been looking backwards to the turn of the century legacies of Jaurès and Guesde, rather than finding a credible way of achieving a Marxist-inspired revolution. Blum had theorised the problem in his distinction between the revolutionary conquest of power and the reformist exercise of power, but all that seemed possible in practice was the latter. Experience of the Popular Front and during the Fourth Republic suggested that even when opportunities arose, as they did in the wake of the liberation in 1945, the exercise of power improved the lot of working people through the creation of the welfare state and improved bargaining rights for trade unions but the capitalist system remained firmly in place. Even an extensive nationalisation programme seemed to have little effect upon the distribution of economic power. Furthermore, the Socialists became committed in practice to the existence of a mixed economy, although one in which the public sector was the senior partner. Its loss of the support of most of the industrial workers and its reliance upon the support of teachers as the backbone of the party meant that it came to stress anti-clericalism on the school issue, which reinforced its backward-looking character. The advent of the Fifth Republic led to further losses of support and the emergence of attempts to rejuvenate socialism from outside its ranks, notably in the so-called Unified Socialist Party. However, attempts to mobilise the non-Communist Left in dissociation from the PCF failed and the future looked hopeless. The Socialists could not come to power with or without the Communists because, being too weak, the voters would assume that the Communists would dominate any alliance and manipulate it to serve their purposes.

The salvation of the PS was to come principally from outside its ranks: from François Mitterrand, who had never been a Socialist, and Michel Rocard, who had abandoned the party in favour of the Unified Socialist Party. Having become discredited by compromising its Socialist principles and programme, the innovators decided that a precondition of its revival was not to abandon its fundamentalist rhetoric but to modernise its style and change its political behaviour to conform with its principles. This was done by bringing in some of the new rhetoric developed by the Unified Socialists, notably the mobilising myth of worker self-management and the decentralisation of power to the groups making up civil society. This did not fit in very well with the traditional aim of the conquest of state power, socialism being implemented from the top down rather than from the bottom up. Mitterrand's main contribution, when he simultaneously joined the new PS and took over its leadership in 1971, was to secure a compromise between the traditional and innovative elements within the PS. Ideologically pragmatic, he used the PS as an instrument for re-establishing social reformism as a major and then the dominant political force, first on the Left and then in the country generally. Mitterrand's own supporters were initially few in number but he had the politicians's capacity to build a winning coalition. Taking advantage of the 1968 cultural themes of the need to 'change life' and reduce the arrogance of power, strengthened by the acquisition of Rocard and part of the Unified Socialist party in 1974, as well as Left-wing Catholics from the CFDT, Mitterrand also used those – such as Chevènement's CERES faction inside the PS – who were capable of restoring the party's Left-wing ideological credentials, while ridiculing them for wishing to make the PS into a fake Communist party with a membership of real petty bourgeois. Mitterrand succeeded as First Secretary of the PS from 1971 to 1981 in making it into a vehicle for his narrowly unsuccessful 1974 presidential candidacy and his successful candidacies in 1981 and 1988, using ideology to win over and motivate the party activists but diluting it for electoral purposes.

The 1980 *Projet Socialiste*'s (party programme) commitment to a 'break with capitalism' had the advantage of implicitly suggesting that social revolution in the sense of a new beginning, a total reversal of the old order, was back on the agenda. Furthermore, it could be achieved by structural and cultural reforms that would not threaten the liberal democratic form of government or the commitment to civil liberties, which the PCF could not be trusted to preserve. This blurring of revolutionary Utopianism and reformist realism was helped by the composite character of the PS, whose diversity lent credibility to its appeal as a catch-all party. However, the Socialists were to demonstrate after 1981 that they had not found the 'third way' between the disappointing compromise of the social democrats and the repellant imposition of the Communists. They increasingly resembled what, in opposition, the activists had described as past failures and betrayals but the French voters did not seem to hold this against them. On the contrary, Mitterrand's capacity to subordinate the ideological proclivities of the activists meant that the social reformism which had previously been regarded in the party as anathema was now widely accepted as common sense. He achieved this without the ballast of a strong, affiliated trade union movement, which in the social democratic tradition was the way of keeping the ideological extremists under control.

Both the aggressive advocacy of state interventionism identified with the 'Left wing' headed by Chevènement and the pleas for action through voluntary associations of which Rocard has been the main protagonist, have been moderated to the point at which they can uneasily coexist. The PCF was first compelled in 1981 to enter a Socialist-dominated government on its knees and then allowed in 1984 to leave office as an enfeebled shadow of its former self. Class reconciliation, not class conflict, was the objective, even if the Left naturally had its own clientele to cultivate. Private business was rehabilitated and public ownership ceased to be on the agenda, while modernising national economic planning was confined to adapting France to face the single European market. The acceptance that international market forces cannot be resisted with patriotic slogans about 'defending the home market' or resisting Americanisation has meant that whereas Mitterrand's election to the presidency in May 1981 led to the Stock Exchange suspending dealings, with his re-election in May 1988 stocks rose. Stripped of its sectarian ideology socialism, far from provoking panic, is reassuring to a French population that has reservations about doctrinaire economic liberalism. The mixed economy and welfare state were considered to be safe in Socialist hands. Chastened by its extended experience of power, the PS in 1988 was prepared to position itself in the Left–Centre, rather than wait for circumstances beyond its control to push it rightwards.

Pseudo-liberalism and the Fragmented French Right

Traditionally, the French Right was anything but liberal. Liberalism was identified with the values that inspired the French Revolution at its outset, even though liberals quickly criticised the threats to liberty consequent upon the radicalisation and concentration of state power. Individual rights, democracy and nationality were regarded by the Right as disruptive forces that had to be repressed in the name of both spiritual and secular authority. However, as the old monarchical and religious order was replaced first by a bourgeois monarchy and then a bourgeois republic, liberalism became a defensive rather than a revolutionary force. Liberals became more concerned to defend private property rights and less preoccupied with civil liberties. Nevertheless, the cultural hegemony of the Catholic Church still had to be fought, especially in education, and political power had to be kept weak for fear of its abuse, so liberalism could not be relied upon to preserve order. Moreover, patriotism, initially identified with national liberation, was taken over in the late nineteenth century by the Right, while the Left became inclined towards pacifism. The predominantly agricultural economy and slow industrialisation meant that British liberalism's free-trade ideas were only popular with a small minority, notably of economists, the rest of the population being protectionist. The politically fragmented character of the French Right meant that it was difficult to organise effectively. Described as *indépendants* and *modérés* they prided themselves upon rejecting discipline and concentrated on resisting the extremist forces that threatened the political, economic and social status quo. It was only with the recent emergence of a more modernist, managerial and internationally-oriented Right that the economic liberalism of Guizot's 1840s call to 'Enrich yourselves by work and saving' could attract interest after its long neglect. Before then, the mid-twentieth-century Gaullist capture of part of the French Right delayed the resurgence of liberal values and still remains as a factor complicating attempts to unite the French Right itself.

In some ways Gaullism was profoundly opposed to the traditional French Right which had its apotheosis in the defeatist Vichy regime of 1940–4, in whose overthrow de Gaulle played a leading part, together with the predominantly left-wing Resistance. His mystique of national unity was aimed at asserting the military and economic power of the French state, to ensure that its independence was respected and its influence acknowledged. He had no patience with those who sought to restrict state power by liberal juridical, political and economic limitations, and neither did he have any particular respect for the private profit-making concerns of business people. The transition from the old fragmented and reactionary Right took the form of a nationalistic movement and a technocratic leadership which prevented Christian Democracy acquiring in France the place it secured in West Germany and Italy. Service of the nation state became the legitimising ideological principle, it being assumed that there was a general interest that transcended partisan interests (whether of Right or Left). However, as the effects of industrialisation made themselves felt in the 1960s and the impact of the European and international market forces became ever more difficult to manage, the Gaullist ideology was increasingly adulterated. Under Pompidou's influence, first as Prime Minister and later as President, a business-oriented liberal-conservatism increasingly came to the fore. Although it had required state support and guidance to build French firms into national champions capable of sustaining the national interests in an increasingly open and competitive international environment, they were now inclined to cast off the leading reins and assert their independent pursuit of their own pecuniary interests. The nationalistic allergy towards attempts to develop a supranational European community rather than a confederation of European states began to wane, particularly with the accession to the presidency of Giscard d'Estaing in 1974.

Giscard's partial contribution to unifying the Right was to bring together in a fragile Right–Centre alliance (the UDF) the forces of the traditional 'independent and moderate' republican Right, with the residue of the Catholic Christian Democrats and the more conservative among the Radicals. However, although this appeared to increase the coherence on the Right–Centre of French politics, it challenged the hitherto dominant position of the successor Gaullist movement which, in its latest incarnation as the RPR under the leadership of Jacques Chirac, was necessarily involved in competitive cooperation with the UDF and its components. The appeal to an economic liberalism that owed something to the fashionable attractions of Thatcherism and Reaganism was coupled with a revival of interest in Frances's own liberal political traditions and with a rediscovery of the neglected Constant and de Tocqueville, as well as the prestige of the hitherto isolated Raymond Aron. However, in political terms these theoretical concerns were very superficial, the prime motivation being to find a counterpoise to the advocacy of state socialism. The ideological reversal was especially great in the case of the ex-Gaullists and came most easily to the members of the PR component of the UDF. Calls for reductions in taxation and the privatisation not merely of firms nationalised by Mitterrand but also of those nationalised under de Gaulle appealed to business-financed movements which increasingly saw themselves as future components of a single party of the Right that dared to speak its name.

In any case, Gaullism was difficult to use as a distinctive political trade mark, thanks to its successes more than its failures. It was hard to defend political institutions which the Left no longer threatened, or make an issue of a defence and foreign policy that its opponents largely accepted. Those aspects of Gaullism that had failed – such as the neo-corporatist 'association between capital and labour' – were not popular with either the workers or employers. Still, they could be given a symbolic place in privatisation schemes with a small minority of shares initially reserved for employees. The period in power (1986–8) when the Right indulged most in liberal rhetoric was not characterised by liberal behaviour outside economic policy and even there partisan statism bulked larger than market forces in the implementation of the privatisation programme. The UDF component that found it most difficult ideologically to accept the pseudo-liberal revival was the CDS, out of waning loyalty to the values of social Catholicism and a commitment to a Centrism seeking its independence from the emerging party of the Right. However, even more serious threats to the ideological and political unification of an anti-Socialist coalition had appeared in the 1980s in the unprepossessing shape of the FN.

Populist Nationalism: A Resurgent Extreme Right

While it is often the case that the extremes feed on and favour each other and the FN is at the forefront of anti-communism, it was during a period in which the PCF was in steep decline that the FN made its spectacular breakthrough. The exhaustion of the revolutionary impetus on the Left seems to have coincided with a re-emergence of a counter-revolutionary focus on the Right that had been buried prematurely. Xenophobia was discredited by its association with the defeatism and anti-semitism of the Vichy regime, the authoritarian Right rallying after the Second World War to a Gaullist movement that repudiated such attitudes. However, while Gaullism's reassertion of national grandeur and power were attractive to the extreme Right, it was repelled by key aspects of de Gaulle's policy when he returned to office in 1958. Decolonisation was regarded as national betrayal, particularly when it came to Algeria. It was no accident that Le Pen, leader of the FN, was personally involved in the repression of the Algerian independence movement and has received strong support from areas – especially in south-east France – in which former Algerian settlers are concentrated. The extreme Right also resented the process of economic modernisation (begun before de Gaulle but pushed further by him) that was destroying the peasant and small shopkeeper traditional society. There was always an important element of

populist anti-capitalism and anti-technocracy in the French extreme
Right and once again Le Pen was associated with it, being elected
a deputy of the small Extreme Right party led by Pierre Poujade
in 1956 after returning from Algeria. However, while bitterly
opposed to de Gaulle, Le Pen did not take part in the movements
that sought to overthrow de Gaulle by terrorism, carefully remaining within the bounds of the law. He devoted himself to unifying
the highly fissiparous extreme Right in the FN in 1972, but for a
decade his attempts at making this a significant political force were
miserable failures. What accounts for the transformation of the
'France for the French' xenophobia from a traditional phenomenon
of political culture into an organised political movement capable
of influencing policy?

Clearly it could not just be a matter of the size of the immigration problem because France had for many years absorbed a
particularly large number of immigrants. While the North African
and Black African element had increased at the expense of
migration from other European countries, this too long predated
the increase in electoral support for the extreme Right in the
1980s. Because this resurgence coincided with the presence in
power of the Left, it has been too readily assumed that it was in
reaction to the Mitterrand presidency and Socialist governments
that the FN was able to build up its spectacular increase in support. Why was the RPR's and UDF's 'civilised Right' unable to
capitalise on anti-Socialist sentiment? It was the failures of the
Right rather than of the Left that provided Le Pen with his
opportunity for a political breakthrough. He used a wider range
of appeals than the single issue of immigration, although he clev-
erly linked that with the issues of unemployment, crime and the
loss of national identity. The shift away from Gaullist nationalism
and the pursuit of socially disruptive policies of economic modernisation and exposure to international market forces have meant
that part of the Right's clientele felt abandoned. Furthermore, the
process of liberalisation and modernisation within the Church
meant that traditionalist Catholics also felt abandoned. While the
FN cannot rival the main parties of the Right – especially the
CDS – in attracting support from mainstream Catholics, it has
appealed both to the ultra-traditionalist Catholics and to the
dechristianised, who do not feel bound by the humanitarian and
moralistic injunctions of the Catholic Church.

Although the immigration 'invasion' was undoubtedly a potent
issue in acquiring mass support, combined with resentment against
increasing insecurity and high taxation, all of which were amalga-
mated with increasing unemployment, the FN's ideological and

political appeal had a more than circumstantial and protest basis. While its political opponents seemed to resign themselves to the constraint of the forces beyond their control, Le Pen seized the strongly assertive role of the vehement and demagogic proponent of simplistic and draconian solutions to complex and intractable problems. Although the 1988 presidential and assembly elections marked first an upsurge and then a setback for the FN, Le Pen had forced the leaders of the Right to accept – some brazenly, some shamefacedly – that he was one of them and that they could not win elections without his support. The question that remained problematic was whether the Right could win national elections with his support because, although the FN and RPR activists have much in common, this is less true of their voters. What seems clear is that the FN is not a flash in the pan. Attempts by the Right to incorporate homeopathic doses of anti-foreign rhetoric and policies into their party programmes have not so far succeeded in exorcising the spectre of a national populism seeking crude remedies to assuage their resentments and insecurities.

1992: A European Mobilising Myth

As the grip of partisan ideologies has weakened, what if anything has taken their place? While there has been a general political disenchantment, less partisan themes have come to the fore. Part of the revolutionary impetus imparted to France and the world 200 years ago was the idea of nationality as the basis of the political community: the context within which legitimate and binding political decisions would be taken. France's pioneering role was conveniently combined with the assertion that her values – assumed to be shared by all French citizens – were of universal validity, so that what made her political culture distinctive also made it a model for all other nations. France was to be envied even if it could not always be imitated. However, de Gaulle was probably the last major figure, splendid in his self-confident anachronism, who was capable of sustaining even the pretence of dismissing any claimant to authority other than the French nation-state as an impudent intruder to be dealt with summarily. Not merely has France had to resign herself to not being a superpower; she must struggle to retain her place among the few states entitled to share in world political and economic leadership. France has reluctantly faced the humiliation of seeing her language increasingly subordinated internationally to English, having been accustomed to regard French both as the symbol and substance of her cultural identity and of her cultural dominance. France's status appears to be inexorably reduced to global insignificance by rapidly accelerating shifts in population; in economic, political and military power; and in intellectual, artistic and scientific achievement. A desperate search for a solution seemed to offer the emerging EC as a viable framework within which to express the identity which the national community was no longer able to embody successfully. Defeat in the Second World War was regarded by de Gaulle as a challenge to restore the French state and equip it with the capacity to be distinctive, independent and influential in global terms. Jean Monnet, on the contrary, drew a different lesson from national humiliation. With meaningful national independence no longer an option, it was vital for France to find European partners, not as an act of collective resignation but of constructive realism. The EC was the way of acquiring the extra scale, strength and resources which would allow French values, ambitions and assertiveness to be in some measure preserved and imparted to others.

While the PCF remains hostile to the EC out of a combination of loyalty to the Soviet Union, nationalism and an identification of the EC with capitalist values and practices, most of the PS has been warmly disposed to the EC from the early days of the Treaty of Rome. Having condemned the PCF as 'not on the Left but to the East', the PS wanted to avoid being simply identified with the American alliance ('not on the Left but to the West') and the European option was the way forward. While the Centrists remained the most ardent champions of a united Europe in association with Christian Democratic Germany and Italy, leaders of the Right–Centre – such as Giscard d'Estaing – played an important part in resuming the task of post-Gaullist European institution-building. Through the establishment of the European Council and its regular summits, support for the direct election of the European Parliament and the launching of the EMS, Giscard's presidency marked a major shift away from Gaullist nationalism, relying mainly upon bilateral Franco–German collaboration.

The major problem was faced by Chirac's RPR, reluctant to abandon the Gaullist legacy but deciding to do so for the 1984 European elections as part of the price for the RPR–UDF unity of candidature. What began as a tactical concession has since continued with greater momentum, primarily for economic reasons, with Chirac's Finance Minister, Balladur, advocating the creation of a European central bank. A common Euro-currency is another idea that has been discussed. With the FN accepting the process of unification through a conviction that France could not otherwise resist being submerged by the Muslim South and the Communist East, there has been an almost total consensus (bar the PCF) on increasing European collaboration.

Mitterrand, an early and enthusiastic supporter of the European cause from the 1950s, has used his presidential office actively to encourage the achievement of the single European market as a way of unifying the French people. With the waning of the past mobilising myths of both Left and Right, which in any case were divisive, Mitterrand has tried to promote a sense of collective national purpose in economic modernisation so as to become competitive. He has managed not to neglect cultural collaboration in the pursuit of technological and financial prowess. His former Finance Minister, Jacques Delors, was appointed President of the EC Commission and has been concerned to continue in the Monnet tradition of steering towards a more united and effective EC under French leadership. It was the former planner Delors who had the inspiration of fixing a target date for the completion of the single market, arbitrary in itself but stimulating in imparting a sense of urgency to public and private economic actors. The year 1992 has become the symbolic objective of European economic effort and nowhere has it been adopted with such widespread enthusiasm as in France. Preparing France to take full advantage of the unified market, the attempt at a Socialist revival of French planning will be focused on this objective. Continuing to appeal to nationalism – the desire to avoid West German economic dominance – and patriotic pride – the refusal of a process of relative economic decline after the spectacular resurgence of the post-war years – this mobilising myth can be pushed to unrealistic lengths. In his desire to reconcile his new-found Euro-enthusiasm with his vestigial Gaullism, Chirac asserted that France would become dominant economically within the EC under his leadership by 1995. Giscard is more concerned that there should be a President of the European Council and that he should occupy that office. With less national or personal pretentiousness, Mitterrand is content that France and he should play the most active part in the process of European unification. This policy has the virtue of combining a domestic desire to widen the basis of his political support with an extrovert concern to achieve by association the additional strength necessary to carry weight internationally. Having acquired power as the leader of an ideologically backward-looking Left against the Right, Mitterrand's second presidency has been placed under the emblem of a reforming, forward-looking Left–Centre, dedicated to maximising national consensus against the archaic constraints of a pseudo-revolutionary Left and a posturingly counter-revolutionary Right.

The Scope and Limits of French Consensus

If we are to show that the dualistic imprint imparted to France two centuries ago is now becoming blurred, it is necessary to consider how far the notions of 'Left' and 'Right' still seem valid to the political leaders, activists and the mass public. One would expect that those remaining most committed to this dichotomy would be the activists, whereas the leaders and the public would be less inclined to bipolarise political attitudes. Furthermore, even if the activists try to persuade the voters and leaders that what divides is more important than what unites, that consensus (like compromise) is a prelude to betrayal of the convictions and interests of one's own side, in a liberal democratic system the decline in ideological fervour among the public will compel even the zealots to moderate their polarising passions on pain of condemnation to electoral extinction. It is the stubborn reluctance of the PCF to adapt, accustomed to believe that it is the party professionals who should dictate to the public what to think and how to act, which has forced the most dramatic loss in public support. In contrast, the Socialists, despite their lack of 'ideological firmness' and greater willingness to sacrifice doctrinal intransigence for pragmatic flexibility, have prospered. They constitute the party which in the 1970s and 1980s has consistently enjoyed the highest public regard, partly because they are more tolerant of dissent and are generally more willing to take their cue from public opinion than to bully it into acquiescence. The Socialists are closest to presenting an image of themselves with which the plurality of the French population can identify.

Let us consider the results of some opinion surveys which suggest that while the Left/Right split has been losing its bipolarising power, it nevertheless continues to have explanatory power. In 1985, when asked whether the dichotomy still held true, 49 per cent said it was out of date, 37 per cent still valid, with 14 per cent expressing no opinion. Those most inclined to consider the dichotomy dated were bigger business, managerial and professional people, as well as UDF voters, among whom the numbers reached 61 and 60 per cent respectively. Over the period 1981–4 (that is, roughly the first three years of the Mitterrand presidency), the number who thought the dichotomy dated had increased from 33 to 49 per cent, particularly among supporters of the Right, while those who thought it still valid declined from 43 to 37 per cent. Only one in five refused to identify themselves with either the Right or the Left, so even if the hold of the traditional categories was weakening, it still made sense to four out of five people.

As far as the content of these denominations and how they changed over the period 1981–4 are concerned, there was general agreement about patriotism and European unification, although Right-wing supporters were more inclined to identify with these. The most distinctive demarcators were the notions of private property and inheritance on the Right and social justice and full employment on the Left. Over the early Mitterrand years, the Left lost its lead in the belief that it was identified with full employment and the preservation of living standards, while it improved its identification with the rights of women (and to a lesser extent of men) and of tolerance (Duhamel, 1985, pp. 93–5). The abandonment of the attempt to unify and secularise the education system demonstrated the Socialists' willingness to give up one of their cherished ideological commitments, rooted in the struggles of the French Revolution and reinforced a century later. While the Left remained identified with the welfare state, to which the majority of French people were attached, they were harmed by their association with state economic intervention and nationalisation at a time when public opinion was swinging towards market liberalism and many of the Socialist leaders were themselves lionising the entrepreneur, the firm and the private sector.

The moral legitimation of capitalist enterprise by its erstwhile opponents, against the ideological traditions of both social Catholicism and of socialism, initially favoured the parties of the Right. However, the willingness of the Socialists to manage capitalism, after having mismanaged it, has been retrospectively rewarded. Even before their electoral successes in 1988, their economic performance was being favourably compared with their Right-wing successors. Although stern competitiveness displaced smiling conviviality, the public was impressed by the Socialists' ability to reduce inflation, even if they had not reduced unemployment. 'Competitiveness' was by 1988 accepted as desirable by four out of five French people, even though 'capitalism' still had predominantly negative connotations. Both liberalism and socialism were favourably regarded, the former enjoying a 73 for, to 19 per cent against, rating (66 per cent among stable Left-wing supporters, 82 per cent among stable Right-wing supporters). However, socialism only mustered a 59 for, to 32 per cent against, rating (95 per cent among stable Left-wing supporters but only 21 per cent among stable Right-wingers). A similar but smaller Right-wing bias is evident in public opinion on nationalisation and privatisation. While opinion was equally divided for and against nationalisation, there was a 10 per cent margin in favour of privatisation; mainly because Right-wingers were more strongly inclined to favour pri-

vatisation than Left-wingers were prepared to favour nationalisation. Nationalism continued to be favourably regarded by 57 per
cent of the population with 33 per cent against, the Right predictably being more nationalistic (70 as against 21 per cent) than the
Left (49 as against 43 per cent).

Even if the fires of ideological fervour are burning somewhat
lower, France cannot be said to have established a quietist ideological consensus. Quite apart from the revival of ethnic xenophobia on the extreme Right (with calls to put the French first),
on issues such as fiscal policy or the restoration of the death
penalty the old conflicts re-emerge. Nevertheless attempts in 1988
to resurrect past battles, which even recently could still mobilise
millions (such as the Church schools issue), were not effective.
One of the reasons that Chirac lost the 1988 presidential election
was that he tried to fight it as a Left–Right duel, while Mitterrand
– more in tune with the times – was able to transcend the traditional dichotomy. Yet if in 1978 it could be said that a Left-
wing France voted for the Right, in 1988 a Right-wing France
voted for the Left. The electorate is less ideologically rooted, and
more volatile. Although the PCF and its trade union ally, the
CGT, persist in trying to give industrial disputes a wider ideological significance, they are hampered by the fact that the PCF's own
decline has been (more modestly) matched by that of the CGT,
so that class conflict has largely moved off the agenda. Political
argument, despite desperate attempts at infusing it with ideological
passion, has become concerned with incrementally more or less
rather than fundamental differences of kind. It is in this sense
that when France celebrated the bicentenary of its Revolution in
1989, it appeared at last to have accepted the reality of piecemeal
reformism, although it is too much to ask its politicians wholly to
renounce an inherited revolutionary rhetoric as a way of keeping
up appearances.

2

Changing Patterns of Party Competition

HOWARD MACHIN

During the 1980s, the number of parties, their organisations and memberships, their relative electoral strengths, their alliances with each other and the ideological diversity of party political competition have all changed considerably. There has been a transformation of the parties and the entire party system. Both have become increasingly hybrid: parties with different objectives, styles and strategies now coexist rather than form a coherent party system. Not all parties even share the same strategic aims, for while the PS and the RPR compete for power at all national and local levels, the PCF and FN contest only for the possibility of parliamentary leverage, influence on public opinion, seats in the European Parliament, organisational self-preservation and control of some local councils. Different parties are sensitive to different external influences. All suffer increasing internal divisions, but the nature and intensity of the conflicts vary considerably. The UDF no longer operates as a single political force and its component elements have adopted conflicting strategies. The Greens, however, have yet to form an effective party organisation or gain national representation, but they are already established in local government (largely as allies of the PS) and in the European Parliament. Presidential and parliamentary coalitions no longer always coincide. As the March 1989 municipal elections demonstrated, national control of local and regional party organisations is often ineffective. Living with such tensions inside each party is not easy. Coalition fragility is increased and the whole party system has become intrinsically changing and changeable.

In the 1978 parliamentary elections two coalitions, both compris-ing two similar sized parties, had fought for a majority. The coalitions were the same at all electoral contests – presidential, parliamentary and local – and the parties were all national, disci-plined forces, with mass memberships and organised structures and finances. The Centre–Right alliance, the 'majority' of incumbent President Giscard d'Estaing, included the RPR ('neo-Gaullists', called the UNR–UDT until 1968 and the UDR thereafter until 1976) and the UDF (a federation of small parties including the Christian Democrats [CDS], Republicans [PR], and the Radicals). In 1978 this narrowly defeated the 'opposition': the PS (virtually merged with the tiny Left-Radicals [MRG]), and the PCF. All four parties had won similar shares of the votes and the margin between the two coalitions was very small, but this apparent sym-metry was misleading. As Bartolini (1984) noted, differences between the RPR and UDF were about tactics and personalities, whilst those between the PS and the PCF reflected an ideological gulf. The two-bloc system concealed three distinct ideological pos-itions on a Left–Right axis: Communist, Socialist and Cen-tre–Right.

TABLE 2.1 *The Parliamentary Parties*

(a) % first ballot votes

	PCF	PS + Radicals)	Other Left	Green	UDF	RPR	Other Right	FN
1978	20.6	24.7	4.4	2.1	21.5	22.6	3.0	0.9
1981	16.1	37.5	2.0	1.1	19.2	20.8	2.8	0.4
1986	9.8	31.6	2.6	1.2	← 42.1 →		2.7	9.8
1988	11.3	35.9	2.0	0.4	18.5	19.2	2.9	9.7

(b) Seats in the National Assembly

	PCF	PS + Radicals)	Other Left	Green	UDF	RPR	Other Right	FN
1978 (491)	86	114	1		139	150	1	
1981	44	283	6		62	84	11	
1986 (577)	35	214	1		129	146	14	35
1988	27	277			130	129	13	1[1]

Note:
1 Expelled from the FN just after the elections for indiscipline.

Since 1978 things have changed dramatically, as Tables 2.1, 2.2 and 2.3 illustrate. The first stage of evolution, in 1981, involved both the electoral defeat of the Right and a shift in party strengths on the Left. Mitterrand defeated Giscard d'Estaing to win the presidency by a wide margin, whilst in the parliamentary elections the Left gained over 50 per cent of the votes for the first time since 1956. With 37.5 per cent of the first ballot votes, the PS emerged with a single-party majority in the Assembly, a feat achieved only once before (by the UDR in 1968). In 1984 a second stage of transformation began. On the Left the coalition of the PS and PCF collapsed: in July the PCF left the alliance when the Mauroy Government resigned. In opposition the Centre–Right parties faced a new challenge on the Right from Le Pen's FN: in the June European elections the FN broke their monopoly on representing the Right, and the party system thus gained a fourth ideological position on the extreme Right.

TABLE 2.2 *Parties and power since 1979*

	President & Prime Minister	Governing parties	Oppositions
1978	Giscard Barre/UDF	RPR + UDF(PR–CDS–Rads) (Two-bloc system)	PS + PCF
1981	Mitterrand Mauroy/PS	PS(& MRG) + PCF (Dominant-party system)	RPR + UDF
1984	Mitterrand Fabius/PS	PS(&MRG) (One-party majority)	PCF RPR + UDF (FN)
1986	Mitterrand Chirac/RPR	RPR + UDF (Cohabitation)	PCF PS FN
1988	Mitterrand 2 Rocard/PS	PS(&MRG) (Minority)	PCF CDS RPR + UDF (PR–Radicals)

In 1986 *cohabitation* brought a new stage of party development, with the temporary non-coincidence of the presidential and parliamentary majorities. After the President's promise to stay in office unless the new majority blocked his constitutional powers, the RPR–UDF alliance won a three-seat majority. Chirac, the RPR leader, was appointed Prime Minister with a Centre–Right government. Opposition now came from three parliamentary groups (the PS, still the largest single party, the PCF and the 35 FN deputies), but also, intermittently, from the president. The re-election of Mitterrand in 1988 ended *cohabitation*, and another phase began with the presidency and dominant group in Parliament again controlled by the same party, but no majority. The new Prime Minister, Rocard, began discussions to form an alliance between the

PS and the CDS or other elements of the UDF. But only a handful of UDF leaders and a few 'new men' from outside the parties joined the government, so the President dissolved the Assembly. In the June elections, however, the optimistically titled 'presidential majority' alliance failed to live up to its name, winning only 277 of the 577 seats. The PS and its new friends reacted by making a pact with the PCF (to allow the Communists to form a parliamentary group) and a number of policy deals with the CDS (notably over New Caledonia and the budget). The results of the 1989 European elections, however, showed that the FN had not lost its electoral appeal and that, if the CDS was the main loser, Giscard d'Estaing had not scored the sweeping victory he had hoped for. Divisions in the Centre–Right had clearly not diminished.

TABLE 2.3   *The presidential and European party systems*

(a) **Presidential (% votes at first ballot)**

	PCF + MRG	PS + Left	Other	Green	RPR	UDF Right	Other	FN
1974	← 43.2 →		3.7	1.3	15.1	32.6	3.8	0.9
1981	15.3	28	5.6	3.9	17.9	28.3	3.0	–
1988	6.8	34.1	4.4	3.8	19.9	16.5		14.4

(b) **European (% votes)**

	PCF + MRG	PS + Left	Other	Green	RPR	UDF Right	Other	FN
1979	20.5	23.5		4.4	16.3	27.6	–	1.3
1984	11.2	20.8		3.4	← 43.0 →			10.9
1989	7.7	23.6		10.6	← 28.9 →		8.4[1]	11.7

Note:
1 CDS list.

What then brought about these many changes? Whilst some seemed to reflect institutional modifications, and others developments in public opinion, yet others were more related to the internal dynamics of the parties themeslves.

Party Changes in Response to Inter- and Intra-Party Pressures

During the 1980s, one of the main sources of change has been the parties themselves. The basic characteristics of many parties had made them ill at ease in their roles and uncomfortable in existing coalitions before 1981. As a consequence of that victory tensions were exacerbated and new problems arose. The RPR and

UDF blamed each other for defeat, whilst the PCF greatly resented relegation to junior partner status. The parties of the Left were accustomed only to opposition, whilst those of the Right had experienced over two decades in power. The FN, having broken through to win European, National Assembly and regional council representation in 1984 and 1986, sought to consolidate its position and win recognition from the RPR and UDF as a legitimate partner on the Right. By the end of the decade all were facing problems of leadership renewal. In many cases the challenges to existing leaders reflected the dissatisfaction within the ranks at continuing electoral failures.

The PS wanted to reinforce its new dominant position by a successful period in government. It sought not only to provide a competent government, to carry out many electoral promises and to remain united and disciplined, but also to woo support for the 1986 parliamentary elections. In 1981 wielding power and dominating the Assembly was no easy task for the PS, in part because it had a radical programme, but only ten years of existence as a united force and few leaders with ministerial experience. One source of tensions was the dominance of the presidency within the political system, since some Socialist deputies had believed that their party rather than the president should guide the government. Mitterrand showed more sensitivity to feelings in his party than any of his predecessors, but some PS deputies were distressed that in power their party seemed to be run by presidential breakfast meetings.

Other problems reflected the fact that in 1981 the PS was still a highly factionalised body. Before 1981, this very diversity had helped its growth by providing an ambiguous, catch-all identity. Factions had originally represented the distinct groups which had merged at or after the 1971 conference at Epinay to form the new party. Later they became voices for different ideological, policy and strategy options. The CERES faction, led by Chevènement, with centralist and statist Jacobin views and a strong attachment to the Communist alliance, was often contrasted to the 'second left' group, which was loyal to Rocard, had Christian-social, CFDT origins, participatory preferences, and was reluctant to concede much for good terms with the PCF. Increasingly the factions became clans around prominent leaders struggling to assume the role of heir-apparent. This leadership contest had even dominated the 1979 party conference at Metz, when it seemed that Mitterrand might not run in 1981.

After his 1981 victory, factional strife arose over the distribution of governmental posts and policy priorities. At the 1981 party conference at Valence, only months after the election, there were calls for more radical changes of policies and administrative personnel. In the government, factional disputes over policy choices even led to ministerial resignations, as in 1982 (Questiaux) and in 1983 (Chevènement). A party leadership competition restarted in 1984, as Mitterrand seemed too unpopular to be re-electable. This new race, however, was largely conducted by informal political 'clubs', including Rocard's *Convergences*, Fabius's *Démocratie 2000*, and Chevènement's *République Moderne*. All claimed to be merely think-tanks for new policy ideas. As Mitterrand's popularity increased again after 1985, the leadership contest was called off and the rivals closed ranks.

A further difficulty for the PS between 1981 and 1984 arose from its determination to maintain both voter loyalty and credibility as a radical force. The mild reflation of 1981, the nationalisations of 1982 and the balance of payments and devaluation crisis of 1983 were followed by a major change in economic policy. Although the 1983 municipal elections and opinion polls showed a dramatic loss of support, many Socialist activists still wished to carry out the mandate for sweeping reforms. Many PS members were teachers and the main goal of the anti-clerical teachers' unions for over a century had been to abolish the private (mainly church) schools, so it was not surprising that the PS pressed on with plans to merge them into the state system. Opinion polls indicated that this idea was very unpopular, and there were several huge hostile demonstrations in early 1984. The poor performance of the PS in the European elections (20.8 per cent: down from 23.5 per cent in 1979) confirmed how far the Socialists were out of step with the electorate.

This crisis was not resolved by the party but by Mitterrand, who scrapped the Schools Bill, accepted the resignation of the Mauroy Government and appointed the young, moderate Fabius as Prime Minister. The new government again included the leaders of every faction within the PS but no Communists, and the entire party closed ranks behind it. The Fabius team, by projecting a modernising and managerial image, hoped to demonstrate that a real change in sensitivity to public opinion had taken place. The 1985 party conference at Toulouse confirmed that most activists supported the new approach. The PS realisation of and reaction to its own electoral fragility came in time for survival, but not for victory in 1986.

The 1986 election campaign was not made easier for the PS by the involvement of Hernu, the Defence Minister and close friend of the president, in the Greenpeace–*Rainbow Warrior* scandal (see

Chapter 15). Furthermore, after the elections evidence of corruption emerged (the Nucci and Luchaire scandals), which made it difficult for the PS to repeat its 1981 claims of moral superiority over the corrupt, clientelistic RPR and UDF: Socialists too seemed corruptible. Once again, Mitterrand saved the situation by suggesting an all-party agreement on public funding for political parties and the publication of party accounts.

In contrast, after 1981 PCF leaders were primarily preoccupied by regaining an electoral strength equal to that of the PS. This meant finding a way to stop and reverse their own dramatic decline. The Communists found their new role painful: they had always attacked presidentialism (ideologically they preferred collective leadership, yet they also knew that a PCF candidate would never win), but had become the ally of a tough Socialist president. In 1981 the party lost 25 per cent of its 1978 vote, much of it to the PS. It was humiliating that the PS now represented the votes of twice as many workers as the self-styled 'workers' party'. Worse, the industrial working class (its traditional base) was shrinking, and the CGT, its trade union link to the workers, was in rapid decline. Opinion polls showed that many remaining PCF voters favoured participation in government. The Communists, however, were given only four ministries.

Adopting a governmental approach was very difficult as leaders' and activists' instincts, since 1947, were to protest by demonstrations, political strikes and attacks on governments and capitalists. To share governmental responsibility – no easy choice – was the only option for survival and a chance of revival, at least until the Socialists became unpopular. The PCF strategy was necessarily schizophrenic: it sought to gain from the Government's popular successes by loyal support and the demonstrated competence of its ministers, whilst assuming the lead of the discontented by discreet but public criticisms. The Communist position was also complicated by loyalty to its Soviet big brother, an inherited role which had been temporarily neglected during the 'Eurocommunist' phase of the mid-1970s. PCF support for such Soviet initiatives as the invasion of Afghanistan did little to facilitate coalition cooperation, especially as Mitterrand was notoriously suspicious of the pre-Gorbachev Soviet leaders.

Yet another complication for the PCF was internal pressure for renewal of policies, strategies and leaders. The revolt of the 'renovators', as the would-be reformers became known, led to internal dissent on a scale hitherto unknown, and to many resignations. In 1984, six members of the central committee actually abstained rather than vote their approval of the leaders' report;

an unprecedented event in PCF annals. Several local party organisations went even further and dared to reject the report. The
criticisms came from 'liberals' and 'Stalinists' alike, and the only
common factor was a demand to censure those responsible for the
decline, and in particular the General Secretary, Marchais. He,
however, survived, but his party continued to lose members and
activists.

As the Mauroy Government lost popularity, the PCF appeared
to act increasingly incoherently with its governmental and opposition personalities barely in coexistence. By 1984, when unemployment and governmental unpopularity were both growing at alarm-
ing rates, Communist leaders decided that remaining in office
could only cost votes. They left the ruling coalition, and attempted
to take over the leadership of the discontented. This decision was
no more fruitful for their revival plans than their previous choice:
in 1986 the Communists lost almost a third of their 1981 voters.
Furthermore, after the Communists' departure the Socialists
started to regain popularity. The return to opposition did not even
restore any internal unity in the PCF itself. New dissidents
appeared to replace those who had left, and they in turn were
driven out. At the top level in the party Pierre Juquin emerged
as the leading 'liberal' critic of Marchais; he was first marginalised
and later excluded. He did not go, however, without a fight at
the party congress. After leaving he stood, unsuccessfully, against
the lack-lustre official PCF candidate, Lajoinie, in the 1988 presidential contest.

The continued decline of the PCF was again clear in 1988. Even
many who had voted Communist in 1986 opted for Mitterrand at
the first ballot, showing loyalty to the notion of unity of the Left,
and awareness of the futility of voting PCF in a presidential election. The party could no more direct its voters than control its
members. After the elections, with only 27 seats, the PCF had
not even enough to form an independent group in the Assembly.
To avoid total marginalisation in debates, it made a truce with
the Socialists: the PCF voted with the PS to elect Fabius as
Speaker of the Assembly, and the PS responded by changing
Assembly rules to allow a group to be formed with only 25 deputies. The 1989 municipal and European elections brought no solace:
the PCF was surviving but not reviving.

In opposition the situation for the Centre–Right parties was very
different, although relations between the RPR and UDF were no
more cordial than those between the PS and PCF. The parties of
the new opposition sought to reconstruct for an eventual electoral
revenge by simultaneously competing against each other and toge-

ther against the Socialists. Both aspired to presidential and domi-
nant-party status, although the UDF had additional problems of
holding together its constituent parties.

A return to the 'golden age' of de Gaulle and Pompidou was
the dream of the RPR after 1981: to recapture leadership of
the Centre–Right alliance, the presidency and to dominate both
government and Parliament. The initial frustrations of facing opposition were great after 23 years in office, especially as almost half
its deputies had lost their seats. Nonetheless the situation was not
hopeless. The RPR had at least a clear leader, Chirac, with open
presidential ambitions. With Giscard d'Estaing then disgraced,
there appeared to be no real leadership challenge from the UDF.
Furthermore the economic crisis was unsolved, so a medium-term
increase in both unemployment and voter discontent was probable.
The RPR thus strove to lead the parliamentary opposition, to
ensure that Chirac remained the sole presidential candidate of the
Centre–Right and to win the support of all those dissatisfied with
the PS by offering attractive alternatives.

The RPR also set out to modernise its own organisation and
policy stances. Traditionally, the party had been firm in support
of state interventionism, especially in the economy and the media,
and in support of national independence, notably in matters of
European integration. Indeed, the RPR had fought the 1979 European elections on an anti-integration platform. In 1981, however,
Chirac had distinguished himself from Giscard d'Estaing by his
pro-market stance. Soon afterwards his party formally adopted a
neo-liberal and relatively Europhile programme, marking a break
with its statist and nationalist traditions (despite vain resistance
from several of the old guard). Its adoption both signalled that
Chirac's leadership faced no real internal challenge and brought
the party ideologically closer to the UDF. It was also intended to
enhance the electoral appeal of the party, but opinion polls showed
that these changes had little impact on public opinion: the RPR
was scoring only marginally better than the UDF, and voters could
see little difference between the two.

The RPR's failure to regain alliance domination also reflected
the unexpected resilience of the UDF. After the defeat of 1981,
many PR, CDS and Radical leaders had agreed that, whatever
their differences, continued coexistence within the UDF federal
structure was essential in order to avoid becoming mere acolytes
of the RPR. Some, ambitious or far-sighted, saw that the UDF
could provide a base for a presidential candidate in 1988. There
was also agreement on the need for policy and leadership renewal,
but the various parties approached this in different ways. Both

the CDS and the PR chose new party leaders (Mehaignerie and Léotard, respectively), and the UDF group in the Assembly picked a new chairman (Gaudin). The UDF also adopted a neo-liberal platform and made vitriolic attacks on 'the overmighty Socialist state'. The resuscitation of the presidential hopes of the UDF, however, was mainly the work of old leaders rather than new men. In 1983, as the PS Government set new records of unpopularity, its immediate predecessors, Giscard d'Estaing and Barre, staged their own political come-back (as rivals to each other) after months spent avoiding publicity and rebuilding networks of allies. Each saw himself as a future president and strove to win the support of the entire UDF to that end. Whilst the policy differences between the two were small, their intense personal rivalry became a divisive factor within the UDF. Barre was backed by the CDS whilst Giscard d'Estaing, despite the reluctance of Léotard (who himself had presidential dreams), regained the support of his old party, the Republicans. This leadership rivalry thus reinforced the inter-party competition within the UDF but, as both men hoped eventually to harness the electoral support of the whole federation, neither sought to dismember it.

Within the UDF, neo-liberals in the PR liked the RPR's conversion to market economics, whilst CDS leaders were pleased by its new pro-European sentiments: hence, in 1984, it proved relatively easy to agree on a joint RPR–UDF list for the European elections. The results of those elections, however, confirmed that PS popularity had declined but also showed that traditional Centre–Right forces were regaining few sympathisers. The increasingly public 'war of the chiefs' between Chirac, Barre and Giscard d'Estaing seemed to have reduced the electoral appeal of the Centre–Right, despite growing PS unpopularity. On major strategic and policy questions the three presidential aspirants differentiated themselves and their parties. In the 1986 election campaign Barre differed from both Chirac and Giscard d'Estaing by his demand to force the resignation of the incumbent president in the event of an RPR–UDF victory. Rivalry continued during *cohabitation*, although only Chirac and Barre were serious candidates for the presidency. The result was that Chirac, as Prime Minister, campaigned on his record in power, whilst Barre ran against him on a platform explicitly critical of that record.

The campaigns of both 1986 and 1988, however, were singularly complicated by the competition from the FN, after its electoral breakthrough in 1984. The failure of the RPR and UDF to regain support when the popularity of Mitterrand and the PS plummeted after 1982 partly explains the take-off of the FN, as its leader Le

Pen showed remarkable skill in exploiting the weakness of the old parties and the worries of the electorate. Having inherited a fortune and taken professional advice on his image, Le Pen led the great FN electoral upsurge (see Chapters 12 and 14). After 1984 the Front found that holding itself together and growing were real challenges. At the elite level, several deputies who had defected to the FN from the RPR or UDF were ill at ease with Le Pen's anti-semitic comments and authoritarian leadership, and his closest lieutenants had different strategies for expansion. The 1986 vote was high, but over a third of the 1984 FN voters had moved to other parties. The 1988 presidential first ballot also brought more new voters, but the parliamentary elections again showed that voter loyalty was weak. In the 1989 European elections, however, the FN still won more votes than the PCF, the CDS and the Greens.

The rise of the FN destroyed the RPR–UDF monopoly of representation of the Right and Centre and reduced their chances of returning to power in 1986 or 1988. The RPR and UDF were tempted to compete with Le Pen on such issues as immigration control and law and order in the hope of winning back voters. A more risky alternative was to offer no compromise with FN ideas but to combat them at every opportunity. A third strategy was to attempt to dilute FN extremism by involving it in coalition in exchange for moderating its racist and authoritarian tendencies. All three strategies required joint action by the RPR and UDF, but the choice of strategy divided each group internally. The approach adopted from 1984 to 1986 mixed the first two approaches, for the RPR and UDF stressed their firm law and order platform and promised responsible controls on immigration whilst declaring total hostility to Le Pen, his party and its ideas. Polls at this time suggested that the RPR–UDF alliance would win a comfortable majority in 1986, and that most of its voters approved of this distancing from the FN. They also showed that the FN had gained what the PCF had lost: a 'repulsion effect'. Any party associating too closely with it risked losing liberal, moderate voters to abstention or even to the PS.

The narrowness of the 1986 RPR–UDF majority in the Assembly and the fact that the FN held the balance of power in five regional councils caused many to rethink their tactics. In both the RPR and UDF, leaders disagreed as to what should be done. Pasqua, the RPR Minister of the Interior, seemed intent on winning back the FN voters by actually carrying out some of that party's policies. He pushed a new immigration control act through the Assembly, reduced the appeal rights of those accused of illegal immigration and increased police powers. His actions, however, did not receive full support from all his colleagues. The health minister made a blistering attack on Le Pen's attempts to blame immigrants for Aids, whilst the trade minister openly opposed any concession to the FN. Within the UDF there were similar splits. Barre himself initially expressed 'understanding' of the frustrations of FN voters, but later moved towards opposing any deal with Le Pen. CDS deputies voiced total opposition to any links with the FN. The PR was itself divided, with Léotard strongly anti-FN, whilst Gaudin, whose Marseilles election hopes looked increasingly doubtful without FN support, favoured local deals. By 1988, the issue also divided the two presidential candidates of the Centre–Right; Barre opposed any concession to the FN on the grounds that it would push moderate and liberal voters to back Mitterrand, whilst Chirac seemed more worried about the defection of FN voters into abstention. The RPR and UDF had failed either to destroy or to coopt the rival on the Right; their own supporters had been divided and weakened, and in 1988 some were scared back to Mitterrand and the PS.

The FN and the 'war of the chiefs', however, were not the only problems for the RPR and UDF during the period of *cohabitation*. Rivalry was exacerbated by Chirac's choices of ministers and policies. RPR members were given almost all the key posts in the government, notably Finance and the Interior, which went to Chirac's two closest lieutenants, Balladur and Pasqua. The top UDF minister, Léotard, was given only Culture and Communications. Furthermore, the prime minister regularly employed the 'question of confidence' procedure (discussed in Chapter 7) for bills which some UDF deputies disliked. In the first few months Chirac's distribution of political spoils was so blatantly pro-RPR that Barre and other UDF leaders voiced public criticisms. In these circumstances it was scarcely surprising that the UDF should have been so unenthusiastic about Chirac becoming president.

In the months following the 1988 elections various RPR and UDF leaders drew very different conclusions about the causes and consequences of the defeat. Several (including the RPR ex-Finance Minister, Balladur, and the Republican leader, Léotard) suggested that to avoid such destructive public rows the RPR and UDF should merge as a single party. In contrast, CDS leaders, encouraged by Barre, rejected this idea and called into question the need to keep the UDF united. The CDS deputies formed their own group in the Assembly and expressed willingness to support any policy of the Rocard Government with which they agreed. Criticisms of the top leaders of both the RPR and the PR also came from a group of younger leaders within the two parties. These 'renovators' of the Centre–Right included successful former ministers (Séguin and Noir), and all were in their mid-forties. They expressed support for the moderate ideas of the CDS and a strong desire to keep it within the Centre–Right alliance. When Chirac announced a compromise deal with the UDF remnant (essentially the Republicans) for a joint list, led by Giscard d'Estaing, in the European elections, they openly opposed this proposal within their respective parties. Baudis (the UDF mayor of Toulouse) even dared to make a public plea to Giscard d'Estaing to withdraw to leave the way open for a younger and less divisive leader. Their failure meant that the CDS presented its own list for the European elections. The dissent in the RPR and PR ranks was not silenced, however. In 1989 the parties of the Centre–Right seemed further away than ever from the 'unity behind a single leader' which so many saw as essential for their reconquest of the presidency and a majority in the Assembly.

This internal pressure was only one element in determining the patterns of change. Parties may have sought to regain their past glories, to maintain their present advantages, or even, like the FN, to become a major national force, but the electorate on which they depended was itself being transformed. The external context of party competition was changing and the parties had to adapt or face stiff penalties.

The Parties and the Changing Electorate

During the 1980s, there have been a number of changes in the ideological climate and social conditions of the electorate which have had a considerable impact on the party system through the reactions of individual parties. Like all West European countries, France had high rates of inflation (until 1985), of unemployment (rising to over two million by 1984), of disillusionment with a state which could not control the economy or even its own expenditure, of crime rates and of demands for better protection of the environment. How much and in what ways public opinion and voting behaviour were influenced by such changes depended in part on how the parties reacted, their interpretations of the changes and their proposed solutions. The main beneficiaries of these developments, in very different ways, were the FN and PS.

Opinion polls indicated that, after 1979, there was a general fall in the level of public confidence in political parties and a similar decline in personal identification with individual parties. The number of those who identified with any party fell from 29 per cent in 1978 to 17 per cent in 1984, according to *Eurobarometer* polls. Whilst this fall was in line with West European trends, there were several reasons for voter dissociation from specific parties in France. The 1981 elections showed that the RPR, UDF and PCF alike had suffered massive losses of support. Party membership stagnated or declined in almost all parties except the FN. Membership figures for French parties are notoriously unreliable, as there are no published records, or even any agreed definition of what constitutes membership. The PCF admits that its membership dropped from 650 000 in 1979 to 608 000 in 1989, but informed PCF-watchers estimate that the real figures are 450 000 (1979) and 230 000 (1989). The Socialists claimed 195 000 members in 1981, the same number in 1986, and 200 000 in 1989: scarcely a success story for the dominant party of the decade. Within the UDF, the PR calculated its own membership totalled 190 000 in 1986, but only 130 000 three years later. It admitted that over one-third of this membership was renewed each year. The RPR claimed a total of 850 000 members in 1986 but in 1989 refused to provide any figure on the grounds that the party had no definition of membership! Only the FN claims real growth in members and activists, although it admits that many members do not stay for very long. The membership figure given by the Front in 1989 was 100 000. There have also been many newspaper reports of falling party activism but little clear evidence has been provided to confirm this. The PCF has fewer poster-stickers or participants at its meetings, and street sellers of *Humanité-Dimanche* (its newspaper) are fast becoming an endangered species. The FN, however, now has no shortage of leaflet distributors.

This decline in party identification and membership has not been accompanied by a decline in public interest in politics. In these circumstances an increase in voter volatility seemed likely, and post-electoral analyses showed that a substantial increase did indeed occur after 1979. When the voters turned away from the traditional parties, they did not all adopt the same replacement. Some simply abstained from voting. After the presidential elections of 1981 there was a big increase in abstentionism. In the 1981 assembly elections 29 per cent abstained, in 1986 21.5 per cent, and in 1988, 34.3 per cent. Even in the 1981 and 1988 presidential elections turnout was lower than in the previous two decades. At the European elections of 1984 and in the 1988 referendum abstentions attained positively Anglo-Saxon levels (63 per cent in the November 1988 referendum). Abstention was not, however, the only alternative.

Another possibility was protest politics, although many traditional organisers of demonstrations, notably the trade unions,
were in decline and felt constrained by the presence of their
friends in the government from 1981 to 1986 (or 1984 in the case
of the PCF). There were, however, other social groups hostile to
the Socialists who had none of the inhibitions of the unions.
Hospital consultants and junior doctors, travel agents and supporters of private schools were amongst those who marched
through the streets of Paris. Lorry drivers did not march, or even
drive, but in January 1984 their sit-in created a Calais-to-Chamonix
traffic jam, the largest in European history. Whilst RPR and UDF
politicians sometimes joined these protests, they rarely led them
and their presence inspired little enthusiasm. Even in the massive
demonstrations of May and June 1984 against the Socialist proposals on private school reform, the RPR and UDF participants
were followers rather than leaders. Such protest however, were
often short-lived and did not lead to the creation of lasting organisations. Frequently the demonstrators or strikers elected an informal team of leaders (called a *coordination*) but this group disappeared once the protest was over.

Yet another option was to support a political organisation distinct from the traditional parties. In this context one party, the
FN, made great gains on the Right, as discussed above. Whilst
its extremist sentiments were not new in 1984, the sudden electoral
success of the hitherto unknown party espousing them was a shock
to all the other parties. But Right-wing extremism has been found
throughout Western Europe as a consequence of unemployment
and xenophobia at the end of a long prosperous period, but the
electoral success of the FN was exceptional. The public relations
skills of Le Pen, the worsening of unemployment and crime figures, the growth of popular discontent with the Socialists before
the Centre–Right alliance had lost its unpopularity gained during
the Giscard presidency; all these provide partial explanations of
this success. But French rulers differed from those of other countries in providing, by institutional tampering discussed below, the
opportunities for the FN to exploit these advantages.

It is striking to compare the record of failure of the Centre–Right parties to stop the rise of the FN with the relative
success of the PS in dealing with a new ideological challenge to
its position from the Greens. With only a loose national organisation, the Greens could barely be said to constitute a party but
there was no shortage of local Green candidates at elections.
Furthermore, there was clearly a growing voter sympathy for
Green politics. In the 1977 municipal elections Green lists had

scored over 10 per cent in a number of towns including Paris and, in 1979, at the European elections Greens won 4.4 per cent of the vote, just short of the 5 per cent needed to get a seat. These results encouraged some PS leaders publicly to proclaim their sympathy for certain Green policies. The goal was to identify capitalism and its RPR–UDF servants as the enemies of ecological balance, and hence to steer second ballot votes of Greens towards the PS. This was not simply electoral opportunism, for the Socialists shared many Green opinions (notably on equality, citizens' rights, local democracy and participation). Furthermore, it did not facilitate their contacts with the Communists, who were strong supporters of the nuclear power programme and generally hostile to Greens.

The plan to build a nuclear power station on a sea-shore site at Plogoff, in Brittany, was one test case by which the PS proved its 'greenness'; it supported the weekly demonstrations held at the site, and promised that Mitterrand, when elected, would scrap Plogoff and review the whole nuclear programme. In the 1981 elections, many first-ballot Lalonde (Green) voters switched to Mitterrand at the second ballot and again voted PS in the subsequent parliamentary elections. Mitterrand kept his promise to cancel Plogoff, but the report of the nuclear review, which recommended continuing a reduced building programme, disappointed many.

Nonetheless the PS remained the least 'environment-destructive' and most friendly of the big parties, and some Greens could still make pacts with the PS in the 1983 local elections for the second ballot. In the 1984 European elections an independent Green list ran, albeit with little success (3.4 per cent). For the elections of 1986 and 1988 the Greens were not united. Some, led by Lalonde (who became a junior minister of Rocard in 1988), advocated alliances with the PS. Others, and notably in Alsace (encouraged by frequent contacts with the neighbouring West German Greens and their own local hero, Waechter, the 1988 presidential candidate), sought to establish a new 'ecological pole', neither on the left nor the right. The 1989 municipal elections showed that the Greens were divided, but many were still willing to rally to the PS at second ballots. There were some striking Green successes at the first ballot: 24 per cent in Colmar, 23 per cent at Le Puy and 15 per cent at Cahors. In Alsace there were few second-ballot deals with the PS, but elsewhere these were more numerous. The Greens emerged from these local elections with over 1,400 council seats, some 400 more than the FN, and part of this success was explained by local cooperation with the PS. The success of the

Green list in the June 1989 European elections showed that the relationship with the Socialists was facing increasing strains.

The Greens were not, however, the only new sociopolitical movement with which the PS managed to create ties. Three others of importance for winning new voters were the feminists, the pro-immigrant group *SOS-racisme* and the 1986 student movement. These were quite distinct but mutually sympathetic groups. In all cases the PS, by policies and deliberate overtures, successfully established itself as the party closest to their goals and most likely to win their votes.

There was certainly nothing inevitable about the rallying of feminists to the Socialist banner. The feminist movement, a loose network of organisations and individuals striving to enhance women's rights and political consciousness, had hopes of sweeping reforms when Giscard d'Estaing appointed first a 'special delegate' and later a junior minister 'for the feminine condition'. The illusions were soon shattered and Mitterrand attempted to outbid his predecessor by promising, and creating, a ministry for women's rights. This title and the choice of a dynamic minister, Yvette Roudy, suggested a more radical approach. Within a year of taking office the Socialist Government proposed changing the municipal electoral law to ensure that women candidates occupied one-third of the places on all party lists. It was prevented from implementing this measure only by a ruling from the all-male Constitutional Council. The new ministry gradually built up contacts with the feminist movement, and the PS and Mitterrand gathered the electoral fruits.

SOS-racisme, an organisation founded to oppose the FN and to campaign for equal rights for immigrants, grew rapidly after 1984. Its symbol, an open hand, and its slogan, 'Don't touch my mate', were soon widely known. It won massive support from young people of all ethnic origins, but especially from the *beurs* (North African immigrants' children with French citizenship). Many immigrants and *beurs* had already shown Socialist preferences before 1981, in part because both the RPR–UDF coalition and the PCF had gained the reputation of hostility to immigrants. The Socialists' liberal measures on illegal immigrants in 1981 won further support, as did the authorisation of local radio stations (*Radio Beur* soon became very popular, and not just with the *beurs*). The PS links with the CFDT also helped, since the concern of the CFDT in organising and protecting unskilled immigrant workers, especially during the strikes at Citroën–Peugeot in 1983, contrasted very markedly with the indifference of the Communist-dominated CGT unions, which strove to defend the interests of their French skilled workers. PS governments have certainly not solved all problems faced by *beurs* in education, housing and employment, and support for immigrant rights has often seemed aimed at dividing the parties of the Right as much as aiding the immigrants. The Socialists have often discussed (but done little towards actually enacting) voting rights for immigrants in local elections, although some PS mayors have experimented with consultative committees to represent local immigrant communities. Nonetheless when Pasqua introduced tighter immigration controls, the PS led the opposition. In 1988 Harlem Désir, the charismatic leader of *SOS-racisme*, openly supported Mitterrand, and on the night of his re-election the celebrations were often led by *beur* activists. Furthermore, the Rocard Government soon modified the immigration law and circulars of its predecessor. The PS thus remained the party with the strongest links to the *beurs*.

The Socialists also made great efforts to establish close links with the *UNEF-ID* student organisation, which provided the main leaders of the 1986 strikes, sit-ins and demonstrations. These led the Chirac Government to scrap its university reform plans and the minister responsible for the project to resign after a student had been killed by a police baton. The student leaders were openly pro-Socialist, and the PS in turn attacked the government's project and its handling of the demonstrations. Student demonstrators hailed the president as their hero. In due course Mitterrand coopted Isabelle Thomas, an articulate, photogenic student leader, to his 1988 campaign team. Hence, whilst in 1986 the RPR–UDF had overtaken the PS in winning the support of younger voters, by 1988 the situation had been reversed.

Indeed, the Socialist net was being cast increasingly wide. The president's proposal for a new wealth tax to provide a guaranteed minimum income was designed to appeal to those who supported the winter soup kitchens, *les restaurants du cœur*, created by the comedian Coluche to feed the 'new poor' of the age of industrial restructuring. Rocard stressed that his proposed 'opening' of the governing coalition was not just aimed at Centrist politicians but also at any elements of 'civil society' not actually hostile to the PS. His new ministers included Bernard Kouchner, leader of an international humanitarian doctors' movement, Roger Fauroux, a successful industrialist, and Pierre Arpaillange, a respected magistrate who had previously worked with four Centre–Right justice ministers in the 1960s. Whilst this policy was not a complete success, it represented a real contrast with previous governments and an effort towards widening the social coalition of the PS.

In short, it was this ability of the Socialists, through social and political 'networking', to adapt to changing ideological and social conditions in the electorate and to adopt new social movements which allowed them to retain their dominance within the party system. The failures of the RPR, UDF and PCF in this respect facilitated the electoral success of both the PS and the FN. The breakthrough of Le Pen's party, however, depended on proportional representation in the 1984 European elections, and in the 1986 parliamentary and regional elections.

The Parties and the Changing Institutional Environment

The evolution of the parties and the party system was in part determined by the changes in electoral systems and institutions. In particular, the introduction of proportional representation for some, but not all, elections has been crucial. As Bartolini (1984) emphasised, institutional constraints, and especially electoral rules, had played a key role in streamlining the party system into two blocs and four parties before 1981. Since then changes to electoral systems considerably reduced these pressures, and allowed the PCF to survive, the FN to grow and prosper, and the Greens to gain seats on municipal councils and in Strasburg.

Before 1979, there had been a high degree of consistency between the presidential, parliamentary and municipal electoral systems. All involved second ballots with restricted access, which encouraged the parties to form alliances at least for the second rounds. The presidential rules, which allowed only the two front-runners at the first ballot to contest the second, pushed the parties to line up into two blocs. Similarly, in parliamentary elections the raising of the threshold of first-ballot votes needed to qualify as a candidate at the second ballot (from 5 per cent in 1958 to 10 per cent in 1967 and to 12.5 per cent in 1976) increased the pressure on the parties to form into broad coalitions. For local elections the 1964 law provided a 'winner-takes-all' system for the second ballot in larger towns, thus encouraging local as well as national coalition-building. In short, all these electoral systems penalised isolated and small parties, especially if geographically evenly spread, and stimulated coalition formation and centripetal competition between coalitions.

The first element of incoherence was the adoption of proportional representation for the 1979 European elections by Giscard d'Estaing. In the 1984 European elections the FN, by clearing the 5 per cent hurdle, became the main beneficiary of this proportional system. The Greens followed in 1989. In 1982, the municipal electoral system was also modified by the introduction of an element of proportionality. Hence, small parties which refused to form coalitions were no longer doomed. In 1985 the Socialists further complicated electoral structures by a triple innovation. A single-ballot, proportional representation system was introduced for the 1986 parliamentary elections, the same system was adopted for the first-ever elections of regional councils and the two elections were scheduled for the same day. The 96 *départements* were taken as the multi-member constituencies for both elections, a 5 per cent threshold for representation was fixed, the 'highest average' principle was chosen for the distribution of seats and the membership of the National Assembly was increased to 577. The result was a curious mixture, as many rural *départements* with small populations were given only two or three seats. RPR–UDF leaders, however, condemned the reform as an attempt to reduce their chances of winning an overall majority by allowing the FN to win seats. The election system itself became a campaign issue and the RPR and UDF promised to restore the old system if they won. The new rules did allow the FN into the Assembly and the Communists to survive, but did not prevent the Centre–Right from getting a majority. An early act of the Chirac Government was to restore the single-member constituency, second-ballot system with a 12.5 per cent threshold, as before 1986. The number of seats was kept at 577, so many of the new constituencies could not have the same boundaries as in 1981. Opportunities for electoral gerrymandering were not entirely neglected. There were no changes of rules for the municipal or regional elections, so the 1989 municipal elections were contested under the semi-proportional rules and the 1989 European elections under proportional representation.

The difficulties for political parties created by these inconsistent changes were that elections were too numerous and frequent, whilst different systems encouraged different, sometimes conflicting competitive strategies. Small and extremist parties, the victims of the coalition-building pressures of the two-ballot, single-member (or list), winner-takes-all rules of the pre-1979 period, could now not only survive but also win seats in proportional elections. They could also hope to draw concessions from big parties by fighting first ballots of presidential and parliamentary elections with no hope of winning but simply to show their hold on a proportion of the voters.

This tampering with electoral rules has been complemented by other institutional changes, the most important of which was the choice of Mitterrand, Chirac and Giscard d'Estaing to cooperate

in *cohabitation* between 1986 and 1988. The relative smooth operation of that system of government and the satisfaction of the
public, as shown by opinion polls, meant that non-coincident
majorities became a real alternative to the presidential, dominant-
party system of the 1960s and 1970s. In 1988 Mitterrand expressed
his preference for a sympathetic and supportive majority, but could
not argue that a 'presidential majority' was vitally necessary to
avoid chaos. The RPR and UDF even proposed a new bout of
cohabitation. The Rocard Government, however, showed that
stable and effective government may also be provided by a Parliament with no majority.

A second type of institutional tampering was the introduction
of European elections by Giscard d'Estaing in 1977. The decision
to elect the members of the European Parliament by universal
suffrage had a much greater impact on domestic party competition
than on European integration. There were very few issues on
which Europe-wide coalitions could form so election campaigns,
in France as elsewhere, were fought as purely national contests.
Their inconsequential nature made these elections the ideal channel for the FN and Greens to establish national legitimacy simply
by getting a large share of the votes and a number of seats in
Strasbourg. Party competition in 'irresponsible' European elections
was thus disconnected from that in presidential and parliamentary
elections, where the results determine who governs and responsible
voting is at a premium.

Other institutional changes also affected party competition. The
imposed reduction (to two 'important' posts) of the accumulation
of elective offices (*cumul de mandats*) weakens the nationalising,
disciplining effect on parties of participation by deputies in local
councils at all levels. In 1989, party leaders stressed that the
municipal elections were *not* a test of national politics and opinion
polls showed that most voters believed that local politics in 1989
was about local men and issues. The decline of national party
discipline and differentiation between national and local party
elites was seen in the triumphs of such dissidents as Vigouroux
(ex-PS) at Marseilles and Jarry (ex-PCF) at Le Mans. Finally, the
1988 law on the public financing of political parties has also had an
impact on the parties. Its net result was to facilitate the continued
operations of small parties.

The overall impact of these institutional changes has been to
reinforce the conflicting pressures created by the electoral system
innovations: the reduction of the nationalising, moderating, disciplining and pro-coalition pressures of the first two decades of the
Fifth Republic.

Conclusions: Changing Parties and a Hybrid Party System

The last decade has witnessed major changes in the parties and party system. Relations between parties and governmental institutions have been profoundly modified. Alternation in power now poses few problems, coincident majorities are no longer a precondition for government, and even the possibility of minority government creates no panic. There is still a dominant party, the PS (thanks to the divisions of its opponents), but it no longer possesses the 'court' party status of pure presidential legitimacy. The PCF has moved into a 'semi-ghetto' position and, after losing half of its 1978 support, no longer inspires hatred or fear. The FN in 1989 retained enough support to provoke repulsion and weaken the RPR and UDF who might otherwise win power. In 1981 the UDF parties survived in federation despite the defeat of Giscard d'Estaing, but they seemed unable to remain together in the conditions of 1990.

Parties still share some common characteristics, but are also very different in nature. All claim to be mass-membership participatory bodies, but there is no common definition of membership and very little similarity in formal structures. All parties contest all elections but, whilst some retain traditional goals of presidential and parliamentary coalition-building, others seek merely an impact on opinion or a share of power in local or regional politics. The discourse of major parties has changed markedly: Socialists no longer promise swiftly to end capitalism, and the Centre–Right has toned down its 1986 market liberalism. The anti-capitalist and anti-immigrant diatribes of the PCF and FN are still heard, but even their own voters do not take them too seriously.

This schizophrenia of parties and the party system has been explained in many ways, but theories stressing the importance of institutional changes seem the most plausible. Economic, social, technological, ideological and international factors have been influential, but institutions do matter. The alacrity of presidents to modify their own role and of parliamentary majorities to tamper with new, inconsistent electoral systems have been key factors in this complex evolution of party competition.

3

Public Opinion and Electoral Change

FRANÇOIS PLATONE

The 1989 European elections brought to a close a year in which the French electorate had been called out to vote no fewer than eight times: twice each for the presidential, parliamentary and municipal elections and once each for the November referendum on New Caledonia and the European Parliament poll. After all that it was hardly surprising that the normally civic French were showing signs of voter fatigue. But there were also indications that other, more profound changes might be taking place in the attitudes and behaviour of the electorate. Was a new phase opening characterised by volatile if not capricious voting behaviour and a real modification of the long-term trends? Certainly there was change: the re-election of Mitterrand and the return of the Socialists to a governable position of minority dominance in the Assembly meant the third major change of party in power in eight years. Furthermore, the 1981 elections had not only ended the 23 years of continuous electoral domination of the Right, but had also marked a dramatic fall in support for the PCF. The 1984 European elections saw the rise of the FN, and the 1986 parliamentary elections confirmed this and brought the first FN deputies into the National Assembly. In the 1989 municipal and European elections, however, yet another new party, the Greens, emerged as a sizeable force. The aim of this chapter is to examine whether or not an analysis of the elections of the late 1980s indicates that existing accepted interpretations of voting behaviour since the late 1950s are still valid. It will argue that only a modest re-appraisal is needed and that most long-term trends identified during the 1970s were still in evidence in 1989.

Lond-Term Trends in Voting Behaviour since 1958

The Nationalisation of Politics

Since 1958, there has been a clear trend towards an increasing national uniformity of approach by parties and voters and a sub-sequent decline of diversity in local as compared to national elections. Local elections, referendums and European polls alike tended to be treated as national confidence tests for the governing and opposition coalitions, or even as mid-term elections. As shown in the previous chapter, this trend reflected the evolution of economic, social and cultural conditions as well as the impact of changes in national institutions, and notably of electoral systems.

The Development of a Two-Bloc Electorate in the Political System

The two-bloc electorate is founded on the traditional cleavage between Left and Right, which has been transformed by party politics and electoral tactics into two alliances each in search of a majority (Lancelot, 1983). The two alliances occupy almost the whole electoral spectrum and thus frustrate attempts to form an independent centre group. The Left–Right division was strongest in the mid-1970s and especially in 1974, when at the presidential election the Giscardian coalition – in alliance with the inheritors of Gaullism – mopped up the last survivors of the 'centrist opposition' before forming the UDF in 1978. The political system had at that time its neatest two-fold form with four political formations arranged in two pairs of similar electoral strength.

The traditional division between Left and Right is reflected in geography, religion and social class. A long-established electoral map shows the French Right as dominant in the north-west (especially away from the coast), in the east (notably in Alsace and Lorraine), in the south and east of the Massif Central, as well as in Paris and its western suburbs. The Left is traditionally strongest in the north, the south-west, the Midi and the Paris suburbs. The electoral map for the second round of the presidential election of 1974 (Map 2) gives a good picture of this classical territorial structure of the vote. The geographical Left–Right cleavage is influenced by the religious cleavage (Map 3), which opinion polls confirm as one of the fundamental bases of division, whether of views or of vote, a conservative inclination being very strongly related to the degree of religious practice. Social status appears as the other classical determinant of voting behaviour: Left-wing voters are more frequently young, male and wage-earning (especially workers and public-sector employees) than Right-wing voters.

Change and Evolution in the Major Trends

The traditional representation of the ideological divides has been subject to political change and social evolution over the last 30 years. In politics the Gaullist phenomenon in its original version (1958–69) upset the previous arrangement of electoral forces. The vote for de Gaulle did not coincide exactly with the social and geographic frontiers of Right-wing voting, and made large inroads into the sectors which were usually the province of the Left, notably in the urban working-class of northern France, where Gaullism established itself at the expense of the Communists. But the successors and inheritors of the General have now returned to a more traditional conservative base. More lastingly, three basic movements have affected French society: dechristianisation (or at least the decline in religious practice), the growth of the middle-class salariat (middle management, technicians and white-collar workers); and the Leftward trend of women voters. These three phenomena are in principle so favourable to the Left that the 'Rightward vote' of a predominantly 'Left-wing France' in 1978 could be seen as a paradox.

A Relatively High Level of Electoral Participation

In spite of the increased frequency of elections in the Fifth Republic and only a modest level of interest in politics and party identification, electoral participation is high. Thus, in 1978, 38 per cent of French citizens questioned in a public opinion poll declared themselves to have 'no interest at all' or 'very little interest' in politics (and 27 per cent 'little interest'), while 50 per cent said they were normally 'not a close supporter' or 'not a supporter' of any political party (Capdevielle *et al.*, 1981). However, before 1988 the abstention rate was rarely more than 20 per cent of registered electors at presidential or parliamentary elections. The number of people who never vote is much less than that, taking into account irregular voting patterns. Participation rates are higher when the poll has great influence on the exercise of power at national level. Participation is highest for presidential elections

Départements with a majority vote for Giscard d'Estaing

Départements with a majority vote for Mitterrand

MAP 2   *Left-Right voting by* département *in 1974: voting in the second round of the presidential election*

but the trend towards a common national pattern of political life is bringing about a harmonisation of participation rates for the different types of election. The elections of national importance which have particularly high absention rates are the polls which follow a crucial ballot (such as the parliamentary election after the 1962 referendum and the parliamentary election after the 1981 presidential election), or where there is no candidate for one of

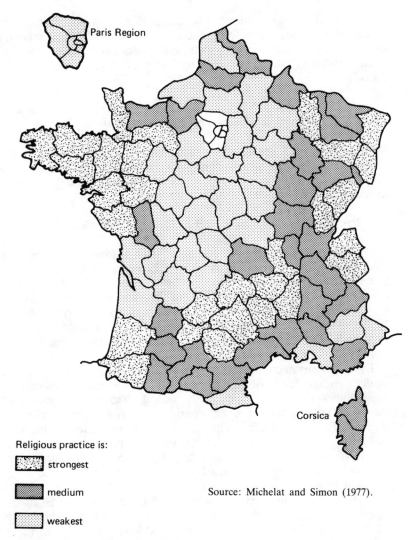

Paris Region

Corsica

Religious practice is:

▦ strongest

█ medium

▒ weakest

Source: Michelat and Simon (1977).

MAP 3 *Religious attendance by* département

the major parties (for example, there was no candidate of the Left
in the second round of the 1969 presidential election).

Apart from the type of poll or its national importance, the
factors which have traditionally affected the level of participation
are of a sociological nature. The highest rates of abstention occur

in urban areas and among the categories least integrated into
ociety: the young, the elderly, the unemployed and, until recently,
women. Like Left–Right orientation, gender has since the late
1970s ceased to be a distinguishing factor in electoral participation
rates.

The First Alternation of Government and Cohabitation

Mitterrand's first presidential term (May 1981–May 1988) was
characterised by four phenomena which introduced important innovations into French politics, as much in the institutional system as
in ideological views or voting behaviour.

The Return of the Left to Power (May 1981–March 1986)

When François Mitterrand conferred the leadership of his first
government on Pierre Mauroy, it was 22 years since the Socialists
had exercised ministerial responsibility (in the de Gaulle Government, June 1958–January 1959) and 24 years since they had led
a government (the Guy Mollet Government, February 1956–May
1957). As for the Communists, who were given four ministries,
they had been permanently excluded from government since May
1947.

   The 'opposition mentality' which burdens the French Left, their
leaders' inexperience of government, the high expectations of Left-
wing voters and their hopes for a radical change in policies were
soon confronted with the economic crisis and stifling economic
climate. The government's change to 'economic realism', and even
austerity, brought in its wake the departure of the Communist
ministers in 1984, disillusion with politics and an ideological re-
orientation of a large section of the electorate. The success of the
Right in the local elections (the departmental elections of 1982
and 1985 and municipal elections of 1983) and at the European
elections of 1984 expressed the discontent of voters disappointed
by socialism. More generally, the modifications in government
policy and priorities encouraged a resurgence of liberal ideology,
a lowering of expectations with regard to political power and a
certain withdrawal into private values. New areas of ideological
consensus (foreign policy, institutions, the market economy, the
value of enterprise and the priority to be accorded to the major
economic constraints) started to emerge in public opinion, except
for the Communists and the extreme Left.

   The Left–Right cleavage nevertheless has not been erased and the crisis in the summer of 1984 over private schools showed the persistent sensitivity of one of the most traditional issues of French political debate. Even if certain dividing lines are tending to fade, new issues are emerging (such as immigration and security) which add to those advanced in the 1970s concerning 'social problems' and 'cultural liberalism', so that a more authoritarian Right now confronts a Left which is more permissive in matters of education, sexuality and the treatment of minor criminal offences. What we are really observing is a renewal and shifting of the political and ideological battlefront between Left and Right rather than a disappearance of cleavage.

Cohabitation (March 1986–May 1988)

Cohabitation is another innovation in the institutional practices of the Fifth Republic. After the victory of the Right in the 1986 parliamentary elections, a Left-wing president and a government supported by a Right-wing parliamentary majority had to coexist for the first time. The change of political power in 1986 (like that of 1981) was followed by disillusion. The confrontation of the ideological discourse of liberalism and the expectations which it aroused with the realities of the crisis and the absence of any miracle cure for the crucial problem of unemployment produced 'voters disappointed by liberalism' and, more generally, deepened scepticism about the results obtainable from changing the political leadership. The day after the presidential election of 1988, 52 per cent of people questioned by SOFRES considered that the result of that election would have 'practically no effect' on their everyday lives or their standard of living. This opinion was shared by only 27 per cent of people interviewed after the presidential election of 1981. The scepticism was even more widespread after the parliamentary elections (67 per cent of people interviewed, as opposed to 31 per cent in 1981).

At the same time, the more or less seemly functioning of institutional *cohabitation* removed some of the drama from political confrontation and consolidated consensus. It also modified the image of the President of the Republic, who acquired the aura of a neutral referee from which he benefited in 1988, while at the same time being associated in the public mind with the positive aspects of government performance.

The Decline of the Communist Party

The brutal and unexpected drop in electoral support for the PCF at the presidential election of 1981 (20–22 per cent of votes cast between 1959 and 1979, then 15.4 per cent for Georges Marchais in 1981) inaugurated a period of sharp decline for the party (16.1 per cent in the parliamentary elections of 1981, 11.1 per cent in the European elections of 1984, and 9.6 per cent at the parliamentary elections of 1986). The PCF, which had been the largest party in France throughout the Fourth Republic with more than 25 per cent of votes, received its first major reverse in 1958 when de Gaulle came to power, and it has never recovered. The setback of 1981 therefore occurred within a long-term downward trend but gave the decline a dramatic and probably irreversible impetus. The municipal elections of 1989 showed a continued drop in Communist support in spite of the PCF's claims of some recovery. The PCF party list in the European elections of 1989 received only 7.7 per cent of votes cast.

The circumstances of this decline allow little prospect of real recovery and show all the signs of sclerosis in activist or electoral support for the PCF. The regions where the Communist vote is receding least are predominantly rural, relatively old-fashioned and undynamic (in economic, demographic and social terms). The electoral decline of the PCF is greatest among young electors. Its capacity to resist is mainly linked with its power bases in municipal government – which are becoming fewer – and support from some elected *notables* (local leaders) with strong personal positions. Finally, the CGT (the PCF-led trade union movement), its natural working-class constituency, a prime element and relay of Communist influence, is also in persistent decline (Platone, 1986).

The decline of the PCF is blamed essentially on its non-adaptation to social change, its hidebound ideology and errors in strategy which have built up in the absence of any real political project. It constitutes the major modification in the last decade to the system of electoral and party forces, and is the concomitant to the steadily increasing hegemony of the PS within the Left.

The Electoral Rise of the FN

Until the beginning of the 1980s the French extreme Right had minimal electoral impact, if we discount the Extreme Right surge in 1956 (11.7 per cent) and the demonstrations of support for *Algérie française* in the 1960s (9.3 per cent 'No' votes in the April 1962 referendum; 5.3 per cent of votes for Tixier-Vignancour (the presidential candidate of the Extreme Right) in the presidential election of 1965). In the presidential election of 1974 Jean-Marie Le Pen obtained only 0.8 per cent of votes, and in 1981 he could not even obtain the signatures required to qualify for candidature.

After some early indications at local elections and by-elections in 1983, the FN, founded by Le Pen in 1972, gained its first success at the national level in the European elections of 1984 with 11.1 per cent of the vote. This success was brought about by the radicalisation of some Right-wing voters who were hostile to the Socialist Government and regarded the UDF–RPR common list, led by Simone Veil, as too 'Centrist' and moderate. It was also based on the response in urban areas, which were seriously affected by the economic crisis, to one of the themes of the FN campaign: an attack on immigrants based on the fusion of three ideas: immigration, 'insecurity' and unemployment.

The geographical distribution of the FN vote, strongly concentrated in the eastern half of France (and especially along the south-east coast), as well as the social structure of its electorate (much more male, urban, young and cross-class than those of the RPR or UDF), do not correlate in any way with the supporters of the traditional Right or with a resurgence of the extreme Right movements of the 1950s and 1960s. On the other hand, the resemblance of its geographic distribution to that of immigrants, as well as the motivation of FN voters as stated in exit polls, establishes a link between the vote for Le Pen's party and the immigration phenomenon. This link must not, however, be taken at face value. The correlation between the FN vote and the presence of immigrants – apart from the fact that it is much weaker when the figures are broken down more closely – relates in fact to an urban crisis, to the deterioration of housing, health and education services, and to anxieties expressed subjectively and focused through the imaginary prism of immigrant rejection.

The *département* elections of 1985, and especially the parliamentary elections of 1986, confirmed the existence of the FN as a new electoral force (9.8 per cent in the parliamentary elections). In 1986 social protest was more prominent than specifically political motivation in the make-up of the FN electorate. The consequence was a relative proletarianisation of this electorate, while some of the 'bourgeois' voters nearer the UDF, and especially the RPR (who had been won over to the FN in 1984), returned to their party of origin in 1986.

The simultaneous decline of the PCF and the electoral rise of the FN led many people to think that a large part of the votes lost by the Communists had gone to the FN. In fact, even though the FN did receive support from some former Communist voters – it had gained from all the parties – this support seems marginal and made only a modest contribution to the success of Le Pen. FN voters came mostly from the Right-wing parties (especially the RPR), from new voters and previous abstainers as well as, in lesser measure, the non-Communist Left. There is nevertheless a relationship between the weakening of the PCF and the surge of the FN. The FN benefits from the collapse of the social networks, notably at municipal level, which the PCF used to organise but no longer has the activist means to lead, or the institutional power to control.

The Presidential Elections of 24 April and 8 May 1988

As in 1981, the Right-wing parties, in spite of winning a plurality of votes in the first round, lost the 1988 election as a consequence of their internal divisions, although these were different in character from those in 1981.

The Candidates and the Campaign

On the Left, François Mitterrand was certain of participating in the second round on account of the Socialist predominance over the Communists. He announced his candidature very late (on 22 March) blocking once again Michel Rocard's path to the presidential contest. From the start Mitterrand adopted a strategy of posing as the catch-all candidate, profiting from his position as outgoing President and the mastery he had shown in managing *cohabitation*. The only possible aspirations for the other Left-wing candidates were to show the flag and use the election as a platform for their views. Trotskyist candidates (Arlette Laguiller and the newcomer Pierre Boussel) are accustomed to this role, while the PCF's representative, André Lajoinie – one defeat was enough for Georges Marchais – was used, without much illusion, to limit the damage by presenting himself as the defender of the rejected and the only real candidate of the Left. Pierre Juquin, the final Left-wing candidate, just expelled from the PCF for trying to organise its renovation, tested the ground for a new mobilisation of forces uniting disillusioned Communists, Trotskyist militants and supporters of the 'new' issues (such as ecology and anti-racism).

On the Right, the situation was much less clear, with a real American-style 'primary' taking place between the Prime Minister, Jacques Chirac, and the ex-Prime Minister, Raymond Barre. Their competition was, however, affected by the presence of Le Pen, which weighed heavily on the campaign; not so much because of any chance he had of winning but more because of the arbitration role his voters would play and because the other candidates needed to choose their position on the FN carefully. In this Right-wing competition, the trump cards held by Chirac related to his position as Prime Minister, to the support of a party organisation – the RPR – of which he was the uncontested leader, to the goodwill of a large part of the press (especially the Hersant group) and to his image as an efficient and dynamic politician. Yet this image cast an ominous shadow, since its authoritarian side worried moderate voters.

Barre was able to profit from popularity in public opinion and the view that he would be a competent and worthy president, little compromised by party politics. But the other side of the coin was that he had no real party apparatus to support his campaign. The UDF, and particularly its PR component, (whose leader, François Léotard, was nearer to Chirac than to Barre), was far from being solid behind him. The press and the opinion polls were much more dubious about his chances than those of his rival. Finally, his campaign, launched too late and not really focused on his potential electorate, was a failure.

As for the ecologist, Antoine Waechter, practically unknown at the national level, he intended (like his predecessors) to place himself outside the 'traditional' political debate by attacking both Left and Right, on whom he urged proposals for democratising society and fighting unemployment as well as the conventional ecological themes.

On the whole, the campaign was characterised by moderation and by a lessening of real ideological confrontation, the successive changes of political power in 1981 and 1986 with their respective 'disappointments' having made the promises of any party and the credibility of a choice between two models of society seem less convincing. In the event, the media concentrated their attention on the personalities and images of the candidates and on the development of the campaign itself, giving more importance to the competitors' tactics than to their ideas. In this context the opinion polls, more numerous than ever, acted like a daily barometer reading and, without influencing the voters noticeably, affected the behaviour of the candidates.

The Results

The votes collected by the Right-wing candidates (50.8 per cent of the votes cast in metropolitan France) were clearly greater than those of the Left (45.3 per cent). Although the proportion was less unfavourable to the Left than at the parliamentary elections of 1986 (54.7 per cent compared to 44.0 per cent), it was more unfavourable than on the first round of the presidential election in 1981 (48.8 per cent as opposed to 47.2 per cent). The two candidates who qualified for the second round were Mitterrand and Chirac, with Barre coming third. The surprise came from the high score of Le Pen (14.4 per cent: see Table 3.1).

TABLE 3.1   *Results of the 1988 Presidential Election*
(for the whole of France)

	First Round		Second Round	
	Votes	% registered voters	Votes	% registered voters
Registered voters	38 179 118		38 168 869	
Votes cast	31 059 300	81.35	32 085 071	84.06
Valid votes	30 436 744	79.72	30 923 249	81.02
	Votes	% valid votes	Votes	% valid votes
Arlette Laguiller	606 201	1.99		
Pierre Boussel	116 874	0.38		
André Lajoinie	2 056 261	6.76		
Pierre Juquin	639 133	2.10		
François Mitterrand	10 381 332	34.11	16 704 279	54.02
Antoine Waechter	1 149 897	3.78		
Raymond Barre	5 035 144	16.54		
Jacques Chirac	6 075 160	19.96	14 218 970	45.98
Jean-Marie Le Pen	4 376 742	14.38		

Source: Constitutional Council.

The result obtained by Mitterrand constituted, as a percentage of registered voters, the best score ever for French socialism and, as a percentage of votes cast, the second best score (the best being in the 1981 parliamentary elections). The outgoing President improved by almost 6 per cent on the combined score achieved in 1981 by Mitterrand himself and the Radical Left. In 1981 the outgoing President, Valéry Giscard d'Estaing, lost 5 per cent compared to his result of 1974. So, unlike his predecessor, Mitterrand did not suffer from having been in power and, despite the defeat of 1986, he was able to modify and thereby restore his image.

This development was accompanied by a significant change in the profile of groups voting for Mitterrand, both geographically (with advances in northern and western France, especially in traditionally conservative areas) and socially (with increased support from the young, women and senior managers), which gave a catchall dimension to the Socialist candidate. The development confirmed the hegemony of the Socialists within the Left and was the result of picking up the votes of former Communist supporters as much as from winning over Right-wing voters. The score of André Lajoinie (6.8 per cent) constitutes the lowest-ever result for French communism. It confirmed the trends observed in 1986: a withdrawal to the rural bastions of central France, and a deepening disaffection of young voters (see Map 4).

Chirac succeeded in beating Barre but, with less than 20 per cent of votes in the first round, he seemed to be in a difficult position for the second round. It was the first time that a second-round candidate in the presidential election had had such a low first-round score. He was therefore totally dependent on attracting the votes of Barre and Le Pen supporters, who had conflicting expectations. As the principal victim of the surge of votes for Le Pen, Chirac was not able to present himself in electoral terms as the leader of the Right. His electoral base, already modest in terms of size, was qualitatively mediocre. It was founded on personal clientelist relations, especially in Corrèze (which Chirac represented in Parliament) and in Paris, of which he was Mayor. Sociologically and politically, the Chirac electorate is typical of traditional conservatism.

Barre, beaten by Chirac, was supported by an electorate with the geographical base of the moderate Right but which differed from the Chirac electorate in having certain modern characteristics, as much in the sociological sphere (the young and the middle-class salariat) as politically (an interest in education, the economy and Europe). It also differed in that it was much more hostile to the FN and its ideas. Even so, could this group of voters be regarded as evidence for 'the persistence of a Centrist temperament' which would open the way to an organised centre group independent from the rest of the Right?

Le Pen's score was the most striking result of the first round. It denoted a marked increase in support and a national spread of his appeal. His progress was particularly marked in the urban areas of eastern France (especially in Alsace) but also in the normally moderate rural departments where support had pre-

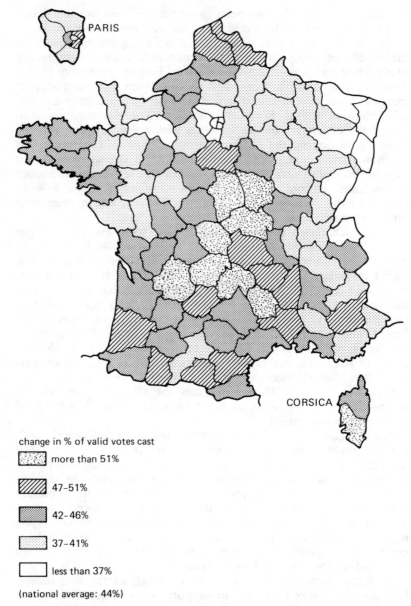

change in % of valid votes cast

more than 51%

47–51%

42–46%

37–41%

less than 37%

(national average: 44%)

MAP 4   *Decline in Communist party vote by* département, *1981–8:*
voting in the first round of the presidential election

viously been thin. The growth in votes came from diverse social and political groups, which emphasises the heterogeneity of FN voters, mobilised by the old themes of anti-immigration, insecurity and unemployment and the new ones of anti-Europe, anti-tax and anti-state.

In all, compared with the first round of the 1981 presidential election, that of 1988 witnessed quite significant changes in the distribution of votes. The Left was dominated by the Socialists, the Right was split and there was a new political movement on the extreme Right.

In the second round Mitterrand came in well ahead of his opponent (54 per cent as against 46 per cent). The consequences which had been foreseen of the first-round split within the Right brought about the defeat of Chirac, who did not manage to attract enough supporters from both Barre and Le Pen. A fifth of Barre's voters and a third of Le Pen's declined to support the prime minister. More of these non-Chirac voters gave their vote to the president than abstained, thus ensuring his clear victory since the Left-wing voters remained faithful and two-thirds of the ecological vote also went to Mitterrand (see Table 3.2).

TABLE 3.2 *Transfer of votes from first to second round of the 1988 presidential election (first-round votes = 100%)*

	Vote in second round		
	Mitterrand	Chirac	Abstained, or did not reply
André Lajoinie	87	2	11
Extreme Left	80	6	14
François Mitterrand	98	1	1
Antoine Waechter	68	16	16
Raymond Barre	14	81	5
Jacques Chirac	1	97	2
Jean-Marie Le Pen	19	65	16
Abstained or did not reply	23	18	59

Mitterrand beat Chirac in an overwhelming majority of *départements* (77 out of 96). The electoral map for the Socialist candidate (Map 5) shows both the persistence of the geographic structure of the Left (although weakened in the south-east) and the national spread of the president's vote. Mitterrand's ability to attract votes

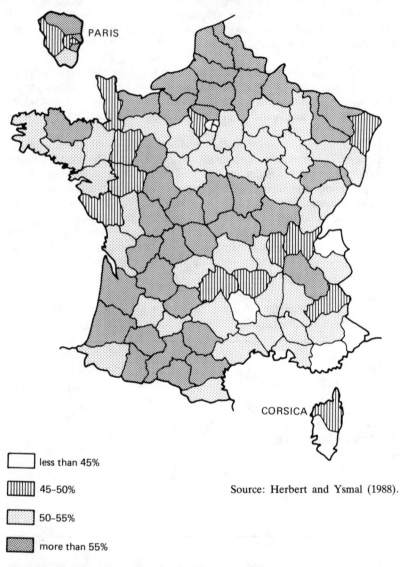

less than 45%

45–50%   Source: Herbert and Ysmal (1988).

50–55%

more than 55%

MAP 5   *Voting for Mitterrand by* département, *8 May 1988*

was enhanced by an increasingly tough campaign, dramatic in its final days (gendarmes held hostage by New Caledonian autonomists were liberated with much bloodshed) and by a fear of the extreme Right. Unlike previous experience, it was the Left-wing candidate, now relieved of the Communist albatross, who provided more reassurance than the Right-wing candidate. On 11 May 1981, the day after Mitterrand's first election as President, prices on the Bourse tumbled; on 9 May 1988, the day after his re-election, prices rose by almost a point (Capdevielle, 1988).

The Parliamentary Elections of 5 June and 12 June 1988

The elections were noteworthy for the record number of abstentions in parliamentary elections this century. In the first round the voters split fairly equally between Left and Right (see Table 3.3). Unlike 1981, victory in the presidential election did not help the PS in the parliamentary elections. The PS suffered from a confused campaign, loosely focused around the idea of 'opening towards the centre'; from a lack of strong commitment by Mitterrand to the PS; and from the demobilising effect of opinion polls and forecasts which in the aftermath of the presidential election were forecasting a 'pink high tide'.

TABLE 3.3 *Results of the 1988 National Assembly elections: first round (the whole of France)*

	Votes	% of registered votes
Registered voters	37 945 582	
Votes cast	24 944 792	65.74
Valid votes cast	24 425 095	64.37

	Votes	% of valid votes
PCF	2 765 761	11.32
Extreme Left	89 065	0.36
PS	8 493 702	34.77
Radical Left	272 316	1.11
'Presidential majority'	403 690	1.65
Ecologists and unclassifiable	104 810	0.43
UDF	4 519 459	18.50
RPR	4 687 047	19.19
Various Right	697 272	2.85
FN	2 359 528	9.66
Various extreme Right	32 445	0.13

Source: Ministry of the Interior.

The PCF experienced a substantial recovery from Lajoinie's score (it polled 11.3 per cent), less substantial compared with its 1986 result (9.7 per cent). However, this advance could not easily be interpreted as the beginning of a real return to its former level. It was due essentially to the *notable* effect which benefited outgoing deputies and local leaders, systematically chosen as their candidates by the PCF. The moderate Right benefited from their *notables* but also from having single RPR–UDF candidates standing as *Union du Rassemblement et du Centre* candidates. They thereby recovered some of the voters they had lost to Mitterrand and Le Pen. The vote for the FN fell back to approximately its level and distribution of 1986 but, while in 1986 proportional representation had allowed the FN to obtain 35 seats, the return in 1988 to majority voting in two rounds practically deprived it of representation in the National Assembly. Only one deputy was elected and she was excluded from the FN a few months later for having disagreed with Le Pen.

Generally, June 1988 marked a return to 'classical French voting' giving a plurality of seats (not an absolute majority as in 1981) to the PS, after universal two-bloc confrontations in the second round. It also showed the limitations of the Centre's hopes of independence. Even though the CDS formed with other 'Barristes' an autonomous parliamentary group, the *Union du Centre*, the two-bloc logic which has dominated elections affected Parliament just as strongly as it affected the subsequent local elections (for the *départements* in September 1988 and the municipal elections in March 1989), although the June 1989 European elections, using proportional representation, allowed the re-emergence of a Centrist list. The European elections confirmed the FN's place in French politics and witnessed the entry of French ecologists to the European Parliament at the expense of the Socialists.

The Lessons of the 1988 Elections

With the sharp increase in Le Pen's vote, the division in the moderate right and the geographic shift in votes for Mitterrand, the first round of the presidential election had suggested that change was about to occur in the alignment of political forces and views. The second round, and the parliamentary election in particular, modified this impression. The results showed the persistence of opposition between Left and Right, reinforced by the bipolarising effects of these elections. Certainly the transfer to Mitterrand of some of those who had voted for Barre and the ideological difference between Chirac's and Barre's supporters is evidence of some heterogeneity among 'those on the Right' and of the absence of an insuperable divide between the two main poles of French political life. But, for the most part, the funda-mental cleavage persists. The voting analysis for the second round of the presidential election (Table 3.4) clearly shows – as does the analysis for the parliamentary election – the role which social and cultural status still continue to play in the choices voters make. Although the analysis confirms that the Left-wing candidate is likely from now on to receive at least as many votes from women as from men, it can also be seen that a large majority of wage-earners, and especially factory workers, still prefer the Left-wing candidate, while two-thirds of the self-employed (farmers, entrepreneurs, shopkeepers, artisans, liberal professionals) voted for Chirac. In the same way, age and religious affiliation are still influential in determining the distribution of votes.

As for the ideological cleavage, its continued existence was also confirmed (see Table 3.5), even if some of the criteria for defining it have evolved. Attitudes to privatisation – notably that of tele-vision – or to immigration or the death penalty now separate Left and Right just as much as do views on trade unions or private education.

Under these conditions the possibility of forming (or re-forming) an independent Centre could certainly be envisaged, either as a party or in Parliament, on the basis of the fairly distinctive charac-ter of Barre supporters: but it risks being jeopardised at the elec-toral level whenever the two-bloc constraints of decisive ballots operate. Equally, the occasional desire of certain Centrists to col-laborate with, or even join, the Socialist Government must not make us forget that these leaders owe their election to voters who have long regarded them as opponents of the Left.

Finally, the repeat performances of alternating governments, and the substantial changes in electoral support which characterised the 1988 elections, have again attracted attention to the phenomena of electoral volatility which were already evident in the 1970s. It started a debate on the interpretation of electoral behaviour and the respective influence of sociological determinants and the response of electors to what the parties had to offer. Playing down the role of structural factors (both cultural and socioeconomic) in explaining voting behaviour, some authors have emphasised the specifically political conditions in which voters have to make their choice. They have therefore given pride of place to the influence of the political situation, as well as to what and whom the parties offer (the purpose and issues of the particular election, the particu-

TABLE 3.4 *Voting analysis of the 1988 presidential election:*
second round (by social categories, all France; %)[1]

	Mitterrand	Chirac
Gender		
Male	53	47
Female	55	45
Age		
18–24	60	40
25–34	63	37
35–49	51	49
50–64	51	49
65 or more	47	53
Occupational status		
Farmer	33	67
Artisan, shopkeeper, employer	36	64
Middle management, professional	31	69
Intermediate and clerical	63	37
intermediate	62	38
clerical	63	37
Manual worker	70	30
No profession/retired	53	47
Employment status		
Self-employed	33	67
Employee	62	38
public sector employee	66	34
private sector employee	60	40
Unemployed	53	47
Left–Right orientation		
Extreme Left	100	0
Left	97	3
Centre	45	55
Right	6	94
Extreme Right	3	97
Religious practice		
Regular attending Catholic	27	73
Occasional attending Catholic	44	56
Non-practising Catholic	58	42
No religion	75	25

[1] Mitterand achieved 54 %, Chirac 46 % of the total votes cast.
Source: SOFRES (2,000 interviewed, 19–25 May 1988).

TABLE 3.5   *Ideological Profile of Left- and Right-wing voters,*
24 April 1988 (%)

	Left-wing voters[1]	Right-wing voters[2]
Left–Right scale		
On the Left	50	2
Nearer the Left	29	3
Neither Left nor Right	16	25
Nearer the Right	1	30
Religious practice		
Regular attending Catholic	6	23
Occasional attending Catholic	11	21
Non-practising Catholic	40	38
No religion	33	12
Another religion/no answer	10	6
In favour of:		
Right to strike	78	51
Trade unions	69	41
Nationalisation	57	33
Privatisation	29	70
Stock Exchange	39	59
Employers	38	71
Private television	29	61
Right to an abortion	70	49
Multiracial society	57	33
Death sentence	33	59
Private schools	36	76

Notes:
1 Those voting for Laguiller, Boussel, Lajoinie, Juquin, Mitterrand.
2 Those voting for Barre, Chirac, Le Pen.
Source: Dupoirier (1988).

lar array of candidates and their personalities) and of the new individual dimension to voting behaviour.

Following this line of reasoning, the hypothesis of 'the rise of the new voter' was advanced after the 1988 elections.

Less constrained by the play of partisan and ideological determinants, having to rely on personal choice because of the gradual disappearance of traditional structures, acquiring the logic of electoral individualism by turning to personal values, new voters assert their growing autonomy by taking political decisions and modulating their choices according to a strategic response to the variation in electoral supply and the issues of that election.

According to this interpretation of electoral behaviour, the increase in votes for the French Greens in the municipal and

European elections of 1989 is to be explained by voters making their choice in response to current preoccupations with the environment rather than along traditional socio-economic and cultural cleavage lines.

Minimising, perhaps too much, the influence of 'traditional' determinants which have been shown here to have persisted in 1988 as in 1986, and founded on the analysis of a minority of 'floating' voters – 10 per cent of the franchise – this hypothesis seems rather shaky at the moment. It will need to be subjected to more detailed analyses and judged by the future evolution of the French electorate. In any case it proves the importance for French political sociology of analysing situations in which power changes hands.

4

Pluralism and Pressure Politics

PETER A. HALL

Between the state and society in every industrialised nation stands a network of interest organisations, established to express the views of various social or economic groups to the governing authorities. Along with political parties, this network of organised interests is one of the principal features of the political system whereby the interests of social groups are defined, represented, and pressed upon the government. In most countries, this system of interest intermediation is a widely accepted and well-understood component of the political system. In France, however, the operation of organised interests has always been the subject of suspicion and controversy. It is closely bound up with major debates about the capacities of the French state and the character of French politics as a whole.

Our contemporary understanding of the role of organised interests in France is still derived, in large measure, from studies of French politics that concentrated on the Fourth Republic (1946–58) and the years when Charles de Gaulle and his followers dominated the Fifth Republic (1958–74). Two influential images emerged from these studies. The first portrayed France as a nation with a weak associational life. The French were said to be reluctant to join organisations and the few existing organisations were believed to have weak ties to their rank and file. The second saw France as a nation with a strong state. If other governments made policy in response to pressure from organised interests, the French state was portrayed as a strategic actor, capable of imposing its own

77

preferences on society, even in the face of resistance from organised interests.

Both of these images are rooted in the Jacobin ideology associated with the French Revolution of 1789. In reaction to the many corporate bodies that seemed bastions of privilege under the *ancien régime*, the revolutionaries agreed with Jean-Jacques Rousseau that 'if the general will is to be able to express itself, it is essential that there should be no partial society within the State and that each citizen should think only his own thoughts'. Accordingly, they outlawed secondary associations and proclaimed that the state alone was the legitimate interpreter of the public interest. Even today, this aspect of Jacobin doctrine continues to have an impact on French political discourse. Pressure from organised interest groups, which has generally been seen as a legitimate part of public policy-making in Britain and the USA, is still viewed by many in France as a source of bias, injustice and inefficiency (compare de Closets, 1985). Negotiations may occur among organised interests and the state, but state intervention is often seen as the ultimate means for resolving such conflicts. Many French officials relish their position as guardians of the public interest.

Together with the residual impact of Jacobin ideals on political discourse and behaviour in France, a number of factors lent credence to this image of French politics in the 1950s and 1960s. An administrative elite pushed the boundaries of state intervention forward during these decades, in pursuit of socioeconomic modernisation. Armed with increasing presidential powers and a growing Gaullist party, Charles de Gaulle seemed to rise above even the most powerful of sectarian interests. In comparative terms, it was possible to see France as a special case, marked by the presence of a strong state presiding over a weakly-organised society.

Today, however, this image no longer fits the contours of contemporary French politics. A series of developments, which began in the 1950s and 1960s but were often hidden behind the façade of Gaullist hegemony only to gain increasing momentum in the 1970s and 1980s, have undermined many of our conventional views of French politics. On the one hand, they reveal that France is quite similar to other nations in a variety of unexpected requests. On the other, they suggest that we must recast our understanding of what is distinctive about the politics of organised interests in France.

To begin with, it now seems apparent that associational life in France is alive and well. By 1977, over half of all French men and women belonged to at least one voluntary association, and over 45 000 new associations of one sort or another were being created each year (*Conseil National*, 1987, Wilson, 1987, p.14). Most of these groups are non-political; they range from cycling clubs to tenants' associations, from charitable organisations to housing cooperatives, but their growing numbers suggest that French society is highly organised rather than purely individualistic.

To be sure, there are sectors in which French organisations seem less robust than their foreign counterparts. French trade unions, for instance, still have a relatively tenuous relationship to their rank and file. The proportion of the workforce that belongs to a union has fallen from a peak of about 24 per cent in 1975 to around 13 per cent by an optimistic estimate in 1989, partly in response to rising levels of unemployment. In crucial sectors like education, health care and small business however, French providers are more fully organised than their counterparts in many nations; and such catch-all parties as the RPR and the PS have built up a respectable mass membership. There seem to be few grounds for arguing that the French are less organised, in social or political terms, than the population of most European nations.

Similarly, the strength of the French state *vis-à-vis* organised interests looks considerably different now compared with 20 years ago. One distinctive feature of these relations remains the same: French interest groups are unusually dependent on the state for financial support and official recognition. All formal organisations are required to register with the authorities in France and the government grants some of them official recognition which brings with it membership on a range of consultative bodies. Moreover, the state subsidises roughly half to three-quarters of the operating budget of many organised interest groups; as many as 4,000 public employees may be seconded to such groups as the trade unions (Wilson, 1987, p. 136, *L'Express*, 2 September 1988, p. 19). For instance, it is estimated that, in 1979, the national agricultural association, received almost as much in public subsidies (8.6 million francs) as it did from membership dues, its youth wing receiving another 13.3 million francs (Keeler, 1987, p. 233).

These are substantial sums in comparison to the negligible levels of support provided in Britain or the USA. It is tempting to assume that they give public officials considerable leverage over the activities of organised interests. However, there is little evidence to support this. France's largest trade union, the CGT, was granted state subsidies only after it helped to quell the social disturbances of May 1968, but their receipt seems to have had no discernible effect on the CGT's subsequent behaviour. Conversely, many beneficiaries of state subsidies have entered into bitter conflicts with the state. Over time, state subsidies seem to have done more to sustain such groups than to tame them.

In addition, the Jacobin image of public officials making policy in relative isolation from organised social interests has been belied by the proliferation of consultative bodies associated with policy-making. As public policy stretched into more and more spheres of social life and became increasingly complex, French officials found that they needed information, advice, and at least tacit agreement from the affected social groups in order to design and implement their policies effectively. This is a universal problem in the contemporary world. The French have coped with it by sub-sidising organised interests and establishing an extensive network of consultative organs designed to elicit advice and acquiescence from those interests.

The notion of consultation was embodied in the early modernis-ation commissions of the economic plan and later built into the constitution of the Fifth Republic in the form of the Economic and Social Council which was powerless but positioned, like a latter-day Estates General, to bring the views of social and econ-omic groups to bear on legislation. Moreover, there are a range of representative organisations in many spheres of the French economy, associated particularly with the administration of social policy. Representation on these bodies brings resources and influ-ence to many interest organisations. Regular elections for such representatives provide a benchmark of support among the rank and file and a focal point for much organisational activity. This is another distinctive feature of interest group politics in France. In recent decades, however, the number of consultative bodies has grown steadily. By 1971, there were over 500 such councils, 1,200 committees, and 3,000 commissions attached to the French state. The 1970s saw another wave of expansion, as successive govern-ments sought consensual solutions to the intractable fiscal problems posed by slower rates of growth and an expanding welfare state (Ehrmann, 1971, p. 178; *L'Express*, 3 July 1987). By 1987, for instance, the peak family association in France, UNAF (National Union of Family Associations), sat on 92 national-level committees alone.

However, many of these consultative bodies exist primarily for show, and French policy-making now reflects a rather uneasy compromise between Jacobin ideals and pluralist politics. Before many major policy initiatives, elaborate soundings are now taken, involving the establishment of new commissions, reports from dis-tinguished groups of experts, and canvassing of the relevant organ-ised interests. Precise policy proposals are then frequently formulated quite independently by public officials and unveiled, only to meet a new chorus of complaints from the affected interests. Depending on the strength of that chorus, the proposals may be changed at the last minute or even withdrawn; but there is often a radical disjunction between the vague consultation that precedes a policy announcement and the hard politicking that follows it. Hence, French interest organisations rarely feel fully involved in policy-making, despite the proliferation of consultative organs. There is still an element of fiat in the behaviour of the public authorities and a great deal of public posturing on the part of organised interests. If France no longer has a state that is above society, this process of policy-making by consultation-fiat-revision is still some distance away from one based on intensive and ongoing negotiation with social groups.

Moreover, there are two distinctive aspects of organised interests in France themselves that tend to militate against the kind of intimate negotiations which often mark relations between the state and organised interests in nations like West Germany or the USA. The first is the divided, and relatively politicised, character of French interest groups themselves; the second is the continuing salience of a tradition of direct protest.

Organised interests in France are often much more factionalised internally than their counterparts in other nations. These internal divisions run along lines of partisan political allegiance as well as functional sub-interests. The labour movement, for example, has never been united under one umbrella organisation, such as the British TUC or the West German DGB. Instead, it is divided among competing confederations, many of whom have well-known affinities for particular political parties. Even individual unions, like the FEN, are themselves divided into subsidiary unions along partisan lines, and these subsidiaries, in turn, contain a variety of factions that support one political tendency or another within the major political parties. Farm and business associations are typically less divided along partisan lines but, even here, multiple organisations compete for support. As a result, when public officials seek a body with which to negotiate, it is difficult to find one that can speak for an entire constituency of related interests, and many interest-group conflicts take on a partisan tone.

For the most part, French interest groups operate as their counterparts do in all the industrial democracies. They disseminate their views in pamphlets and the press, lobby legislators when the outcome of any bill is in doubt, and maintain regular contacts with bureaucrats in the relevant ministries. However, pressure politics in France has always moved readily from the corridors of power to the streets. As a result of precedents set in the 1789 Revolution, the events of July 1830, the days of June 1848 and the Paris Commune of 1871, mass demonstrations have become a potent and oft-utilised weapon in the tactical repertoire of organised interests in France. They are used to reinforce rank-and-file solidarity within the organisation itself at the same time as they pose a threat to public order which the regime has difficulty ignoring. Out of one sample of interest group leaders, fully a third reported that they used demonstrations, strikes or other forms of direct action to get their views across with at least some frequency, 18 per cent expressing the view that this sort of power struggle was their most effective means of action (Wilson, 1987, pp. 150–3). As a result, mass demonstrations, often accompanied by some form of public disruption, are a regular feature of pluralist politics in France.

In short, French society is now more organised than ever before, and the French state seems less strong or aloof from societal interests than it was once thought to be. Indeed, through a system of public subsidies and a network of consultative bodies, it helped to create the matrix of organised interests with which it now has to deal. Most of those organisations behave much as their counterparts do elsewhere, yet at times their highly factionalised character and propensity for direct action can render them particularly intractable intermediaries.

Pluralist Politics in the 1980s

These observations are confirmed by the course of interest group politics in the 1980s. The election of a Socialist president in 1981 followed by a solid Socialist majority in the legislature was an event of major significance for post-war France. The new government set out to change the balance of power among organised interests in France, away from big business, the large farmers and conservative groups that had been privileged during the years of Gaullist rule, and towards the trade unions, small farmers and Left-leaning organisations in the polity. Here was a natural experiment. Could a new administration use the power of the state to reorganise societal interests in France? The results are apparent in each of the major realms of interest politics.

Agriculture

The French agricultural sector has long been dominated by the FNSEA, a powerful confederal organisation that, with the help of Gaullist allies, had been taken over by a modernising leadership in the early 1960s and given a powerful position as the privileged intermediary between French farmers and the state. By according the FNSEA representation and influence on the network of local committees that administered agricultural subsidies and land policies crucial to the fate of local farmers, French officials handed the organisation a set of selective incentives with which to consolidate its support in the countryside. In return, the FNSEA and its affiliates, like the *Centre National des Jeunes Agriculteurs* (National Organisation of Young Farmers), lent support to the modernising policies of successive conservative governments which were designed to increase the size of land holdings and promote agricultural business in France. Both sides gained. Indeed, relations between the state and the FNSEA began to approach a system of interest intermediation known as neo-corporatist collaboration, in which a single interest organisation is accorded responsibility not only for representing the views of its constituency to the state, but for implementing a variety of public policies as well. Although common in nations like Sweden and Austria, this sort of relationship is relatively rare in France.

The 1981 Mitterrand Government set out to break up this cosy relationship between the state and the FNSEA and give more support to the small farmer. In her first speech, the new Minister of Agriculture declared that: 'It is necessary to end the confusion between the role of professional organisations and that of the state. The former must negotiate and contest if they feel necessary; the state must make the decisions' (Keeler, 1987, p. 219). In this spirit, she promptly accorded privileged status to three organisations competing with the FNSEA: one dominated by the Communists, another on the far Right, and a hastily-formed amalgam of six Socialist-leaning farmers unions. Most important, the network of committees administering local agricultural policy was to be restructured so as to reduce the influence of the FNSEA and increase that of the Left.

If the French state were as powerful as some suppose, this might have worked, but the FNSEA fought back. After many years of holding back peasant protests against the Gaullists, it gave open support to practices of confrontation that became known as the 'peasant revolt'. Week after week, in 1981–82, groups of peasants demonstrated in Paris and the countryside with the acquiescence of the FNSEA. In Perpignan, they ripped up half a mile of railway track and carried it to the steps of the local *préfecture*. In Calvados, they bombarded the Minister of Agriculture with eggs until she was forced to an emergency airlift; on 23 March 1982, they filled the streets of Paris with 100 000 angry farmers demonstrating against the new regime.

The Socialists looked in vain for some way to stem the rising tide of agricultural protest. However, the new organisations they hoped would challenge the FNSEA were still too small to exert much influence over farmers. In the prevailing climate, even they saw advantages in attacking the government. In many regions, the authorities had to reappoint FNSEA supporters to local agricultural committees because their competitors had no mass base there and could not agree about whom to appoint to the few positions available. By 1983, the FNSEA still took almost 70 per cent of the vote in elections to the important Chambers of Agriculture. Long-standing organisational relations could not be replaced overnight.

Accordingly, Mitterrand was forced to come to some accommodation with the FNSEA. His next Minister of Agriculture was a conciliator who toned down the proposals for reform and restored collaboration with the FNSEA. Following the 1986 legislative elections, his successor was none other than the former President of the FNSEA himself. In a sphere where local discontent was endemic, the FNSEA had made itself so indispensable as a guarantor of social order and conduit for information and advice that the government could hardly do without it.

Industry

Relations between the state and organised interests in the industrial sphere have been more chaotic but no less significant. In this case, the state has to deal with both employers and labour. Moreover, each of these is represented by a large number of organisations that stretch from plant and firm level to sectoral and peak-level associations.

There are active organisations representing small and medium-sized businesses in France as well as local chambers of commerce and trade associations in most sectors of the economy. Some can be very powerful. In steel, for instance, a powerful trade association became the conduit through which the state channelled billions of francs in successive efforts to rationalise the industry. At the peak level, French employers are grouped together under a general confederation, the CNPF. But collaboration at this level has always been limited by the decentralised nature of the CNPF itself: it is an umbrella organisation representing about 800 separate trade associations. With widely disparate interests, these associations have been reluctant to concede real negotiating power to the CNPF; and, while it makes frequent representations to the government, it only occasionally makes concrete bargains on behalf of industrialists.

When issues of industrial rationalisation are at stake, public officials have found it more useful to deal with sectoral organisations or large firms directly. Each ministry generally develops a *tutelle*, or supervisory relationship, with the industries in which it is most interested, whereby the industry responds to the suggestions of the ministry in return for the latter's support inside the government itself. In addition, there is a much more extensive flow of personnel from the senior Civil Service to leading managerial positions in the private sector in France than in Britain or the USA, relations between industry and the state gaining cohesion from this network of personal relations.

Relations between the state and the trade unions are more difficult, for several reasons. First, France has no single or unified union confederation. Only about 13 per cent of the workforce belongs to a union, and five separate confederations compete with each other at plant and national levels: the CGT (supported by about 18 per cent of those eligible to vote in enterprise committee elections), the CFDT (with 11 per cent support), the FO (10 per cent support), the CFTC (4 per cent support), and the CGC (5 per cent support). Second, most of these organisations have weak organisational ties to the rank and file. They can bring thousands of workers into the streets for a 24-hour strike, but their capacity to enforce collective bargains or even collect dues from their membership is limited. Third, many of the French unions are highly politicised; the CGT has close ties to the PCF and the CFDT is known for its Socialist sympathies. Although favoured by the RPR, the FO has tried to maintain an apolitical profile. These factors make cooperation among the unions themselves difficult. As a result, although the French state accords the unions an official role on the agencies that supervise health insurance, old-age pensions and unemployment insurance, it has rarely been able to bargain with them effectively about national economic or incomes policies.

The election of a Socialist Government in 1981 was a watershed for French business, and the CNPF in particular. It had gradually come to support the relatively interventionist policies of the Gaullists in the interest of economic modernisation. It continued to do so even in the face of slower rates of growth, a rising tax burden, and stiff regulations regarding lay-offs during the 1970s in order to stave off any challenge from the Left. Once the Socialists were elected and embarked on policies of nationalisation, reduced working hours and workplace reform, however, the CNPF became ambivalent about maintaining close ties to the government. Instead, under a new leader, it retreated to a more aggressive rhetorical stance, based on neo-liberal demands for deregulation, lower taxes and denationalisation. This was to have a significant impact on French political discourse. Entrepreneurialism, flexibility and the market became the watchwords of the day.

The Mitterrand Government countered by according de facto recognition to a traditional rival of the CNPF, the SNPMI (National Union of Small Industry). Once again, it hoped to break the privileged position of organised interests that had long been sympathetic to the Right, but once again its strategy backfired. The SNPMI gained support rapidly and began to mount demonstrations against both the CNPF and the government. Not to be outdone, its own rivals for the support of small business, the CGPME (Confederation of Small Business) and CID-UNATI (National Artisans Organisation), took to the streets as well on three successive days in May 1983 (Berger, 1985). The government was ultimately forced to disown the SNPMI and respond to the neo-liberal climate of opinion that the CNPF had helped foster. After 1986, the CNPF softened its stance somewhat under a new leader, but the Chirac Government took up the neo-liberal rhetoric with enthusiasm.

Relations between the Mitterrand Government and the trade unions were more positive but less straightforward. Mitterrand hoped to strengthen the position of the trade unions *vis-à-vis* business and the state; but he hesitated to go too far in this direction because the most powerful trade union was the Communist-dominated CGT, and Mitterrand did not want to enhance its power in relation to the government or the other unions. Accordingly, some trade unionists were brought into ministerial offices; frequent consultations were held with the unions; and the Auroux laws, designed to strengthen union representation at the plant level, were passed. However, neither the unions nor the government wanted to be seen as the prisoner of the other. Accordingly, consultation was only rarely followed by substantive negotiations; as a result, relations gradually cooled between the government and the unions.

Even worse, rising levels of unemployment were sapping union membership, which fell dramatically during the 1980s. When the

Socialist Government turned toward austerity policies after 1982, the unions most closely associated with the government, like the CFDT and CGT, began to lose support among the workforce to such organisations as the FO and CGC, which forswore politics in favour of a focus on material benefits and collective bargaining. Hence, even with the Auroux laws, the unions were barely able to strengthen their hand at the plant and firm level. Meanwhile, the PS did little to build a lasting base for cooperation with the unions at the local level and, when the government left office, labour organisations were even weaker than usual. In yet another sphere, those at the helm of the state had been unable to reorder the underlying patterns of interest organisation in society.

Armed with the neo-liberalism that had become popular in business circles, the 1986–8 conservative government continued to reduce industrial subsidies and remove regulations governing lay-offs, despite union opposition. The trade unions were left struggling for members and relatively demoralised in the face of a revival of market rhetoric to which even the Socialists seemed to subscribe. In many cases, employers used these conditions to turn the Auroux laws to their advantage, and industrial relations became considerably quieter in the private sector as the focus turned to collective bargaining and issues of workplace flexibility.

The most important developments at the end of the 1980s, however, were an escalating series of strikes in the public sector, led in this case not by the unions but by *ad hoc* coalitions of militants drawing on widespread rank-and-file discontent with five years of wage austerity. Informal coordinating committees of workers took the initiative away from the trade unions and led industrial action by railway workers in 1986, nurses and transport workers in 1988, and prison guards in 1989, often in defiance of statutes forbidding strikes in such sectors. This posed a potentially serious problem for the unions: were they losing their influence over the rank and file? The CGT quickly tried to lend support to these efforts, but the others rushed to keep up. These strikes were also a major problem for the Rocard Government. As economic growth revived, so did the long-standing militancy of the French working class. As new leaders took office in several of the major union confederations, they were faced with the problem of defining new lines of action capable of tapping this discontent.

Individual Issue Areas

There are organised interests operating in most spheres of French policy-making. By and large, they are of two sorts. In areas that have been the subject of policy for many decades, such as education and health care, there are dense networks of organised interests with deeply entrenched positions. In spheres that have become the object of intense concern only more recently, such as those of environmental policy, immigration and women's issues, many of the relevant interests tend to be grouped into much more loosely organised social movements.

Education policy, for instance, has been a highly controversial subject in France since the 1790s when advocates of secular schooling were first aligned against the supporters of Catholic education. Today, policy-makers confront a powerful set of teachers' associations grouped together into the FEN. Representing two-thirds of all school personnel, the FEN is a virtual empire, linked to 53 service agencies, including savings banks, insurance companies, publishing firms, tourist agencies and old-age homes, worth at least ten billion francs (Ambler, 1985a, p. 26). In addition to the many factions inside the FEN and their Catholic equivalents, policy-makers must also deal with a miscellaneous set of national student organisations and powerful parent–teacher federations, divided between the *Fédération des Conseils de Parents d'Elèves*, representing 650 000 families in state schools, and the *Union Nationale des Associations de Parents d'Elèves de l'Enseignement Libre*, representing 860 000 families associated with the Catholic schools.

Although there is no single organisation as powerful as the FEN in the sphere of health care, policy-makers there must also deal with a bewildering network of agencies and consultative committees on which health-care providers are strongly represented. The doctors belong to a public organ, the *Ordre des Médecins*, and a variety of unions like the conservative CSMF, linked with others under an umbrella organisation, the *Centre National des Professions de Santé* (National Organisation of Health Workers). Nurses, medical students, hospital administrators and others are likewise organised into a variety of associations. Each has a different set of vested interests to defend. Many other traditional policy spheres display a similar pattern.

Any attempt to reform one of these spheres, therefore, is likely to meet stiff opposition from some or all of such groups. The classic case is that of education, where reform has often seemed necessary and notoriously difficult. The experience of the Mitterrand Government provides a typical example of the policy process in such spheres. Alain Savary, the Socialist Minister of Education, made a determined effort at educational reform, including implementation of the traditional Socialist concern to bring private education under state supervision. After his initial proposals met serious opposition from Catholic educators and parents, Savary spent two years negotiating a compromise measure with the affected interests. At the last moment, however, the FEN and *Comité National de l'Action Laïque* (National Committee for Secular Action) persuaded the Socialist deputies to amend the proposals again in favour of secularism; and, in response, the Catholic forces brought a million protesters on to the streets of Paris. Savary resigned with only a few of his reforms in place, and Mitterrand gave up the secularisation plan altogether. Measures designed to render specialised medical training more selective met a similar fate, as protesting medical students and teachers filled the parking meters of Paris with plaster, and agreement on an appropriate set of reforms eluded the government.

The Socialist Government under Michel Rocard which took office in 1988 fared little better. Although Rocard made educational reform one of his priorities, mandated substantial new funds for the field and appointed a senior figure as the new Minister of Education, his early initiatives led to widespread protests from the teachers' unions and had to be revised in 1989. Rocard himself concluded that French 'society is so rigid, sclerotic, full of corporatisms that even to measure the difficulties to be encountered is impossible, since they are so numerous' (*L'Expansion*, 9 September 1988, p. 23).

If the organisations of professional defence in these traditional spheres of policy have served largely as veto groups, the new social movements associated with women's issues, the environment and immigration function more as ginger groups, bringing new issues on to the political agenda and mobilising support for specific actions. These groups are generally weak coalitions of activists, often led by intellectuals, with a shifting base of popular support that makes it difficult for them to veto specific policies but which gives them the opportunity to form at least transitory alliances with major political figures and parties. The feminist movement that emerged from the events of May 1968 grouped around the intellectual circles of *Politique et Psychanalyse* in Paris and a loose association known as the *Mouvement de la Libération des Femmes* (Women's Liberation Movement) had notable success securing passage of a liberal abortion law in 1974 and the appointment of a minister for the status of women when the Giscardians saw that it might be advantageous to woo this constituency.

SOS-racisme, created to counter the rising tide of anti-immigrant sentiment in the 1980s, gained sufficient strength as a result of recognition and financial support received from the Mitterrand

Government to enable it to build broader support for ethnic tolerance as well as resistance to the racism of the FN. In yet another
sphere, French ecologists are represented by about 250 national
and 900 regional associations dedicated to preserving the environment; but they have been notably less successful at securing mass
support or influence over policy than their counterparts in West
Germany or Britain. Despite isolated protests, the government
proceeded with an ambitious programme for constructing nuclear
reactors in the 1970s; and the relatively weak agencies for environmental protection of the French state have rarely been a match
for the well-organised industrial interests they confront. In frustration, the ecologists finally formed their own political party.

Retrospect and Prospect

Two hundred years after the French Revolution supposedly wiped
out the bastions of privilege in the *ancien régime*, French society
again contains a wide variety of organised interests. Indeed, many
of these organisations owe a portion of their resources or privileges
to the French state itself. Once in place, however, these organisations often take on a life of their own. Most now have independent bases of power and, as Ezra Suleiman (1987) and others
have pointed out, the French state is not nearly as strong *vis-à-
vis* these organisations as was once believed. Three features of the
administrative practices of the French state are especially relevant
here.

First, most ministries exercise a quasi-official *tutelle* over various
groups. As noted above, this entails supervision of the activities
of a group but also defence of the interests of that group within
the counsels of state. Hence, there is an element of clientelism
built into the relations that many groups have with particular
ministries or agencies. The two sides exchange favours in such a
way as to give some outside organisations a privileged position
regarding the state.

Second, although the French state is relatively centralised compared with, say, the American state, there are still many competing agencies and organs within it that can themselves be semi-
independent sources of pressure for particular lines of policy and
certain kinds of privilege. Notable in this regard are the *grands
corps*, specific bodies of experts that undertake a range of tasks
and distribute their members widely throughout the administration.
Established in many cases during the nineteenth century, many of
these *corps* have been able to extend their purview to newly-

created fields in recent years. Policy-makers contemplating administrative reorganisation, regional decentralisation or major engineering projects have often had to cope with their demands as well as those coming from outside groups. The presence of semi-independent organisations inside the state itself further enhances the pluralistic tone of contemporary French politics.

Finally, despite its centralisation, there are still many divisions within the French state that interest groups can exploit to secure their objectives. Inside the bureaucracy, they can often play one ministry off against another. The French notaries, for instance, were able to block the Mitterrand Government's attempt to reform their profession by exploiting divisions between the Ministries of Justice and Finance as well as their dependence on the notaries themselves for accurate information about the state of the profession. Similarly, there are times when organised interests can play the legislature off against the Executive. Although the Executive is especially powerful, control over it is divided between the president and prime minister.

In recent years, these divisions have become particularly important. From 1986 to 1988, a Socialist president faced a conservative majority in the legislature led by a Gaullist prime minister. In the face of such *cohabitation*, groups who failed to secure support from the government could in many cases appeal to the president for redress. Moreover, as Gaullist hegemony has waned, factions have opened up in many political parties and the balance of power within the legislature has been much more evenly divided. This offers new opportunities for outside interests. Just as the focus of interest group activity shifted toward the Executive in the early years of the Fifth Republic, we can now expect some attention to shift back to the legislature, as organised interests seek to apply leverage to the fragile alliances there (Berger, 1975).

However, the principal challenge that interest organisations now face comes not from within France, but from the growing influence of the EC. The policies of the EC became vital to French agriculture but Community initiatives in coal and steel, telecommunications and aerospace have also had a significant impact on French business. As the attempt to secure a unified European market in 1992 proceeds, a growing portion of the regulations affecting French society will be promulgated from Brussels. Following the lead of the farmers and major industrialists, many organised interests can be expected to devote an increasing share of their resources and attention to the European Commission. In some cases, this will entail closer alliances between interest groups and French officials aimed at common opponents in Brussels; in others, it will mean greater participation in European-wide organisations designed to coordinate lobbying there.

In sum, a number of convergent trends have enhanced the pluralism of French politics in recent years and shifted some political emphasis away from the state towards civil society. Over the course of the Fifth Republic, interest organisations have become an increasingly important feature of society. The passing of Gaullist hegemony in the 1970s and 1980s has distributed power more broadly among a variety of political parties and undercut the seemingly monolithic character of the state. The gradual internationalisation of French business and the growing influence of the EC has moved the axes of influence over social and economic policy away from Paris while the recent surge of interest in market solutions to socioeconomic problems has enhanced the role of private sector actors in many economic and cultural spheres. Policy-makers will have to come to grips with all these developments during the coming years.

PART TWO

The Governmental System

5

Political Leadership

HOWARD MACHIN

Leadership functions are performed in a variety of different areas (symbolic representation, opinion formation, party organisation, ideological production, agenda setting, brokerage, decision taking and coordination) and at a number of different levels (local, regional, national and European). Who exercises what kind of political leadership, and how, thus depends not only on institutions but also on personalities, on the nature and organisation of the different parties and pressure groups and the balance of power between them, on the effectiveness of control by politicians over other professions, and on the media. The advent of de Gaulle and the Fifth Republic, accompanied by both the resolution of several divisive issues and the rise of mass television precipitated, or at least catalysed, a number of long-term changes in political leadership. The most notable were the presidentialisation of government and party leaderships, the replacement of parliamentary debating skill by television performance technique as a vital qualification for top roles, the dominance of national over local leaders, the cooption of 'outsiders' into political posts, and the sharing of some functions between politicians and experts. Before the 1981 elections, several opponents suggested that a victory for the Left would mean a return to the bad old days of the Fourth Republic. Again in early 1986, some suggested that if a president lost his majority in the National Assembly, the pattern of leadership would be profoundly changed. The aim of this chapter is to assess how the experience of alternation in power between Left and Right and the institutional reforms of the 1980s have modified the changes brought about by de Gaulle, and how a more diversified and balanced leadership pattern has emerged.

Since the developments of leadership politics in the 1980s rep-

95

resent reactions to these earlier transformations, our starting point must be an analysis of those changes brought about by de Gaulle in and after 1958, when the Algerian trauma precipitated the replacement of the constitution. This is of particular importance as François Mitterrand began his political career as a deputy and a minister during the Fourth Republic, and was one of the most outspoken opponents of de Gaulle's return to power and the presidentialisation of the Fifth Republic. In power after 1981, however, he did not attempt to reverse anything which de Gaulle had achieved, and showed no inclination to return to the practices of the previous regime.

The 'de Gaulle Revolution' in Leadership

The major achievement of de Gaulle in the Fifth Republic was to establish strong, stable and respected political leadership. This represented a complete break from the practices of previous regimes. Before 1958 the weakness of presidents, prime ministers, ministers and national party leaders reflected both the institutional subordination of the Executive to the legislature and the fragmentation of political elites. Rivalries within governing coalitions and their constituent parties were inherent. Ministers often viewed the prime minister as a temporary, transitional figure, and themselves as his potential replacements. Apart from those in the Left and Right extremist parties, almost all deputies were potential ministers. Splits in coalitions or within parties did not constitute major crises even when they led to a fall of the government. Instead, governmental 'crises' became a normal part of the political process, as Williams (1964) so eloquently demonstrated. De Gaulle caricatured the Fourth Republic as a 'regime of the parties', but in practice the fragility of party organisations was one of its major problems. The old joke that France was the country where most schoolboys dreamed of becoming prime minister when they grew up, and many of them achieved their dream was inaccurate in one important respect: most children, and parents, despised politicians (including prime ministers) for their weakness.

This prevalent weakness of national leaders in normal circumstances was especially striking by comparison with the apparent strength of other leaders. Some *local* leaders were, and were recognised as being, extremely influential. At first sight this seems paradoxical, since France was often cited as the great success story of Napoleonic centralisation, and the elected councils in the 96 *départements* and 36 000 communes could decide little without legal, technical and financial authorisations given by central government officials, led by the *préfets*. Nonetheless, some local leaders (or *notables*) were very powerful, either simply because of the population or wealth of the city or area they ran, or due to their talents of lobbying or persuasion, or as a result of their accumulation of local and national elected offices (which allowed them to use direct influence as deputies or senators to win funds or favours for their home towns). Not infrequently, the theoretically omnipotent *préfet* was reduced to the role of assistant to an all-powerful city boss (see Chapters 6 and 8). The same men could be weak leaders in national politics, but unchallengeable despots in local government. Whilst this accumulation of local and national offices was common practice, it did not lead to any nationalisation of local politics or harmonisation of coalitions. Instead elites were fragmented, and some men participated simultaneously in national and local alliances with totally different partners.

National political leaders were also weak in relation to the officials who were, in theory at least, their subordinates within the state machine. Not even the generals who ran the armed forces were entirely reliable, as became clear during the Algerian War. Senior police officers also sometimes appeared to operate with total autonomy from the government. Many critics of the Fourth Republic attacked the power of senior civil servants, and especially of those in the prestigious *grands corps* (as will be discussed in Chapter 6). Some suggested that, in the absence of effective political leadership, bureaucrats or technocrats such as Jean Monnet ran the country.

Political leaders were also seen as feeble in comparison to some economic leaders. Before 1945, the economy performed poorly compared with those of its neighbours. For many critics the power and backwardness of French capitalists were the causes. Marxists argued that politicians could do no more than serve the interests of the class – the bourgeoisie – from which they came. Others advanced that the captains of industry effectively ran things for themselves with little reference to (or respect for) politicians. The myths of the 1930s – of '200 families' who controlled France, or of a 'wall of money' which blocked any advance towards socialism – were still widely known during the 1950s. The extension of the public sector, with the nationalisations of 1944–6, and the increase in state powers to direct the economy during the war and reconstruction period did not invalidate such theories. Renault and the EDF (the nationalised electricity corporation) might have been state owned but they still seemed to act as independent forces. Although the French economy grew rapidly during the 1950s, political leaders derived little credit for this;

on the contrary, since the consumer society did not arrive until the 1960s, the mass public did not perceive the economic success, except as 'lining the pockets of the rich'. Whether the economic growth of the 1950s took place because of, or in spite of, the policies adopted by successive governments, political leaders gained no prestige or legitimacy from it.

The return to power of de Gaulle in 1958 at first seemed to fit into the patterns of the past, as he appeared to be a 'saviour figure' necessary to sort out a major crisis. In 1958, with a revolt of the settlers in Algiers, a nationalist insurrection by the Arab population and a declaration of disobedience by the Army high command, the political system seemed near the point of collapse. With no clear majority in the Assembly either to fight the nationalists or to discipline the army and settlers, and with the real possibility that some hot-headed army leaders might stage a *coup d'état*, de Gaulle alone appeared to have the authority to provide a solution. Unlike earlier 'saviour figures' he was able to exploit his temporary advantage to bring about a substantial change in patterns of politics as his price for taking power was the adoption of a new constitution, his own election to the presidency and a free hand to run foreign and defence policy.

De Gaulle, however, did not get everything on his own terms. The old party leaders agreed to vote him into office as the last prime minister of the Fourth Republic and to change the constitution, but they set down clear parameters on the institutional modifications to be undertaken and insisted on their own participation in his government and in the constitutional reform committee. The consequence was a rag-bag constitution, a triumph of committee architecture. The new text clearly provided that the government, led by the prime minister, should decide and implement national policies. There was no provision for presidential government except in a national emergency, when full powers might be assumed under article 16. The only real constitutional basis for a normal leadership role for the president lay in article 5 (which gives the president the duty of arbitration to ensure 'the regular functioning of the organs of government and the continuity of the state' and protecting 'national independence' and 'territorial integrity', and 'respect for treaties').

It was the continuation of the dramatic Algerian situation until 1962 which allowed these vague provisions to be interpreted with such imagination that presidential leadership was gradually imposed. Between 1958 and 1962, in the absence of a real presidential majority coalition in the Assembly, de Gaulle relied on the deference of his prime minister and ministers, who in turn depended on the fear of the deputies that a defeat of the government, especially on a 'question of confidence', would precipitate not only the government's resignation but also de Gaulle's departure; and that might even lead to a military coup. Until 1962, the Algerian War proved to be a substitute for a presidential majority.

Debré, de Gaulle's hand-picked Prime Minister in 1959, may have disagreed with de Gaulle, but he always ultimately deferred to the president on all policy options in those areas (Algeria, defence and foreign affairs) in which the president could claim some constitutional right, however vague, to have a say. Debré also allowed de Gaulle to decide on the choice of ministers, on the whole organisation of governmental decision-making and on any other matter. The prime minister knew that his tenure of office depended entirely on his president's pleasure, since he himself could not make any claim to leadership of a parliamentary majority except as de Gaulle's spokesman and assistant. The president also made it clear that ministers were not chosen as party or faction leaders but for their personal qualities and competence. Indeed, he recruited senior civil servants to top ministries, thus by-passing the parties and the Assembly as the main selection agency.

To assume effective leadership of the government de Gaulle adopted a number of extra-constitutional devices. The first of these was the prohibition of meetings of the government other than the formal Wednesday morning Council of Ministers which the President chaired. He also took over the *de facto* supervision of the General Secretariat of the Government (responsible for organising the work of the Government and the agenda and minutes of meetings of the Council of Ministers) although the prime minister remained its *de jure* boss. With the consent of ministers, he also set up his own presidential staff at the Elysée Palace by 'borrowing' posts of advisers from different ministries; hence, many of the president's advisers in the three main policy units at the Elysée (the General Secretariat of the Presidency, the Secretariat for Community and Malagasy Affairs and his *cabinet*) were not paid from the budget of the Presidency, but from those of the ministries whose work they 'shadowed' for de Gaulle. Many important decisions were no longer made in the Council of Ministers but instead were taken by smaller groups of ministers, brought together as an 'interministerial Council' under the chairmanship of the president. Even in 'interministerial committees' (under prime ministerial direction) the absent president was usually represented by a senior member of his staff. In some policy areas, notably foreign affairs and Algeria, de Gaulle held regular tête-à-tête meetings with the Minister of Foreign Affairs, and the ministry was virtually transformed into an annexe of the Elysée Palace. Finally de Gaulle became the main public speaker for the government:

he travelled widely in France and Algeria to make public speeches defending his government and its policies; he gave presidential press conferences which became the main forum for announcing major policy changes; and he spoke on radio and television.

In 1962, however, with Algeria independent and the Army tamed, de Gaulle realised that he was no longer needed by the leaders of the old parties. Before they could conspire for his departure, however, he precipitated an open conflict: he replaced Debré by Pompidou, a banker from outside politics, and then proposed to amend the constitution to provide for the election of the president by universal suffrage (instead of by the electoral college). Furthermore, to attain this goal he decided to employ article 11 of the constitution (which provided for the use of a referendum on Bills concerning 'the organisation of public powers') instead of article 89 (which stipulated two methods for amendments, both of which involved obtaining the approval of parliament). Almost all the old parties realised that this was a direct challenge to parliamentary supremacy but, as they could not act directly against the president, they voted a motion of censure on the Pompidou Government. De Gaulle at once dissolved the Assembly but kept Pompidou on as caretaker prime minister. The elections were fixed to follow the referendum. The results reinforced presidential leadership: the amendment was adopted, and the disciplined coalition supporting de Gaulle won a majority in the Assembly. Ironically, the amendment did not give the president any additional powers. In 1965 the first universal suffrage elections for the presidency took place and de Gaulle was re-elected. It was then clear that presidential elections had become the key leadership contest.

The creation of a disciplined coalition with a majority meant that a government could last the full life of a parliament unless the president wished to change it. Spared the terrible chore of fighting for survival and confident of remaining in office for at least a few years, the prime minister could play a powerful role in policy-making, parliamentary management and opinion formation in the media. Under de Gaulle any prime minister was inevitably eclipsed, but Pompidou soon began to emerge as an influential leader in his own right. Indeed, with the support of the president and his majority he developed his talents for debating and decision-making and soon appeared as the heir-apparent to de Gaulle.

Pompidou's success as prime minister also symbolised one other element in the change after 1958: the cooption of new men from outside political organisations directly to leadership functions. This was now possible because the government was no longer a delicately balanced mix of party representatives, but a team chosen by the president and his prime minister for their personal abilities. It also corresponded to the idea of 'separating powers' which de Gaulle had insisted should be introduced by means of a constitutional ban on being both a minister and a member of either House of Parliament. Yet another reason for this cooption was his wish to 'depoliticise' some areas of policy-making by appointing experts or 'technocrats'. Hence a number of senior respected civil servants were recruited directly as ministers. In the past civil servants had sometimes entered politics at the bottom level by party activism and then contesting seats to enter Parliament, but this direct access route from top Civil Service posts to ministries was new. It had a paradoxical result: the Fifth Republic, like its predecessor but for totally different reasons, was attacked as a 'technocracy'.

The other real change was in leadership style. Debating skills and talents of brokerage had been essential during the Fourth Republic, but television performance and policy-making effectiveness were even more important under de Gaulle. Mitterrand might still make newspaper headlines by his debating prowess in the Assembly, but the impressive talents of Pompidou and Giscard d'Estaing on television were increasingly noticed. It was difficult, of course, for opposition politicians to get on television at all.

The consolidation of presidential leadership was continued by Pompidou and Giscard d'Estaing after de Gaulle's resignation in 1969. Both men chose their own prime ministers (and replaced them when dissatisfied), and strongly influenced the selection of ministers. They also set major policy priorities, fixed the limits of their party coalitions and dominated policy-making in the 'presidential domain' reserved by de Gaulle for himself: foreign affairs, defence and institutional reforms. Both men also intervened widely in other policy areas, according to their individual interests and the political sensitivity of particular issues. There were, however, major differences of style. Until he became ill, Pompidou had very close relations with his parliamentary coalition, and especially with his own party (the UDR). Giscard d'Estaing not only had problems with his coalition but also developed an increasingly regal style. These factors certainly contributed to Giscard's loss of popularity, although his main problem was the deepening economic crisis. The growing unpopularity of Giscard d'Estaing and some of his policies did not diminish respect for presidential government. By the end of the 1970s the coming presidential election (1981) was seen by everyone as the crucial leadership contest. All the major political parties had come to view the selection of presidential candidates as one of their main functions, and presidential coalition-building as an essential to winning power.

New Variations on a Presidential Theme, 1981–6

When Mitterrand was elected in 1981, a break with previous patterns of presidential dominance seemed quite possible. The new
president was the author of one of the most critical attacks on de
Gaulle's presidentialism, *Le Coup d'Etat Permanent* (1964). He
was also the leader of a party, the PS, which boasted the superiority of its own internal democratic procedures and a programme of
creating a more participatory political system. Furthermore, as a
spokesman of the entire Left under de Gaulle, Pompidou and
Giscard d'Estaing, Mitterrand had denounced, often in strident
terms, the excessive presidentialism of the regime. But whatever
the new president's earlier thoughts on the desirability of sharing
leadership roles at the summit, and however strong the encourage-
ments of his party friends to do so, Mitterrand was to prove a
worthy follower of his predecessors, at least until 1986.

Among Mitterrand's first acts as President were his acceptance
of the resignations by Barre and the government; the appointment
of a Socialist Government; the dissolution of the Assembly; and
an appeal to the electorate to give *his* Government a majority in
Parliament. Like their predecessors, the two prime ministers,
Mauroy and Fabius, were the President's personal choices. If
Mauroy was undoubtedly very popular within the PS and appreciated by the Communists, he still owed his office to Mitterrand's
personal decision. The appointment of Fabius, who had no independent power base in the PS, was a purely presidential choice,
imposed upon, and accepted by, the PS deputies. The nature of
this choice of second prime minister was very similar to that of
Pompidou by de Gaulle in 1962 or that of Barre by Giscard
d'Estaing in 1976.

In many other respects Mitterrand followed the presidential precedents already set. He used his personal staff at the Elysée to
follow policy-making in all fields and to keep him well informed.
Within this team Attali, as Special Adviser, and Bianco, the General Secretary of the Presidential Office from 1982, had special
status and the privilege of daily meetings with him. However, the
composition and work methods of the Elysée staff were slightly
changed. In his staff, Mitterrand included old personal friends, PS
activists and even his own son, alongside the traditional group of
politically sympathetic civil servants. Another innovation was that
of setting several advisers to work separately on the same question
so that he could have several policy evaluations and options from
which to choose. In two other respects, however, continuity
reigned. The first was the closeness of ties between the Elysée

staff and the Foreign Affairs Ministry, and the second was the key role played by the president's adviser on African affairs. De Gaulle had set up a separate Secretariat for running French relations with African states, and although the separate institutional status had disappeared Pompidou, Giscard d'Estaing and Mitterrand followed the pattern set by the first president. Indeed, the first Minister for Cooperation (aid to developing countries) resigned, protesting that all decisions in his policy area were being taken at the Elysée.

In other policy areas, however, another tradition was respected: namely that ministers, not presidential advisers, were formally responsible for policy-making, and a staff adviser who openly intervened in a ministerial jurisdiction, or disagreed in public with a minister, risked dismissal. There were a few notable exceptions. One was Bérégovoy, the first General Secretary, who, when Mitterrand realised that he was far better suited to public ministerial tasks than to the discreet role of an adviser, became Minister for Social Security in 1982. Even in this respect Mitterrand was only following the example of Pompidou who had moved Jobert from the Elysée to become Foreign Affairs Minister. In general, however, the influential but discreet role of the Elysée staff changed very little.

Mitterrand also made few innovations in governmental decision making patterns. The Council of Ministers each Wednesday morning remained a formal reporting session rather than a forum for real discussion and collective decision-making. The meetings were planned carefully, as the General Secretary of the Government prepared everything in advance with the president (although always keeping the prime minister, to whom he was officially subordinate, informed). The president rapidly made it clear that he did not wish to encourage discussion and that ministers should restrict their comments to matters within their ministries' competence. He, however, intervened as and when he liked.

The new president was less enthusiastic than his predecessor about chairing formal sub-committees of the government (the Interministerial councils). The number of meetings of these bodies fell noticeably after 1981. In some policy areas Mitterrand had close contacts with the minister responsible, and the president's constant support and involvement gave the minister high prestige and considerable influence when dealing with other ministers or with the PS group in the Assembly. Lang as Arts Minister (and with special responsibility for following the President's pet building projects, the Louvre extension, the new opera house at La Bastille and the massive arch at La Défense in particular) had such a working relationship. In other areas, Mitterrand left a trusted minister to get on with the implementation of an agreed policy with little or no presidential interference or supervision: Defferres's decentralisation programme and Hernu's defence policy were largely carried out in this way. Men like Hernu, Dumas (at Foreign Affairs) and Bérégovoy were old friends and had much easier contacts than former political rivals such as Rocard at the Planning Ministry or Savary at Education. Indeed, at the time of the *Rainbow Warrior* scandal, Mitterrand was criticised for being far too trusting (see Chapter 15). Nonetheless the president did not attempt to run everything but left a lot of decision-making to his prime ministers and ministers.

Some compared Mitterrand's style to that of de Gaulle, others to that of Pompidou. Like de Gaulle, Mitterrand has often seemed distant, almost regal, aware of his superior status as President of France and conscious of his leading role in international relations and contemporary history. He has travelled widely and made many lofty speeches about grand principles. Like Pompidou, however, he retained direct contacts with ordinary citizens (partly through regular visits to a holiday home in the south west, also like Pompidou) and an especially close loyalty for and from the party he did so much to create. In 1981, however, his whole style seemed to contrast very sharply with the strange mixture of technocracy and monarchism displayed by Giscard d'Estaing in his later years at the Elysée.

In his first five years three distinct periods of presidential styles could be distinguished. In the first, from 1981 to 1982, Mitterrand seemed to devote himself to foreign and defence questions, leaving domestic affairs to Mauroy and the government. By the end of this period some opinion polls were indicating, for the first time in over two decades, that a majority saw the prime minister as the dominant actor in the leadership tandem. The dramatic fall in PS and governmental popularity, the devaluation crisis of March 1983, and the huge demonstrations of 1984 against the bill to integrate private schools into the state system meant that crucial choices had to be made at the very top. Mitterrand not only made the decisions but also took public responsibility for them. Thus, in 1983 and 1984, he appeared to dominate domestic as well as foreign policy-making. The height of this period of apparently unlimited presidential domestic political domination came in July 1984 when Mitterrand scrapped the private schools bill, accepted the resignation of the Mauroy Government, appointed Fabius as Prime Minister to lead a team with no Communists and proposed a constitutional amendment to allow for greater use of the referendum. A third period of presidential withdrawal from the limelight of domestic politics followed. By the 1986 elections, when his PS supporters lost their Assembly majority, Mitterrand had reverted to his role of foreign and defence policy leader: the head of state representing France, rather than the leader of a partisan majority.

To some extent this division into three periods reflects his evolving goals. During the first two years, the goals were clearly set down and the Mauroy Government could be left to get on with the implementation of the president's electoral platform ('110 proposals for France'). The programme was clear, so Mitterrand could devote himself to foreign affairs. By early 1983, however, he was being increasingly drawn into conflicts between ministers over the new policy directions to pursue. The change of direction in economic policy was decided by the president in the March 1983 devaluation crisis. So too was the dropping of the schools law and the PCF ministers in 1984. Once this was done and Fabius had been set to pursue a policy of moderate, modernising management, Mitterrand could return to his preferred role of foreign policy and leave his trusted lieutenant to continue the good work. Throughout the period 1981–6, therefore, whilst retaining the ultimate authority in all policy areas, Mitterrand only exercised it outside his areas of special interest when sensitive political problems arose.

One other innovation of this period was noteworthy: leaders of the main factions within the PS were included in both governments, and regular weekly breakfast meetings were held at the Elysée Palace with the leaders of the party organisation and parliamentary groups. It seemed that the president felt obliged to ensure that the presidential party and its leader stayed in close harmony during his presidency.

Prime Ministerial Leadership: Before and Beyond Cohabitation

The period known as *cohabitation* has been seen by many as the exception to the rule of presidential leadership: the government led by the prime minister ruled, whilst the president reigned. Only in foreign and defence matters did the president remain influential, as the constitution prescribed. It was certainly true that when *cohabitation* began after the 1986 RPR–UDF election victory, Chirac only agreed to become prime minister on condition that the president explicitly accepted his constitutional and democratic mandate to govern. Nonetheless, the experience of *cohabitation* was not simply an island of prime ministerial government in a sea of presidentialism. In fact, prime ministerial leadership had been far from insignificant before 1986, and during *cohabitation* the president continued to play a key role in politics. After *cohabitation* presidential domination was re-asserted, but it remained clear that the prime minister and his government were not mere acolytes.

Even under de Gaulle prime ministers had three important leadership functions. At the level of governmental policy-making it was the prime minister who had the task of coordinating the work of the ministers, arbitrating in interministerial conflicts (especially over the budget) and initiating new policies in areas where the president chose not to intervene. He was also the government's parliamentary manager, with ultimate responsibility for the legislative programme and good relations with the Assembly and Senate. Finally, he was obliged to attempt to coordinate, if not to lead, the president's party and coalition in the Assembly. The extent of his influence depended on his personality, his relations with the president, his interests, his diplomatic and managerial talents and the popularity of his government. Governmental policy-making tasks were carried out with considerable success by Pompidou, Chaban-Delmas and Barre before 1981; indeed, these men appeared to dominate economic and social policy-making at all but crisis moments. Mauroy and Fabius were also effective policy-makers before 1986. Mauroy took many of the key decisions in the nationalisation and decentralisation reforms of 1981–3. Fabius, Minister of Industry from 1983 to 1984, continued to determine industrial policy as prime minister.

To some extent this policy-making and coordinating role is thrust upon any prime minister by the institutional system. The Fifth Republic inherited a framework of government centred on the prime minister's office. Since 1958, the administrative management of the government has remained the task of the 40-strong staff of the General Secretariat of the Government. This involves organising the vast numbers of meetings of formal interministerial committees (often chaired by the prime minister) and *ad hoc* working groups of ministers or top ministerial aides. These include the annual round of budget arbitration committees where the prime minister must either persuade his ministerial partners to agree to a coherent package or impose his own arbitration.

The use of the General Secretariat staff to assist in coordination and arbitration tasks has often allowed the prime minister's personal advisers in the *cabinet* – often 30 or more in number – to focus on policy initiation. This role is not easy since the prime minister's staff, like that of the president, must be both effective and discreet so that he can exercise real influence but avoid offending the sensitivities of his ministers. The *cabinet* also helps with the difficult task of parliamentary management which has not only effects on policy (when decisions on accepting or rejecting amendments have to be made) but also an important impact on public relations (notably in major policy declarations, answering parliamentary questions, and employing such 'guillotine' devices as article 49, clause 3).

Finally there is the thorny and often thankless task of attempting to ensure the loyal support of the president's party and coalition partner(s). Before 1981 only one prime minister, Pompidou, was really successful in this field. Mauroy could not hope to have smooth relations with the embittered PCF but he was very sensitive to, and appreciated by, his own party between 1981 and 1984. Indeed, by pushing ahead with the project – so beloved of PS activisits – to phase out private schools, he led his government into a major crisis. Fabius was far less effective with the PS, partly because he was a purely presidential choice but partly too because he seemed unable to avoid challenging the authority of Jospin, the Secretary of the PS.

Fabius was, however, more generally effective at public relations than his predecessor and made good use of frequent television appearances. During his premiership the popularity of his government and party increased considerably and his own image as an effective leader was enhanced. By March 1986 he was no longer seen as a presidential assistant, but as an effective and dynamic leader of the government in his own right.

Cohabitation, however, produced not only a further 'retreat' of the presidency but also a public recognition of full prime ministerial leadership in domestic affairs. *Cohabitation* was not a system of collaboration or cooperation; instead, it involved continual competitive coexistence, often at the risk of public conflict. All but two of the ministers were chosen freely by the prime minister. Only for Defence and Foreign Affairs could the president claim some constitutional right to be consulted, and there he rejected Chirac's choices. Compromise 'technician' ministers were then agreed. All the major policy options in domestic affairs came straight from the RPR–UDF electoral programme, with Chirac dictating the pace and priorities. The vast privatisation programme, the changes of immigrants' rights and police powers, the tax reforms and the new television control agency (all discussed in other chapters) were decided by the government in spite of the president's hostility. The Council of Ministers still met on Wednesdays with Mitterrand in the chair, but it was completely by-passed as a decision-making body. Chirac met his ministers in advance, without the president, to agree a collective position. Thus the

Council of Ministers merely gave formal legitimation to decisions made elsewhere. So clear was the prime minister's leadership in domestic policy-making that there appeared to be a 'presidentialisation' of Matignon (the Hotel Matignon is the prime minister's official residence and office). Journalists even suggested that Balladur, the Finance Minister and Chirac's closest lieutenant, had become the 'real prime minister'.

All this notwithstanding, the president was not simply relegated to a back seat. This partly reflected Chirac's unwillingness to empty the presidency – the office he hoped to win in 1988 – of its predominant role in foreign and defence matters. It was also partly a consequence of the considerable consensus between Chirac and Mitterrand on many foreign and defence policy options. Hence it was often possible for the president and prime minister to attend international or European meetings together and for them jointly to pursue an agreed line in negotiations. The president's continuing influence, however, was largely due to Mitterrand's political skill in exploiting his situation.

During the period of *cohabitation* Mitterrand presented himself not only as the voice of France in Europe and the world and the true supreme commander-in-chief of the armed forces, but also as the 'arbiter and guarantor of the Constitution', the defender of national unity, and the protector of the poor and the weak. He had the great advantage that the decisions he took in foreign and defence matters – whether to withdraw troops from Lebanon in 1986 or adopt a critical position on Soviet disarmament proposals in 1987 and 1988 – had the full support of the prime minister and the government. Furthermore his frequent official visits abroad inevitably grabbed the headlines and became the lead items of television news broadcasts. Hence although Chirac increasingly attempted to influence foreign policy (by replacing many ambassadors and conducting direct discussions with foreign governments without keeping Mitterrand informed), he gained little public credit for this. His one widely-known foreign initiative, the freeing of the Lebanon hostages in 1988, brought him scant respect as its timing appeared suspiciously electoral (the hostages were released two days before the second ballot of the 1988 presidential elections).

Mitterrand, in contrast, was more skilful in his interventions in domestic matters. He rarely changed the policy outcome, but he established himself as a defender of national interests and fair play. Hence he refused to approve delegated legislation to allow privatisation and to change the electoral system and justified the former decision by the need to protect French industry from foreign take-overs and the latter on the grounds of fair play and equality. In both cases the changes were carried out (by normal statute law) but the president had focused attention on the 'divisive and sectarian' nature of governmental policies. Mitterrand's interventions of this kind were rare because he quickly realised that he could not hope to win re-election in 1988 if he appeared to be responsible for the collapse of *cohabitation*. Nonetheless he made public attacks on the government's decisions to limit social security benefits, to allow university selection, to abolish the wealth tax, to expel Mali citizens with no immigration papers (in late 1986), to restrict the access of immigrants to full citizenship and to protect settlers' interests in New Caledonia. By so doing he helped to create his own image as a true father-figure and to caricature Chirac as sectarian, selfish and partisan. His triumph in this respect came in 1987 when he diverted attacks on the PS for corruption by proposing that the prime minister should bring together all the parties to discuss a joint agreed policy for public funding to political parties.

The opinion polls indicated that *cohabitation* was generally well liked by the electorate, except during the last months when the presidential election campaign led to more public confrontations between the two main protagonists. Most politicians, however, liked it much less and were relieved when it ended. Mitterrand, however, learned several lessons. The first was that it is much easier to be a consensual respected and popular president if the leadership role is restricted to foreign and defence policy areas and occasional interventions in domestic matters to defend national unity goals. The second was that clearly sectarian policies (including the distribution of 'spoils' posts in the public sector) cause unnecessary resentment and hostility. The third was that power sharing between a president from one political family and a government from another does not scare the electorate nearly as much as it horrifies the politicians. Certainly Mitterrand's own popularity in 1988 did not lead to a landslide majority in the Assembly for his followers, as his victory in 1981 had done.

The first year of the Rocard Government saw the president clearly recognised as the supreme authority. Rocard was clearly Mitterrand's choice as prime minister, rather than that of the PS. Rocard's policy of seeking new support from the Centre also followed from Mitterrand's presidential campaign promises. Nevertheless, most of the ministers were chosen by Rocard and only the Defence and Foreign Affairs ministers were purely presidential choices. The solution of the crisis in New Caledonia was clearly Rocard's work and most domestic policy choices appear to have been worked out by him and his ministers with little presidential intervention, although the promises of Mitterrand's re-election campaign have been respected. As long as there is no major crisis, the president seems content to let his prime minister lead, but to continue his own active role in foreign and defence matters. The 'Rocard method' of government by negotiated consensus and long-term incremental policies fits in well with Mitterrand's new approach. In 1989, the 'imperial presidency' of de Gaulle during the Algerian War, of Pompidou in 1972–3 and of Giscard d'Estaing seemed to have been replaced by a more shared leadership pattern with the prime minister as the key domestic figure.

Changing the Limits of Political Leadership: Europe and Decentralisation

The role and functions of national political leaders in France has not only been modified by the distribution of power within national institutions but also by the transfer of authority from Paris to the provinces and to Brussels. The decentralisation reforms of the early 1980s, and especially the legally imposed limit of the accumulation of elected offices (discussed in Chapter 8), imply that urban and regional leaders are now emerging with real leadership opportunities in their respective jurisdictions. Indeed, to be mayor of a big town such as Marseilles or Toulouse may well be much more interesting and influential than being a back-bench member of the Assembly or Senate. If the Rocard Government carries out its promise of reducing the number of regions, the regional council leadership posts (especially the presidencies) will become increasingly attractive jobs in their own right. This is not to suggest that the top posts in national government will cease to be the prime targets for political careerists, but rather that new attractive local leadership positions are being created alongside the old national ones.

Perhaps of more immediate importance, however, has been the impact of European integration. As a founder member of the Coal and Steel Community and the EC, France has a long experience of the ever-growing range of policies which are decided by the Commission or *jointly* in Brussels or which are left to market forces. In the 1980s the impact on political leadership is beginning to become clear. Since 1981 the EMS has not only survived but prospered. The Single European Act was agreed in July 1987 and the Schengen Treaty signed in 1986. These provide for removing the existing controls on capital flows, the removal of border controls on goods and persons, further deregulation and liberalisation measures, and some tax harmonisation. The parameters of policy-making for French governments are gradually being reduced as the European Commission issues more directives and the Court imposes some respect for these rulings. Inevitably there are effects on political leadership.

One consequence is that the policy debates with EC institutions are becoming the locus for important decisions and consequently the focus for the media. The leaders of France's European partners (or at least Thatcher and Kohl during the 1980s) are increasingly familiar figures within France, and all French leaders seek to show their European stature to the voters at home by effective policy leadership in Brussels. The European Commission itself, once despised and derided by de Gaulle, is now presided over by a close associate of Mitterrand, Delors, who was Finance Minister from 1981 to 1984. Not surprisingly it has gained wide respect throughout France. Even the European Parliament has gained in prestige. The two main competing party lists for the 1989 European Parliament elections were led by an ex-president, Giscard d'Estaing, and an ex-prime minister, Fabius, both of whom clearly saw real potential for developing a leadership role even in Strasburg. French political debates now have a distinct European flavour, and the policy preferences of other member states of the EC are discussed in all the media. No national leader is openly opposed to European integration and only Le Pen and Marchais have proposed radically different patterns of European cooperation from those currently pursued.

Promoting New Leadership Styles: Institutions and Media

During the early years of the Fifth Republic the objectives for politicians with ambitions of attaining top leadership positions were completely changed by the creation of the elective presidency and the establishment of stable governments with disciplined parliamentary majorities. The top job was no longer the premiership but the presidency, and the method of obtaining it was by winning popular support rather than by avoiding offending party barons. Although the old political parties initially disliked this personalisation of power, and the Communists (who had no hope of ever winning the presidency) did not change in this respect, there was a gradual change in the ways in which all other parties selected their leaders. In 1971 Mitterrand was chosen as secretary of the PS because of his 'presidential stature'. After 1981 Barre and Giscard d'Estaing contested the effective leadership of the UDF as a base for presidential campaigns against Chirac and Mitterrand in 1988. In turn there was a change in the leadership competition as various approaches to gaining presidential stature were tried. Within the PS some sought ministerial office to demonstrate their competence and others attempted to keep a firm hold on the party machine or a party faction, whilst other pursued the strategy of promotion through the presidential 'court'. For some who wished to participate in national leadership but had no dreams of the presidency (Bérégovoy or Dumas are good examples), posts as ministers became ends in themselves, whereas for others (notably Fabius and Rocard) they were seen as merely steps on the path to higher glories.

The leadership competition was not only changed by these institutional factors, but also by the growing importance of television for conveying political information and forming public opinion. The gradual liberalisation of television from tight control by the government (as under de Gaulle and Pompidou in the latter years), or by its journalist friends placed in key posts within the television companies (as under Giscard d'Estaing), meant that leaders of all political parties were welcome on television. Not only was the period of the 'televisual non-person' closed, but all politicians were increasingly judged by their technique on television. Long interviews with individual politicians (including *l'Heure de vérité, Droit de réponse, Questions à domicile, Sept sur sept*) have become popular mass viewing and thus essential virility tests for would-be leaders. Le Pen and Harlem Désir both passed from being marginal leaders of minority groups to having national stature as politicians by their successful television appearances on programmes of this kind.

The campaign for presidential elections is now largely fought on the television screens of France. In 1988 it was not, however, the candidates' own allotted campaign slots which commanded the public attention; on the contrary, these may have been visually entertaining (Mitterrand's fast moving images were never boring) or worthy but boring (the case for most minor candidates). There was much greater interest in discussions between politicians and journalists, and in the televised debates between the candidates themselves, especially that between the two who contested the second ballot of the presidential elections. If Mitterrand did not win his re-election in 1988 by his 'defeat' of Chirac in the televised face-to-face debate, he certainly exploited the chance to demonstrate his verbal prowess and tactical skill.

The side effects of this television impact on political leaders have been two-fold: almost every serious leadership candidate now employs a public relations consultant and regularly commissions private opinion polls. In 1965, when Lecanuet sprang to overnight fame in a presidential campaign which 'sold him like toothpaste', other politicians derided such desperate tactics (and nick-named Lecanuet Mr Colgate). In 1974, however, after his narrow defeat by the professionally-advised Giscard d'Estaing, even Mitterrand changed his mind. The success of the Seguela campaign posters and slogans for Mitterrand in 1981 was widely remarked. In the race for the presidency all the candidates of the main parties had their own consultants in public relations; it was joked that even Chirac's shirts were chosen by his public relations man. Closely linked with the growth of such consultancy activity was the massive spread of opinion polling. This is by no means restricted to presidential contests, but is widely used in parliamentary and even municipal election campaigns. One of the consequences of these developments is that politics has become extremely expensive and the public financing of the parties has become essential if this professionalisation is to continue.

Concluding Remarks

By 1980, the president, very weak before 1958, had become very powerful in relation to the parties and Parliament; so too had his government. Attitudes towards leadership gradually had changed in response to the new reality, at both elite and mass levels. What has emerged during the 1980s is that leadership remains personalised, but is becoming increasingly diversified. The firmament of French politics no longer contains only one sun, but now has many stars. Most leading politicians in 1989 favour the present dispersal of power-centres and the power-sharing which it imposes: in Europe, between centre and periphery, between president and prime minister, or between government and Parliament. Some critics, however, note that if the stars are now numerous, the present 'star system' still has much in common with that of Hollywood: success depends not only on talent but also on physique, voice, technique, lighting, make-up and, above all, on finding a good public relations consultant.

6

The Administrative Machine: Old Problems and New Dilemmas

VINCENT WRIGHT

Recent developments have created unprecedented tensions and problems for the French administration. Those tensions and problems are related to the self-image of the administration, its functioning and its role. They highlight the fact that whilst the administration may have acquired a certain autonomy, it is nevertheless sensitive to the changing moods and conflicts of the state and society it serves.

The malaise of the administration is the subject of widespread comment and, in 1988, was manifested in widely supported public-sector strikes. One of Michel Rocard's first tasks, when he recognised the sense of disorientation within the administration, was to engage in prolonged discussions with the Civil Service unions. But these discussions merely revealed the depth of the crisis rather than led to any practical solutions. At bottom, the crisis is linked to the accelerating abandonment of the traditional model of French administration, a model which defined the powers, regulated the functioning and, perhaps most importantly, established the legitimacy of the state administrative machine. For that reason it is important briefly to analyse the distinguishing characteristics of the model and its distortion before 1980; after that, we will examine the further destabilising impact of recent developments.

114

The Napoleonic Model of Administration

The French administration – unlike its British counterpart – was forged according to a model: a model which corresponded closely to the ideas and prejudices of Napoleon Bonaparte, its creator. As a general, Napoleon had a clear predilection for hierarchical command structures; as a man of method he was disposed to codification; as a nationalist he was keen on welding together a country which had lived through a prolonged period of civil war, the 'temptations of federation', political and social disorder; as an astute and pragmatic politician he was prepared to absorb some of the practices, institutions and personnel of past regimes. The characteristics of the Napoleonic model of administration clearly reflected the tastes and preoccupations of its founder.

In the first place, the administration was to be an agent of state power. In a divided nation it should embody the continuity of the state and represent the general interest. As such it was endowed with a certain mystique and legitimacy which armed it against the particular interests whose conflicts constantly threatened the nation's harmony. Disinterested, dispassionate, distant and depoliticised, the administration reflected the grandeur and continuity of the state. Top civil servants were given big salaries, splendid residences, titles and rather baroque uniforms, all of which were designed to underline their status as representatives of the state.

The next characteristic of the Napoleonic administration was the power that was bestowed upon it. This power was both functional and territorial. Top civil servants (notably in the Council of State) displaced politicians as the major definers and defenders of legislation, and an army of state officials in the provinces implemented that legislation. Moreover, from the outset the state penetrated policy areas (such as education) which were left to private agents on the other side of the Channel.

The third characteristic was that the administration, given its multiple roles, should be efficient. Technical expertise was required and was to be nurtured in the specialist schools inherited from the *ancien régime* (such as the *Ecole des Ponts et Chaussées*) or the Revolution (such as the *Ecole Polytechnique*): their students were to form the 'technical' corps, including the Mines Corps and the Roads and Bridges Corps. Generalist expertise was to be acquired through training in the *grands corps de l'Etat*: the *Corps préfectoral* and the Council of State (both created in 1800), the Treasury Inspectorate (1801) and the Court of Accounts (1807); all of which had their roots in the *ancien régime*.

Fourth, the administration was to be based on a centralised and pyramidal structure of decision-making, both territorially and within the Paris ministries. Fifth, the administration should be distinguished by uniformity. This may be seen in several ways. For instance, all local authorities, irrespective of their size, whereabouts, resources or traditions were given exactly the same legal powers. Similarly, the structure and functioning of all public services were rigidly to conform to a uniform pattern, and the Council of State was empowered to impose the pattern.

Finally, the administration was powerful but, because of its place and power, was to be controlled: administrative malpractices could only tarnish the image of the state. However, Napoleon was unwilling to confide the function of control to irremovable and politically irresponsible judges, or to representative institutions. Three major methods of control were employed: power of dismissal; a disciplinary code (of almost military rigour); and institutionalised internal mechanisms such as the Court of Accounts and the Council of State; these devices are discussed in Chapter 7.

Statist, powerful, centralised, hierarchically-structured, ubiquitous, uniform, depoliticised, instrumental, expert and tightly controlled; such were the dominant features of the Napoleonic administrative model. Those features were connected in a coherent, systematic and logical fashion, and were designed to provide a machine capable of ensuring social and territorial integration, political order and functional efficacy. It was – and remains – a model attractive to tidy minds in untidy countries. French history has been punctuated by efforts to return to at least some of the principles of the original model. Indeed, the administrative ambitions of the founders of the Fifth Republic in 1958 rested on a desire to resurrect some of the features of the Napoleonic model. However, the constantly reiterated desire to return to the model suggests that it had been undermined: this was the case from the outset. Even during the First Empire military, political and bureaucratic pressures combined to distort the functioning of the model. Those pressures were to increase in number and intensity after the fall of the Empire. However, even now the French administration bears the Napoleonic imprint, a point to which we shall return.

The Distortion of the Napoleonic Model

Several factors combined to ensure that the model was never fully imposed in the country of its inception. Yet it is worth emphasising that some of its features were to continue to shape the institutions, functions and attitudes of the administration and were to create an administration which was quite different from those of its British and West German neighbours. The executant role of the administration, the obsession with uniformity, the emphasis on expertise, the existence of training schools designed specifically for civil servants, the key role of the *grands corps* and the conferment of state legitimacy were amongst the distinctive attributes of the French model.

In some respects, these attributes were to be progressively strengthened by successive regimes. First, the executive role of the administration expanded dramatically with the extension of state activities. Activities left to private agents, elected local authorities or semi-autonomous bodies in other countries were embraced by the interventionist state. Even during the nineteenth century there were frequent denunciations of the proliferating power of officialdom. The creation and consolidation of the welfare state (the 'father' of the welfare state in France was a senior civil servant from the Council of State: See Chapter 10) extended the reach of the administration into new areas, whilst the industrial modernisation of the country rested in part on the massive mobilisation of state resources and officials. By the late 1970s the French Civil Service, with nearly two million members, accounted for some 12 per cent of the active population (although the figure embraces schoolteachers, postmen and the police): since 1900 the figure had increased thirty-fold. With its central administrations and extensive provincial field services, its vast army of other administrative agencies and its extensive public industrial, financial and insurance sectors (which were further expanded between 1981 and 1983 by the newly elected Socialist Government), France acquired the reputation of being an 'administered state'. However, as the scale of state interventionism grew, the multiplication of tasks often led to conflicting roles, with one part of the administration attempting to inhibit or undo the work of another part.

Second, the continued obsession with uniformity was apparent in the 'regulatory mania' which afflicted the administration; the passage of a law was followed by a flood of decrees and instructions designed to ensure uniform implementation. The administration was slowly drowning under a flood of paper: between 1971 and 1981, no fewer than 125 516 laws, decrees, directives and circulars emanated from the Paris ministries. The 1945 legislation on prices was to engender 27 000 implementing decrees in the following 35 years, whilst the 1980 legislation on noise abatement required 636 pages of explanation. Such figures were to be exploited by the neo-liberals in their assault on the administration in the 1980s. The obsession with uniformity continues to be apparent, too, in the definition of the powers of local authorities. Thus, the major decentralisation drive of the Socialists in the 1980s devolved the same powers to all communes whether they had a population of more than 100 000 or less than a hundred.

The third enduring feature of the Napoleonic model – the emphasis on technical expertise – may be seen in the key roles, often of a generalist nature, played by groups such as the highly qualified engineers of the Mines and Roads and Bridges Corps. Indeed, certain posts of the administration are perceived as being reserved for such corps, who protect them with almost legendary vigour.

Fourth, the traditional training schools for civil servants have survived constant changes of regime and political and military upheaval and have acquired even greater prestige than in the past. Moreover, after some experiments and much misgiving, France created the Ecole Nationale d'Administration immediately after the Second World War. Its role is to select and train the nation's top generalist civil servants. The ENA, as it is familiarly known, has gained a great reputation in its short existence, and its students – nicknamed *Enarques* – have now colonised many of the major posts of the state apparatus. Since the 1970s a number of regional administrative institutes have the task of selecting and training intermediate-class civil servants.

The existence and prestige of the *grands corps* (both technical and generalist) provide the fifth enduring feature of the Napoleonic model. Both types have increased their role, power and prestige since their carefully selected and highly mobile members have managed to penetrate major areas of state (and even private) decision-making.

A further instance of the survival of the model has been the elaborate system of internal controls, a response to the extension and detailed nature of state interventions. These controls are of a legal, technical and financial character and are exercised after the event. They are numerous but rarely very effective.

Finally, the administration continues to root its legitimacy in its role as the disinterested agent of the general interest, the guardian of the public good and the promoter of the interest of the state. Of course, some civil servants have learned the politics of accommodation (a point we shall take up later) but state-based legitimacy shapes the myths, traditions, symbols, rhetoric, collective attitudes and reactions of most officials.

If some features of the Napoleonic model have proved tenacious, others were to be more fragile or even fallacious in character. Two principal pressures combined to deform the model. The first was political in nature and had several dimensions. It will be recalled that the Napoleonic vision of the administration posited an essentially depoliticised body. However, the role of the French administration was an intrinsically political one. It was given a key role in the nation-building process and as such became one of the props of French nationalism. In integrating the Bretons, the Basques, the Corsicans and later (from 1860) the Savoyards, the reputation of political neutrality and impartiality could only be sullied in the eyes of regional nationalists. But the integrative role of the administration also involved a persistent combat (especially during the early years of the Third Republic) against other groups whose loyalties to the indivisibility of the nation were considered to be suspect. Thus for certain Catholic circles the administration was then seen as an instrument of secular oppression.

The politicisation of the administration was heightened by its role in consolidating new regimes. Each new regime was suspicious of the administrators it inherited, and indulged in extensive purges of senior civil servants, replacing them with politically reliable officials. Parts of the administration were also given a specific political task of political repression (the Interior, Defence and Justice Ministries) or of distributing patronage in a politically judicious way. But it was not only new regimes which were suspicious of top civil servants and coveted their posts. Any radical change of government provoked purges, as new ministers were hesitant to rely on the appointees of their predecessors. Suspicion of the power and political persuasions of all senior civil servants also led to the creation of ministerial *cabinets*: private offices, each of which was recruited by a particular minister to serve him alone and disbanded when he lost his post. Initially these private offices were recruited from amongst personal friends and political allies, and were seen as a buffer against the administration. However, it soon became apparent that the best way to combat the administration was with professionally skilled civil servants. By the Fourth Republic, the majority of members of the private offices were civil servants.

A final factor enhanced the politicisation of the French administration. During the Restoration Monarchy (1815–30) and the July Monarchy (1830–48), many senior civil servants were also members of Parliament (it was not until the Third Republic that rules of incompatibility were introduced) and took an active part in the political controversies of the time. The tradition of the interpenetration of political and administrative elites was to continue thereafter. Bored or restless civil servants would leave (often temporarily) the administration to pursue a political career, a phenomenon which was to be strengthened during the Fifth Republic. The result of these various factors was that the administration became an eminently political animal and lost its depoliticised mission and reputation.

Political pressures also undermined the substance of centralisation. Of course, centralisation remained anchored in the texts (and, for a long time, in the textbooks): Paris decided, the provinces implemented. Yet, from the outset, the reality was infinitely more complex. Provincial leaders, or *notables* – 'men of granite' as they were called during the First Empire – negotiated their support for the imperial regime, a situation which was to characterise every other regime which followed. Some local potentates, entrenched in their fiefdoms, usurped much of the power of prefects and sub-prefects. An elaborate and subtle game was established depending upon the political, financial and technical resources of the actors involved. The constraining rules of centralisation masked, at least in some areas, the practice of local autonomy. Furthermore, the wide variety of relations which resulted between state officials and local political potentates meant that uniformity – another characteristic of the Napoleonic model – was sacrificed.

Bureaucratic pressures also had their impact on the Napoleonic model. In the first place, the model presupposes a unity of purpose and an overarching rationality which may be present in an army but which is singularly lacking in an administration. As noted above, the state administrative machine became increasingly fragmented and internally divided: between central officials and their field services, between generalists and specialists, between senior civil servants and their subordinates of the specialised bureaux, between Finance Ministry officials and those from the spending ministries, between civil servants in the private offices and those in the rest of the administration, between the active administrators and those who had the task of controlling them and so on. The French administration became like a huge Balkan empire, full of squabbling cliques, each intent on buttressing its corporate self-interest and each generating its own method of functioning, traditions and sources of legitimacy. In this bewildering world of differing ministries, corps, grades, career structures and statute, uniformity (already sacrificed in defining central–local relations) was clearly lacking. The more extended the state became, the greater was the potential for conflicts between the various administrative groups, since almost all policy areas involved overlapping jurisdictions. Attempts to coordinate this fragmented and divided machine were numerous (superministries, integrative horizontally-organised missions, inter-departmental committees) but generally ineffective. Conflicts were displaced rather than resolved. The neat pyramidal power structures which underpin the model gave way to the conflictual and ill-coordinated world of competitive groups.

The second bureaucratic pressure was the internal push to define a certain independence *vis-à-vis* the politicians. From the 1860s, recruitment came to be based on merit – assessed through competitive examinations – and promotion mainly on seniority. Political discretion over appointments was progressively reduced and focused on the politically sensitive top posts of prefects and sub-prefects, university rectors and ambassadors.

Political and bureaucratic pressures led, therefore, to the dilution of the depoliticised, uniform, centralised and hierarchical nature of the Napoleonic model. Four other factors were to distort the model further. The first was the emergence, at the turn of the century, of trade unions in the administration. Their recognition gave rise to debates of theological intensity which revolved around the question of whether a civil servant's loyalty and obligation to the state precluded all others. Slowly and reluctantly, unions were recognised (notably by the 1946 Civil Service Statute) and became powerful in certain sectors of the administration. They introduced loyalties and rigidities which were to attract the critical attention of the neo-liberals in the 1980s.

The second additional factor which distorted the Napoleonic model concerns the erosion of the image of the administration as the representative of the state. As already noted, it was also perceived by many as the representative of the regime and even the government. Moreover, much of the model rests on the assumption of the sanctity of the public domain, whereas the French experience of development has been characterised by the intermingling of the private and public sectors and by widespread complicity between them. Several elements contributed to the blurring of the line between the public and private sectors: the creation of 'mixed' public–private firms, the existence of joint ventures between, and of contracts linking public and private enterprises; the taking of financial stakes by state financial groups in privately-run companies; the acceptance by certain state officials of private interests as an intrinsic part of defining the general interest; and the practice of *pantouflage*, by which state officials resigned from the administration to take up posts in the private sector. Defining the 'interest of the state' in circumstances in which pluralistic premises (however attenuated and vague) prevail and in which state and private interests constantly interact becomes intrinsically more difficult.

A third additional factor which undermined part of the model was the increasing sectoralisation of public policy-making. There was an increasing mismatch between the official hierarchical or vertical system of administrative decision-making and the practice of horizontal decision-making through policy communities (such as agriculture, education and industry). There emerged between state officials and their client groups an extraordinary variety of relationships, ranging from the tightly cohesive to outright hostility. However, the essential point is that these policy communities also became autonomous in their operation, and generally escaped feeble attempts at coordination.

Finally, mention should be made of the increasing juridification of the French administration. The legal stipulation, the codified rule, became the haven of the French bureaucrat. Some form of legal training became an essential component and sometimes a dominant element in the upbringing of the average civil servant. Yet the rigidities inherent in an overcodified system engendered methods of circumventing them: lawyers not only make law, they also interpret it. The loophole became the spiritual home of many French bureaucrats: the law is applied but in a flexible way, since exemptions and exceptions abound. The predictability of the Napoleonic (and Weberian) models, embedded in the notion of uniformity defined by the law, gives way to unpredictability and even arbitrariness. Access to, and influence over, strategically-placed civil servants determines whether objectives are achieved.

What, then, were the dominant features of the French administration until the late 1970s? Briefly, in its institutions, its legal framework, its essential mission and its source of legitimacy, it remained marked by its Napoleonic origins. In its internal functioning, its relations with outside groups and its multiple roles it had moved away from the model. By the mid-1970s it became possible to discern several types of administration: a modernising and interventionist one, often based on mobile and highly trained elites from the *grandes écoles* and the *grands corps*; a heavily bureaucratised one based on lower officials intent on applying the rules; a pragmatic one involved in negotiating incremental changes to the status quo with interest groups. Certainly, the tidy and coherent administrative world depicted by the military mind had given way, under various pressures, to a differentiated and competitive universe. The gap between the model and the reality was clear to all. Pressures since the late-1970s have merely served to widen the gap.

The Impact of Recent Developments

Since the late 1970s, irrespective of the political complexion of the parties in government, several attempts have been made to reform, modernise and rationalise the administration. The general code of the Civil Service's conditions of service was thoroughly revised by the Socialist Government elected in 1981. The formal bureaucratic framework was widened to encompass the numerous part-timers and people working on short-term contracts, as well as local officials. Yet a number of interconnected developments may be discerned which have exacerbated the problems of the administration and which have accentuated the sense of malaise which had been growing since the 1960s.

The first development which has had a damaging impact on the administration has been the calling into question of the role of the interventionist state and a growing scepticism about its efficiency. It is not only the neo-liberals who have been claiming that 'less state means a better state' and have questioned the mission of the interceding and redistributive welfare state. Even the Gaullist Right now claim that the state should retreat from a managerial role to that of a last resort protector, while the Socialists, after 1983, came to recognise the 'limits of the State'. Bestsellers (such as *Toujours Plus!* by François de Closets and *Les Danseuses de la République* by J.P. Gaudard) have helped to articulate and popularise latent suspicions about state activitiy. Public opinion, which was generally pro-state in the 1970s, is now imbued with scepticism or even hostility. Furthermore, authors such as Alain Minc (*L'Après-crise est Commencé* and *La Machine Egalitaire*) have pointed to the role of the administration as a key actor in the distributionist coalition which pushed for state expansion.

The neo-liberal onslaught has had several consequences for the administration. In the first place, as the principal servant of the state, the Civil Service has been pushed on to the defensive about its role. Second, its very *rationality*, rooted in the pursuit and protection of 'the public good' and the 'general interest', no longer confers upon it an unassailable legitimacy. Indeed, it is now argued that bureaucratic rationality spawns irrational bureaucracies. As the French have sought to reconcile the market and the community, competing and conflicting rationalities have come to rival those of the state and its servants. Third, and as a consequence of the previous two points, the administration is uneasy in confronting the reforming zeal of the anti-statists who are intent on a policy of liberalisation and deregulation (to which we will return later). Liberalisation and deregulation were very clearly written into the electoral platforms of the Right in the 1986 and 1988 elections but were also pursued, without the rhetorical flourishes, by the Socialists.

We should, of course, be careful to distinguish between the two basic meanings of deregulation. The first involves a diminution and simplification of that vast regulatory web which, it is alleged, strangles initiative and inhibits enterprise. Since the late 1970s (starting with Giscard d'Estaing's 96 proposed measures) various attempts have been made to reduce administrative formalities in an attack on excessive paperwork. Thus a commission on the reform of administrative formalities of firms has been suggesting means of reducing the vast number of detailed procedures that burden the business world.

The second prong of the deregulating strategy involves the introduction of market objectives and practices into the state machinery. This may take a number of forms. In the first place, there has been a rapid decline in the role and prestige of the so-called state modernising agencies, such as the Planning Commissariat (see Chapter 9) and the DATAR, the major territorial and regional planning agency. Indeed, the Belin–Gisserot Report of 1986, which was commissioned and discussed by the Right-wing government of Jacques Chirac, suggested that many agencies such as the Planning Commissariat, the DATAR and the CESTA (Centre for Advanced Technologies) could be reduced in size or simply abolished. Second, since 1983–4 there has been a redefinition of the role of public-sector industries: their employment, social and local economy functions were replaced by largely market-oriented ones. Subsidies were dramatically reduced, and brutal restructuring and slimming-down operations carried out; modernisation and profitability became their operational key words. Managerial autonomy was demanded and accorded both by the Right and the Left. Socialist governments have appointed commercially-oriented managers to head state industries and have allowed them more or less free access to private capital.

The sub-contracting of certain public services to non-state agents (especially at local level) is a third example of the drive to 'bring the market into the administration'. A fourth example is the introduction of private management techniques, incentives and even personnel into the public service. Market-oriented commercial management is now amongst the subjects taught at the *Ecole Polytechnique* and the ENA. It is perhaps revealing that the French Socialists should appoint Roger Fauroux, the Managing Director of Saint-Gobain, the glass-making giant, as Director of the ENA in 1986, before making him Minister of Industry in 1988. The frontier between the public and private sectors is being further obfuscated by these moves. Finally, there has been a growth of private sector provision in areas such as social welfare, training, broadcasting, monitoring and documentation services.

At its most extreme, deregulation may be seen in the progressive dismantling during the 1980s of the machinery of price controls, the easing of credit controls, the liberalisation of the financial markets (the 'Big Bang' in London was quickly followed by the 'Little Bang' in Paris) and, of course, the policy of privatisation pursued openly between 1986 and 1988, more surreptitiously between 1981 and 1986, and again after 1988. Liberalisation and deregulation are partly imposed by the requirements of inter-nationalisation. They are also made inevitable by the increasing Europeanisation of many sectors (for example, agriculture, steel, ship-building and transport) of public policy-making. Nationally-based institutions such as Civil Services are confronted with complex problems of adjustment in this new situation. The fundamental axiom of the Napoleonic model – the existence of state sovereignty – clearly no longer holds.

The second development which has had a deleterious effect on the administration has been cut-back management. The post-war mission and much envied self-confidence of the French administration was rooted in a steady expansion of the state and its corollary, a steady growth in the number of civil servants. The 30 years of economic growth which followed the Second World War facilitated redistribution and bureaucratic compromises between competing parts of the state machine, each serving a particularistic clientele. However, the luxury of incrementalism (the gradual accommodation of interests within the framework of a slowly expanding budget) gave way to the process of decrementalism after the second great oil shock, and more especially after the Socialist Government's celebrated 'U-turn' in 1982–3. The problem of resources has become acute: revenues have been squeezed through mounting unemployment (which has also increased demands on those resources), low or negative growth and growing political resistance to increased taxation. Yet demands in areas such as health and crises in the industrial heartlands (notably steel) have required increased revenues.

A number of consequences have flowed from this squeeze, including a general attack on the overprivileged civil servants who are cushioned against the impact of the recession. In yet another version of the 'dual economy' thesis, France is seen as being divided between the wealth-producing yet vulnerable private-sector workers and the comfortable and stable public civil servants, safe in their guaranteed jobs, decent working conditions and index-linked wages and pensions. The attack on these 'parasites' (Jean-Marie Le Pen) has taken various forms. For instance, there has been an attempt (not altogether successful) to reduce numbers. The radical proposals of Gérard Longuet who suggested, in 1979, that numbers could be reduced to 400 000, with the remaining 1 600 000 being dispersed to agencies (a recent Thatcherite idea) were discreetly shelved. The Socialist Government of 1981 even expanded the size of the administration by some 100 000 before 1983, but as part of its May 1983 austerity package decided to freeze all further appointments. Since that date, small reductions have been budgeted for (although the reduction in numbers appears to be compensated by an increase in the number of short-contract officials). Significantly, the number of students recruited to the regional institutes of administration has been reduced somewhat, whilst the ENA has been forced to reduce its intake by half, but has subsequently been increased by the Socialists. The result of these various cut-backs combined with the increase in the number of candidates for administrative posts (as a consequence of the general rise in the number of unemployed) has been the recruitment of overqualified people for the posts available. They are frequently more competent than their superiors recruited in earlier years, but see their chances of promotion blocked by the failure to create new posts, the still-entrenched rules of seniority in certain ministries and the rigidities defended by powerful unions. Not surprisingly, this situation has given rise to tensions which compound those analysed below. Since the mid-1980s, civil servants of all ranks and occupation have seen the de-indexation of their wages, and have been obliged to contribute to their own pensions in the name of solidarity.

The resource squeeze has increased tensions between bureaucracies competing for diminishing resources, and has also increased strains in the relations between civil servants and others in their various policy communities (notably in agriculture, health, education and industry). It has, perhaps inevitably, enhanced the administrative authority of the prime minister's office and the financial leverage of the Finance Ministry. But possibly the most unsettling aspect of cut-back management has been the drive towards the modernisation of the French administration in the name of cost-efficiency. Alien notions such as productivity, quality and cost-effectiveness are clashing with traditional concepts of the public good. The demands of cut-back management are intimately linked with, yet distinct from, those emanating from the anti-statists. Together, they are demoralising the once self-confident French civil servants.

A third destablising recent development has been the introduction of new technologies and managerial techniques. The French have been especially sensitive to the explosion of so-called 'convergent information technologies' (computer data processing, telecommunications and office automation products) and many civil servants have been trained in this area. The Modernisation of Central Ministries Task Force, as its title reveals, has been given the role of informing the Paris ministries of new technological advances. In this new situation, acquired skills are being rendered obsolete and traditional demarcation lines between civil servants eroded. Technologically superior but hierarchically subordinate officials are questioning established patterns of authority and more participative management procedures (with the emergence of quality circles in many ministries) are providing the arena for such questioning.

The fourth major recent development affecting the administration has been the policy of territorial decentralisation and deconcentration which was pursued throughout the 1970s but more especially after 1981. Since this is dealt with elsewhere in the book (in Chapter 8) the point will not be laboured. Suffice to note that the post-1981 reforms have affected various parts of the state administration very differently: some not at all (Defence, Foreign Affairs), some very little (Labour and Interior), some slightly (Infrastructure has transferred about 7–8 per cent of its personnel to local authorities), and one (Health and Social Security) quite considerably. It is worth pointing out that a diminution in the personnel and functions of the central administration does not necessarily involve a reduction in its influence. There is more than a suspicion that the devolution of responsibilities in the social and health spheres (where revenues are failing to match rising demands) was greeted with some relief by central administration officials. Nevertheless, the processes of decentralisation and deconcentration require some redefinition of the role of the centre. To the extent that they reflect a view of its inefficacy, they have added to the general sentiment of vulnerability.

Accompanying this *territorial* diffusion of administrative authority there has been its increased *functional* dispersal and this has been a further important factor shaping the contemporary administration. The dispersal, which may be seen in several ways, can once again be interpreted as an indication of the waning prestige of the traditional administration. First, there has been the devolution of administrative responsibility to quasi-independent bodies such as the National Commission on Computerisation and

Freedom, the Competition Council, the Stock Exchange Transactions and the Audiovisual Council. Between 1975 and 1989 fourteen such bodies were created. As in the UK, these bodies raise
delicate constitutional, political and administrative issues. Their
creation frequently corresponds to a number of political imperatives but their functioning gives rise to as many problems as those
they were intended to resolve: for instance, such bodies cannot
be seen as competitive with, or rivals to, traditional administrative
bodies, yet collectively they involve a diminution of their power.
In addition, there has been an increased transfer of administrative
responsibility to horizontally-organised missions, often of an *ad
hoc* and temporary character, which are given the task of coordinating policies in a particular policy area. Furthermore, there is
an increasing tendency to appoint individuals or small committees
of experts to make policy recommendations in particularly contentious policy areas such as drugs, prostitution, pollution, unemployment, housing finance and citizenship rights. The result of these
various developments is to demoralise the administration (since
they reflect the suspicion with which it is held) and weaken it in
its role in the elaboration, implementation and monitoring of
public policy.

The increasing politicisation of the administration provides the
sixth major recent development. Of course, as noted above, the
French administration has always been somewhat politicised. This
is scarcely surprising in a country such as France, given the intensity of certain cleavages, chronic regime instability and the sporadic
polarisation of public opinion. The Fifth Republic, unlike the
Third and Fourth (with their murky and fluid party and parliamentary coalitions), has polarised politics around reasonably well-struc-
tured and disciplined (if divided) coalitions, each competing for
the presidency. From 1958 to 1981 enmities *within* the Right-wing
coalition ensured that the dominant element within the Executive
would forge an administrative elite to its own ideological or political liking (the Gaullist state being replaced by the Giscardian state
from 1974), whilst the deep-seated antagonism between the Right
and Left-wing coalitions ensured that any change of the parties in
power would swiftly be followed by an administrative purge. Of
the 500 or so senior posts made at the discretion of the government, 470 changed hands between 1981 and 1985 under the Socialists, whilst 79 changed in the first six months following the Right-
wing victory of March 1986. People with high partisan profiles or
who were known to be personal friends of members of the ruling
coalition were appointed to prestigious administrative posts. The
result was that parts of the French higher Civil Service by the

mid-1980s came to resemble a patchwork of politicised clans (often centred, incidentally, on powerful personalities). The partisan identification of many top civil servants has been an overemphasised aspect of the administration. Equally under scrutiny has been the so-called 'dominant ideology' of the administration. What has not really been studied has been the impact of function and policy area on the political assumptions and premises of top civil servants. How far are the policy preferences of civil servants shaped by the professional networks and policy communities with which they are in constant contact?

A second dimension of the politicisation debate has been the increasing number of civil servants entering politics, a phenomenon which is widespread in continental Europe. The list of presidents, prime ministers, ministers and members of Parliament who commenced their career in the Civil Service is truly impressive and has kept more than one statistically-minded political sociologist busy. We learn, amongst other things, that the Chirac Government of 1986 contained twelve *Enarques* and one 'X' (the term used for students of the Ecole Polytechnique), whilst that of Rocard in 1988 harboured nine *Enarques* and three 'X'. Although the extent of this type of politicisation has been exaggerated (the vast majority of civil servants remain civil servants and politically neutral), it has undeniably affected some of the upper reaches of the Civil Service. Politics and administration become closely intertwined, thus violating one of the canons of the Napoleonic concept. Moreover, the *image* of the Civil Service has increasingly suffered, since its reputation for political neutrality has been tarnished: it is less and less perceived as the impartial arbiter and defender of the general interest.

A third dimension of politicisation has been the inflation in the size of ministerial private offices. The ministers of the Pierre Mauroy governments were helped by some 500 officially recruited (and many more unofficially recruited) members of private offices: those of Fabius by 530, of Chirac by 580. By November 1988, under Rocard, the figure had risen to over 600. This inflation is partly the result of the increase in the number of the ministries (fewer than 30 until 1960, more than 40 since 1980), but is also due to the increase in the size of each private office. This army of officials, recruited from amongst politically sympathetic allies (often in the administration itself), constitutes a veritable duplicate administration which tries to control or short-circuit the mainstream administration. Not surprisingly, this has irritated and sometimes demoralised the latter.

The final dimension of politicisation relates to the rather feeble attempts to democratise the recruitment of the top administration, with its disproportionately few members from the working class and the provincial schools and universities. A timid, yet controversial, Socialist attempt in 1983 to facilitate entry by outsiders into the ENA was abandoned by the Right which founded its arguments on the need to retain merit as the sole criterion of selection and on the need to safeguard against politically-inspired appointments.

The administration is seen to be unrepresentative of the society it serves: yet another sin is added to the list. That political and social representativeness may be uneasy bedfellows and that either or both may undermine impartiality has never deterred the critics who demand political responsiveness and accountability, policy neutrality and impartiality and social representativeness. In other words, the administration is caught in a trap of conflicting demands.

The seventh major recent development has been the mounting criticism of the administration as insensitive, secretive and inaccessible. There has been a flurry of reforms partially to remedy this situation: the creation of the Mediator in 1973 (see Chapter 7); the requirement that state agencies be more communicative about their future projects; the 'humanising' of contacts with the public; the creation of user committees since 1975; the increase in access (through the laws of 1978 and of 1983) to administrative documents; and the making available of more information to public enquiries. The demand for 'open government' has been met with the creation of certain institutions such as the Commission on Access to Administrative Files (1975). Whilst the results have not matched the scale of the preoccupations or even expectations, there is no doubt that the administration is under increased pressure in this direction. Demands for greater information and for greater access to decision-making raise obvious problems for any administration, since their implementation is time-consuming and potentially disruptive of cosy relationships between parts of the administration and their client groups.

The final major development which has had an impact on the administration is the changing nature of policy-making at the political level, from one based on parliamentary ascendancy to one based on Executive domination. Two perfectly conflicting – and largely false – myths circulate about the French administration. It is argued that, on the one hand, during the Fourth Republic weak politicians created a power vacuum which a powerful and power-hungry administration filled. On the other hand, during the Fifth Republic, with its stronger and more stable executives supported by disciplined party majorities, the administration was able fully to exploit parliamentary weakness and pressure-group defensiveness, and feel less constrained in exercising its power. In other words, both weak and strong executives generate strong administrations. In truth, the administrative is a largely *reactive* body: its responses are shaped by the consequences (sometimes unintended) of ongoing policies or by the pressure of politicians. A weak minister invariably means a weak administration. A strong minister, with political clout, may galvanise and motivate his or her administration. The relationship may move from being mutually parasitic to one of symbiosis. Both the Fourth and Fifth Republic provide evidence of this.

What appears increasingly to be the pattern of policy-making in the 1970s and 1980s is a form of 'pluralistic stagnation'. Not only is scepticism about the state evident but, since the mid-1970s, there appears to be a reluctance to indulge in *any* electorally-damaging radical policy-making. Raymond Barre's tough rhetoric as prime minister was matched by emollient and economically 'irrational' policies; the Socialists' transformative phase lasted a heady eighteen months, being brought to an abrupt halt by its European partners (notably the West Germans), the international marketplace and an impressive domestic coalition of the disgruntled; the Jacques Chirac Government (after the student riots of the winter of 1986) was the first Right-wing government this century to declare *une pause* (the fate of so many previous Left-wing governments). The non-committal banalities of the presidential election campaign of 1988 (Mitterrand's 110 concrete *propositions* of 1981 were replaced by a small number of generalised aspirations in 1988) and the modesty of the ambitions of the Rocard Government bear witness to the constraints on France in the late 1980s. The voluntaristic policies and posturing of the early Fifth Republic has been replaced by a sober prudence: the administration of transformation has given way to the management of marginal adjustments.

Conclusions

Historically, the French administration was shaped to conform to a certain model, and some of the distinctive features of that model persist to this day. However, various pressures revealed the flawed nature of the model and aggravated its defects. Recent events have further distorted the functioning of the original model. The administration still retains a powerful influence in the public policy process, since it is well placed to evaluate, inhibit or even block policies. However, it is going through a period of malaise which is due in part to the worsening conditions of public sector employment. Yet the malaise goes deeper and is linked to a diminution in state sovereignty and to a radical questioning of the internal functioning and ultimate external vocation of the administration. Increasingly, it is being locked into a number of conflicting requirements: demands for access and accountability are accompanied by administrative fragmentation and diffusion; the wish for greater participation in no way diminishes the insistence on quicker decisions; an insistence on efficiency is coupled with cut-backs which render such efficiency difficult to achieve. Contrary to popular legend, some key areas of policy-making and implementation are underadministered: efficient tax collection, control over illicit price-fixing, protection against dangerous work practices, defence of consumer rights, all require more public officials.

The administration is constantly criticised for its inadequate performance. This is scarcely surprising, since it is increasingly vulnerable to the superimposition of differing rationalities: those of the state (the 'general interest'), of the bureaucracy itself, of the market and the private sector, and of the client groups it serves. Consequently assessing performance (an obsession of the reformers) becomes intrinsically impossible because the criteria of evaluation are unclear. Furthermore, the collective unease of the administration has been heightened, as traditional ideas of public service, monopoly, the general interest and the prerogatives of the state – the sources of administrative legitimacy – have come to be contested by notions of deregulation, competition and productive efficiency. Public welfarism is disputed in the name of private initiative.

The administration is far from being totally autonomous, and neither is it simply part of the superstructure. It is, of course, both in some measure; yet it also mirrors, absorbs and articulates the conflicting preoccupations and anxieties of the society it serves. The administration is having acute problems of adjustment and self-perception but this may be more a comment on France of the 1980s than on the administration. Certainly, the comfortable and reassuring premises of the Napoleonic model afford little protection against contemporary uncertainties.

7

The Control of Governments

FRANÇOISE DREYFUS

The 1958 constitution, by introducing what has been called 'rationalised parliamentarianism', substantially modified the relationships which existed during the Third and Fourth Republics between the Executive and legislature by reinforcing the former to the detriment of the latter. A desire to endow France with a style of government which would free it from the stranglehold of the parties and make it capable of restoring the power of the state inspired the provisions laid down in the constitution. Even though the Fifth Republic is a parliamentary system, in which the government is collectively responsible to the National Assembly, the conditions for moving a censure motion are severe enough to inhibit an 'excessive' use of this procedure. De Gaulle's distrust of Parliament was expressed not only by a reduction of the National Assembly's powers of political control, but also by limiting the legislative competence of Parliament and the creation of a Constitutional Council to ensure that the laws made by Parliament conformed to the constitution. These innovations were initially criticised by the Left-wing parties which considered them to be a manifestation of the anti-parliamentarianism characteristic of the French authoritarian Right.

The very strict delimitation of parliamentary powers and the reinforcement of executive powers does not, however, mean that the Executive is unfettered. In fact, although the government is not effectively accountable for its political actions except to members of Parliament, the decisions and workings of the administration are subject to numerous controls, which vary greatly in type and effect.

The concept of control has several meanings which apply to quite different situations. Political philosophers have for more than three centuries worked out theories of 'good government' in which the idea of control occupies a central place. The organisation of powers in conformity with the principle of 'checks and balances' in which the recognition of the right of citizens to resist oppression (article 2 of the 1789 Declaration of the Rights of Man and the Citizen, which is an integral part of the preamble to the 1958 constitution) is, for example, considered as a guarantee against the risk of abuse of power by the Executive. Liberal democracy has elevated into a principle Montesquieu's rule which says, 'In order that no-one can abuse power, it is necessary by the arrangement of things, to check power.' The control of government is one aspect of the application of this principle.

The forms which this control can take vary not only according to the agent exercising it and the formal rituals which generally regulate its exercise, but also with social, ideological and political change. This explains the evolution which in the last decade has affected practices within the state institutions and in civil society.

A four-fold typology of the different methods of controlling governments helps to clarify the subject.

1. *Political control* is exercised on the one hand by citizens in presidential and parliamentary – or even local – elections (see Chapter 3), and on the other hand by the National Assembly over the Executive.
2. *Legal control* combines the different methods by which the state is made to respect the law. In fact, whether it concerns laws voted on by Parliament or regulations made by the administration, it can be submitted to different bodies such as the Constitutional Council, the Council of State and other administrative courts, the European Commission and the European Court of Justice, which examine whether they are in order from a legal point of view and penalise any breach of law.
3. *Paralegal control* concerns the methods of enquiry which can be used by parliamentarians to investigate administrative acts, the various corps of inspectors within the administration, and certain bodies regarded as independent administrative authorities as well. Unlike legal control, these controls do not carry any direct sanction. They are only a possible preliminary finding for subsequent decision by a different body.
4. *Extra-institutional controls* are not laid down in documents but

are expressions of civil society. They include the organised or spontaneous initiatives from interest groups whose demands or pressures are often categorised as corporatist (see Chapter 4) and the French media; although not constituting a fourth power (as in the USA), the media are no longer content just to inform. Investigative journalism is developing, and the press is bringing to light defects in the way the government machine works. The case of the *Le Monde* newspaper is especially significant; the role it played in the *Rainbow Warrior* affair in 1985 contributed to the resignation of the defence minister.

This typology, because it is purely descriptive, does not make clear two elements vital for assessing the means of control. First, to be most effective the control must act quickly. The speed with which an authority external to the decision intervenes is crucial if the aim of the control is to improve the actions of government, as much from a legal point of view as from that of meeting the expectations of the public. Most controls are carried out long after decisions are taken and applied. The exceptions to this rule are few. They concern essentially the control exercised by the Constitutional Council before a law passed by Parliament is promulgated, and on occcasion the protest from some social groups to hinder or hasten the making of a decision. Second, the controls have a highly variable impact, not only because some do not entail any direct consequences, but especially because their influence is directly dependent on the symbolic importance of those who exert it, or even on the publicity from which they benefit.

The purpose of this chapter is not to study all the forms of control previously listed. It confines itself to examining the institutional means which can be used to control the activities of governmental institutions. It is concerned less with describing mechanisms than with indicating the gap between the formal rules which regulate them and the use made of them, and then evaluating their effectiveness.

Parliament: The Controller Controlled

The supremacy of Parliament in any regime of parliamentary sovereignty depends on its two-fold function: to control the government derived from its own majority and to show its approval or otherwise of government policy; and also to act as the representative of the nation, to legislate in all areas and thus express the general will. From this double perspective, the National Assembly and the Senate lost a considerable part of their power with the Fifth Republic's constitution. But although until the mid-1970s Parliament was strictly limited to the narrow role assigned to it by the constitution, some flexibility was introduced during the Giscard presidency. Since the Left came to power in 1981, national representatives have been regarded more favourably: the government has only rarely used the prerogatives at its disposal to restrain the legislative capability of Parliament. For its part, the Constitutional Council has acquired considerable power in relation to that which it had until 1971, to the point where it now seems to be a court for the legitimation or delegitimation of government action.

Control over the Government

The political responsibility of the government can only be challenged in the National Assembly, either on its own initiative or on that of the deputies. When the government is formed, unlike the position during the Third and Fourth Republics, it does not have to be approved by the National Assembly. On the other hand, the Prime Minister pledges the responsibility of the government on its programme, or possibly on a general declaration of policy, which means that the prime minister is asking for a priori approval for the policy which will be applied.

In practice, this procedure was followed irregularly until 1974 and in a more systematic fashion since then. When the prime minister designated by the president has had a clear, united majority in the National Assembly, he has pledged responsibility, as for example Mauroy did in 1981 and 1983, Fabius in 1984 and Chirac in 1986. On the other hand, when the government's support in Parliament is more precarious, the prime minister has refrained from asking for a vote of confidence. Thus Rocard, in charge of the minority government in June 1988, limited himself to making a general declaration of policy not followed by a vote. The Prime Minister can obviously pledge the responsibility of the government in this way at any time. Governments usually have recourse to this practice to reinforce their position and show public opinion, or even the French president (as Chirac did in 1987), that government policy is indeed supported by the majority of deputies.

The prime minister can also pledge the government's responsibility during voting on a Bill. The aim of this complex procedure (article 49-3) of the constitution), used to excess by Chirac in 1986, is less to obtain the confidence of deputies than to proceed more quickly on a Bill, which is deemed adopted unless a motion of censure is put down and passed. Rocard himself twice used this procedure before June 1989 but the purpose was to prevent a discussion revealing divisions amongst Socialists.

Real political control is exercised by the deputies when they themselves take the initiative in a censure motion. However, to ensure government stability, the constitution laid down draconian conditions which tend to limit the use of censure. According to article 49-2 of the constitution, a censure motion needs to be signed by at least 10 per cent of the members of the National Assembly (58 deputies). If the motion is not passed, they cannot sign another such motion during the same session. The high number of signatures required means that, since 1988, neither the Communists (25 deputies) nor the Centrists (41 members) have been able on their own to put down a censure motion. Since 1958, even though more than 30 motions have been put down – against practically all governments – only one succeeded, against Pompidou's Government in 1962. Although the procedure does not encourage censure motions, they do not succeed because the distribution of political forces within the National Assembly hardly allows them to do so. In practice, whatever divisions may exist within Left-wing or Right-wing coalition parties, an alliance with parties of the opposition to bring down a government is virtually inconceivable. This classical means of political control thus remains more theoretical than practical.

Parliamentary representatives have other means of ensuring that the government's policy conforms to their wishes. In this respect, the examination of the Finance Bill should allow them to play an essential role in drawing up policies which will be implemented. Once again the constitutional provisions confine the parliamentarians' initiatives within close limits (article 40). The control they could in principle exercise via the Finance Bill amounts to very little in the end. Even there, however, the margin of manoeuvre which parliamentarians have to influence government plans is related more to the distribution of party political forces than to the strict application of the constitution. The examination of the Budget for 1989 shows this: Rocard's Government accepted numerous amendments which modified the Bill substantially in order to obtain a favourable vote from the Centrists and the Communists, or at least their abstention. The comparative vulnerability of the minority government appointed in June 1988 forced it to compromise with the National Assembly. The Assembly has thereby regained a means of acting of which it had been deprived in practice throughout the Fifth Republic.

This recovering of power can also be seen in the proposals made by the President of the National Assembly, Laurent Fabius, and adopted by the deputies in September 1988 to improve the capacity of Parliament and to control government activity more effectively. These measures concern in particular the work of the parliamentary committees: in the National Assembly and the Senate, six standing committees (Finance, Foreign Affairs, Defence, Production and Trade, Social Affairs and Laws) are charged with examining Bills before they are debated in public session; the Finance Committee has created working groups which may present proposals *before* the Finance Bill is drawn up by the Ministry of Finance; and there is now the possibility of introducing public hearings similar to US Congress committee hearings.

Among the means of control is Question Time (borrowed from Britain), to which an hour each week has been devoted in the National Assembly since its introduction in 1974 by Giscard d'Estaing. In 1982 the Senate, responding to Mitterrand's proposal, followed suit. The value of this procedure is that the Opposition, like the parliamentary Majority, can ask the government to explain its actions on the spot, whereas the procedure for 'Oral Questions' requires them to be put down at least a week in advance. Fabius has also suggested that Question Time should be reorganised to increase its effectiveness.

There is another area in which parliamentary power has formally been reinforced and has also increased slightly in practice. The possibility of creating Committees of Inquiry or Supervisory Committees – the former determining the facts concerning some executive action, the latter concerning the functioning of the administration – has been regulated in a very strict manner since 1958. But an Act of 1977, in which the senators took the initiative, reinforced the powers of parliamentarians by allowing them to take evidence from any person concerned with the subject of enquiry. These committees are created by the National Assembly or the Senate following a vote on a resolution. Until the departure of de Gaulle in 1970, no proposal to set up a Committee of Inquiry had been adopted. Only four Supervisory Committees have seen the light of day (three in the Senate, and one only in the National Assembly). This timidity is doubtless explained by the government's domination over Parliament, and especially the National Assembly. It is really only since 1974 that this procedure has developed.

Interest in its work stems not only from the publicity it receives – the decision to publish the report being the subject of a vote by the chamber concerned – but also from the practical proposals which come from the Committee. These aim to remedy the problems discovered in management or in the functioning of the particular public service, or to end some questionable practice which had been concealed by the administration. An example here is the 1974 report of the Committee of Inquiry concerning oil companies operating in France, or that of 1981 concerning the SAC, a strong-arm organisation originally set up to combat those in France seeking to disrupt the Algerian peace settlement in the early 1960s. The proposal to dissolve the SAC was implemented quickly, particularly because the Left-wing parties had been critical of its dubious activities.

Nevertheless such means of investigation, which allow parliamentarians to obtain information at first hand on the working of the administration and the effects of public policies, are not much used. What is the explanation? Because the real capacity of Parliament to debate and vote on Private Members' Bills is extremely restricted (out of all Bills voted since 1958, only 11 per cent were Private Members' Bills) the work of Committees of Inquiry is likely to end only in the expression of pious hopes which have no practical result other than to bring certain facts to the public's attention. So even if Parliament has certain powers of control over the Executive, their application depends essentially on the balance of political forces. Rocard's minority government is a good example. Exposure to the risk of overthrow has forced the government to compromise with the deputies, thereby increasing their power.

Control by the Constitutional Council over Law-Making

The year 1974 opened a relatively liberalising era within the institutional system of the Fifth Republic, characterised by the desire of President Giscard d'Estaing to loosen the vice in which Parliament was held. This was expressed by a constitutional revision which extended the right to refer cases to the Constitutional Council to groups of 60 deputies or senators. Until then only the president, the prime minister and the presidents of the National Assembly and the Senate had this prerogative. Although the Constitutional Council's task was to verify that laws referred to it conformed to the constitution, this task was initially really a means of ensuring that Parliament did not overstep its legislative powers – narrowly defined in article 34 – and did not encroach on the regulatory domain of the Executive.

From 1971 the Constitutional Council extended its control by examining the content of a law to see if it conformed to the preamble to the constitution and ceased to confine itself to defining the boundary between Parliament's legislative and the government's regulatory spheres. The extension of the right to refer cases gave the Council the chance to develop and refine its body of case-law. Since 1974, the number of referrals has increased considerably, being thought of by opposition parliamentarians as a way of winning a legal battle after having been unable to impose their view in Parliament. The Constitutional Council overturned part or all of 34 laws between June 1981 and January 1986.

As the decisions of the Constitutional Council are universally binding, a law or articles of a law declared not to conform to the constitution cannot be promulgated. Whatever the judgement made on the Council's legal interpretations or the neutrality of a court whose nine members are chosen (three each) by the presidents of the Republic and the speakers of the National Assembly and the Senate, one thing must be stated. Any unfavourable decison made by the Constitutional Council tends to be regarded by the parliamentary majority and the government which introduced the Bill as a betrayal. This feeling is even stronger when the contested Bill is highly symbolic, especially in political terms as with the 1982 Nationalisation Bill or the occasion in 1987 when a Government amendment modifying the Labour Code was annulled on the grounds of procedural faults. In the latter case, the Rightwing majority and the Presidents of the National Assembly and Senate started a polemical campaign against the Constitutional Council. This was absurd since the Constitutional Council was attacked in the name of parliamentary rights, when the Council's decision was protecting those rights against Government intervention. Conversely, governments have sometimes behaved as if they had won a victory when the Constitutional Council appears to say 'the government is right' by declaring that a Bill conforms to the constitution.

This very debatable attitude, which the Socialists dropped in 1982, can be interpreted as a sign of majority dictatorship in which any control exercised by the law is an unbearable attack on government power. Laws adopted by Parliament are at the moment the only acts which are subject to prior legal control, since appeal can only be made to the Constitutional Council before promulgation and thus the application of the law. The constitution-makers really intended to reduce the legislative power of Parliament by restricting closely the area of law-making, by giving the government a dominant role in the legislation process and by introducing the possibility of submitting laws to the Constitutional Council's judgement. The evolution of the Council has now led to a very different opinion of its role. Appealed to frequently, it has been able to develop a body of case-law, broadly based on an extensive interpretation of the constitution and its preamble. In this way it has set out both the basic principles which legislators must respect and the boundaries of acceptable interventions by government in the legislative procedure. It is nevertheless true that the definite increase in the power of the Constitutional Council is balanced by the loss of power to Parliament whose legitimacy, conferred by suffrage, is in competition with that of the rule of law.

The relative 'youth' of the Constitutional Council doubtless explains why the control entrusted to it is not yet universally accepted, whereas the control of the administrative tribunals, exercised for nearly two centuries, rarely arouses such passionate reactions.

The Executive under Judicial Control

The Executive exercises its administrative functions under the control of administrative courts. These bodies, of whatever type and with very rare exceptions, intervene after the event, when the contested decision has already been applied. This does not mean that a decision of the Council of State, for example, will be ineffective or that the penalty for the illegality is purely a matter of form. It will be applied, but with some delay from the time the action went into operation. The same is true of the administrative control exercised by the Court of Accounts on the management of institutions subject to public accountability regulations.

The Control of Legality

The administrative decisions taken by the president, the prime minister or ministers can be referred to different courts so that their legality can be examined. Any individual affected by an administrative decisions believed to be illegal can seek redress through the French administrative courts or, in some cases, at the EC's Court of Justice.

The body of case-law built up over a long period by the Council of State – the supreme administrative court – enables a very sophisticated legal control to be enforced. Given the absence of formal guidelines, the Council of State has been able to determine for itself the extent of controls which it applies to administrative acts. Since any extension of control implies an extension of the controlling institution's power, the Council of State has continually extended its investigation of the legality of decisions referred to it for judicial review. The justification for these practices can be summed up in this way: with the administration intervening ever more frequently in all areas of social life – and the 1958 constitution having substantially extended the Executive's powers – citizens need increasing protection, in particular from attacks on their liberty. Judges should ensure that the balance is maintained between what the general interest requires and the rights of individuals.

It is not, however, our task here to describe in detail the techniques used by administrative judges to attain this objective or to draw a complete picture of this copious body of case-law, but to evaluate the impact of judicial action. The protection of liberties by the action of the Council of State can on occasion be considered by government as the Council setting up in opposition to its policy. The most famous example dates from 1962. The Council of State had annulled, due to 'the gravity of the attack [which it dealt] on the general principles of penal law', an ordinance of the President of the Republic setting up a military Court of Justice which had pronounced sentence on a capital offence. In the emotional context of the Algerian War, this decision – which conformed to case-law – was regarded as an affront by de Gaulle, who later tried unsuccessfully to bring the Council to heel.

Less spectacular but still very significant are the decisions which, since 1975, have reinforced the protection of foreigners subject to expulsion orders. This jurisprudence constrains Ministers of the Interior to respect certain rules, in particular to justify their decisions, knowing that the grounds will be examined by a judge. In this case, the control on legality enables the effects of a too-hurried policy to be mitigated. However, the limits of effectiveness of control after the event take on a particular significance in this type of case, when looked at from the viewpoint of the individuals concerned. From the Executive's point of view, judicial control is perceived differently according to the case over which it is exercised. The immense majority of verdicts, which can be termed 'routine', are given after several years, and simply embarrass the administration which must comply with them. Verdicts concerning more thorny problems which require a fast solution can sometimes appear as a sanction on government policy. The subsequent annoyance for the Executive derives not so much from the judicial consequences of the verdict as from its bad publicity because of the prestige enjoyed by the Council of State.

The effectiveness of legal control is also related to the rapidity with which the judge's decision is carried out. Since 1980, a recalcitrant administration can be penalised by fines, and a specialised division within the Council of State checks that legal decisions are implemented properly. Its interventions in the administration have had a positive effect, but the growing number of appeals to the Council of State is nevertheless evidence of the difficulty which individuals find in obtaining the application of verdicts awarded in their favour at a lower court (Braibant, 1988, p. 524). Finally, the educational value of the jurisprudence is only relative. In facing the possible annulment of an illegal act if an appeal is lodged, the administration hardly hesitates about taking a calculated risk by perpetrating an illegal act. Moreover, the Executive power disposes of various subtle ways of deviating from the spirit of laws which it is supposed to apply, while still escaping judicial censure.

European Legal Controls

A similar attitude has been adopted for a long time by the French authorities regarding the obligations deriving from the Treaty of Rome or the French membership of the Council of Europe. The reservations de Gaulle had towards any supra-national institution which might limit French sovereignty are well known. This explains, for example, the delay until 1974 of French ratification of the European Convention on Human Rights, which had been signed in 1950. It was only on 4 October 1981, moreover, after the electoral victory of the Left, that France recognised the right of individual appeal to the European Commission of Human Rights in Strasbourg, which is responsible for deciding on any violation committed by the states which are signatories of the Convention.

France's position as a member of the EC carries with it much more troublesome consequences. It means for the French Parliament and the government – as for the governments of all member-states – the loss of some of their powers to the Community institutions. It also implies that the national courts must apply Community law. In addition, the refusal of an administrative authority to apply a Community norm which has precedence over internal law can be penalised by the EC's Court of Justice.

The French courts – civil and administrative – have had diverse attitudes towards Community law. The Court of Cassation (*Cour de Cassation*) has since 1975 applied European law in conformity with the dispositions of the Treaty and in particular has admitted its superiority over French law. The Council of State on the contrary, using questionable legal arguments, was reluctant to apply the principle of the primacy of Community law over internal law until 1989.

The protection of sectional interests has led the government on several occasions to engage in delaying tactics to hold up standardising French law with that of Brussels, even after the European Commission has intervened. As to the judgements condemning France by the Court of Justice, they scarcely seem to have had any great impact, at least on the public. Doubtless the legitimacy of the European institutions is still weak compared to that of French courts. In spite of the exhortations of President Mitterrand in favour of a strong, united Europe, the nationalist reflex always produces effects which can be conveniently played upon. Thus the government can attribute unpopular measures to the constraints imposed by the Community's external authority.

The Control of Management within the Administration

The Court of Accounts, which was created in 1807, is an administrative court with a dual function. On the one hand it verifies 'the regularity of expenses listed in the public accounts' and 'checks that the funds managed by the state administration have been correctly spent'; and on the other hand, by virtue of article 47 of the constitution, it is responsible for assisting Parliament and the government in supervising the application of Finance Acts. An annual report of its investigations is sent to the president and Parliament, and is also published.

The first of these functions, especially now that it is more oriented towards control of management, allows it to point out cases of mismanagement in the administration. However, the Court of Accounts possesses only fairly limited powers concerning the follow-up of its findings. In particular, the penalising of finance officers' illegal conduct is the task of other tribunals. In respect of its second function, the text lays down precisely the help which Parliament should receive from the Court. In addition, in its verification procedures, the Court of Accounts also brings to light anomalies in management.

Nevertheless, in spite of the range of work accomplished by the Court of Accounts as shown in its annual report – which also makes detailed recommendations aimed at improving public management – the control exercised by this court is limited. In fact, the Court of Accounts is not entitled either to pronounce on the advisability of government policy decisions or to impede the activities of the administration (Wolff, 1988). The publication of its annual report gives the press the chance to spotlight certain wastages which the public authorities have acknowledged, or defective management in some parts of the administration. For example, in

1987 it was confirmed that the government did not know the exact number of public servants it employed. However, the effect provoked by such 'revelations' ranges no further than short-term media publicity. For several years the problem of good administrative management – the cost-effectiveness of the administration – has been questioned. The Court of Accounts has adapted its methods of control, notably by using audit techniques, to achieve this objective of evaluation. It is still true that this control, however refined it might be, consists of verifying the accuracy of accounting procedures set up by the administration. The control of the Court of Accounts is thus limited to working within the rules of public accounting which are not suitable for evaluating management according to a value-for-money strategy.

Since judicial supervision of the administration is intended to ensure conformity with the law, the changes which affect the political arena have only a marginal influence on their implementation. The same can be said of controls exercised by administrative bodies.

Internal Control

Control procedures within the administration itself take various forms. In the first place, the hierarchical structure of the system implies that ministers effectively exercise control over their administrations, because they are accountable for all decisions taken by their staff. It is not, however, that aspect of the functioning of the administration which will be examined.

The Consultative Role of the Council of State

Since its creation in 1799 by Napoleon, the Council of State – an administrative body whose members are administrators and not magistrates – has been charged with a dual role. In addition to its judicial function, which was considered earlier, the Council of State fulfils a consultative function, essential since its origin but whose current importance is often overlooked. In fact, all government Bills (article 39 of the constitution), all ordinances (article 38) and a great number of regulatory decrees (more than 1,000 in 1984–5) must be examined by the Council of State before being presented to Parliament (for the Bills) and promulgated or signed (for ordinances and decrees). The aim of this examination is to check if the texts are correct from a legal point of view and compatible with those already in force. The prior approval which is thus exercised involves different consequences for the government according to the nature of the text.

With regard to government Bills, the 'opinion' given by the Council of State imposes no obligation on the government. It remans free to keep or reject any or all of the modifications proposed. The position is different for regulatory texts. In fact the government has in principle only one choice to make: to accept or reject the Council's advice. Since the Council of State may subsequently be called upon to review the implementation of the text, the government hesitates to risk having the text annulled later on should it not accept the Council's advice (Dreyfus and d'Arcy, 1987, p. 189).

This procedure, in which the Council of State plays the role of the government's legal adviser (even if it is not very easy to distinguish between the political and the legal aspects of a text), in fact constitutes a fairly effective means of prior control. Conceived as a strictly internal procedure of the administration, the consultation and consequent advice are secret, but this does not stop occasional leaks when controversial matters are examined. This was the case in 1986 regarding a Government Bill reforming the law on nationality, when the Council's very unfavourable advice on proposals put forward by the Minister of Justice was published in the press. After having accused the Council of State of being partisan, Chirac's Government withdrew its Bill and set up a commission to report on the nationality question. A second recent example of a leak happened at about the same time and involved the advice given on the Bill concerning the creation of private prisons. The result was once again that the government withdrew its project. The impact of such leaks is magnified by the prestige of the consultative body, which is supposed moreover to be politically neutral.

The Inspectorates

Twenty-one inspectorates are attached to ministers responsible for civil administration. With the exception of the most prestigious Finance Inspectorate and, in a smaller measure, the Administrative Inspectorate attached to the Minister of the Interior which have an inter-ministerial function, the Inspectors are responsible for controlling the central and field services of the ministry to which they are attached. Although very diverse in the size of their staff as well in the nature of their duties only the common characteristics of their role will be examined here.

Members of each Inspectoral Corps are directly responsible to a minister and are autonomous with respect to the ministry or group of civil servants they are inspecting. The traditional definition of control which they exercise is limited to the financial and legal rectitude of administrative acts. The current concept is based more on principles of administrative efficiency and the end-product of administrative activity.

The purpose of inspection can thus include the functioning of the administration as much as the evaluation of how well ministerial policies have been implemented. The goal of such control, besides the discovery of breaches in legal and financial rules, is a better knowledge of the administration in action, with a view to applying corrective measures. The inspectorates draw up reports containing proposals or recommendations for ministers but they have no power to make decisions, since this belongs solely to the ministers concerned. These reports are, with very rare exceptions (such as the public annual report of the Social Affairs Inspectorate), confidential to the minister or have a restricted circulation within the ministry. The law of 1978 (giving the public the right of access to administrative documents) permits the communication of the reports to any person. Yet the law has laid down limits on the rights of access, notably where it concerns documents that mention named individuals.

As the contents of large numbers of reports remains inaccessible, it is difficult to evaluate their real impact and, in particular, any consequent results. Since the reports are not designed to control ministers but to inform them about the way in which their staff accomplish their tasks, it would be very instructive to discover the number of suggestions followed by action compared with those which remain unimplemented. Some reforms or decisions have been made on the recommendation of the inspectorates. These include reforms in the administrative organisation of the field services of the Finance Ministry; the reform of state subsidies (Marcou, 1983, p. 83); and the reinforcement of controls over joint public–private companies following the 'la Villette' scandal, which was also investigated by a Senate Commission of Enquiry in 1971. The conclusions of the report, which was drawn up in 1976 by the Social Affairs Inspectorate, supported by a report from the Court of Accounts in 1980, enabled in 1981 a Communist Minister of Health to prove, with supporting evidence, that the private sector within public hospitals should be abolished.

The work of the inspectorates provides an excellent indicator of the effective will of governments both to improve the functioning of administration and even, at worst, to put an end to abuses. The more prestige attached to an inspectorate – such as the Finance

Inspectorate – the more likely are its proposals to be acted upon, and its members to be involved in decision-making.

The Independent Administrative Authorities

The 1970s were marked by a growing desire of government to improve relations between the administration and citizens. After the Gaullist period, characterised by a powerful statist ideology and by an interventionist administration extending into the most diverse areas of social life, it seemed essential not so much to enlarge the rights of the individual as to give individuals new means of communicating with the administration.

According to a law which has never been invalidated in France, all problems are solved by the creation of an institution charged with making some response. Since the creation of the Mediator in 1973, many similar authorities have been established. Described as 'independent administrative authorities' in the sense that they are not subordinate to any minister, their role is to protect citizens against the actions – possibly excessive – of the administration.

The Mediator is an authority whose independent status is indispensable to the exercise of his or her functions. This institution, inspired by the Swedish Ombudsman, is novel within the character of the French system, as it is responsible for helping to solve the difficulties which arise between the administered and the administration. The solutions proposed by the Mediator are essentially inspired by a desire for fairness, since frequently it is the strict application of the texts which was the origin of conflict. An appeal to the Mediator is not made directly by individuals who consider that the public service has not functioned correctly; their requests must be channelled through a deputy or senator acting as intermediary. The Mediator acquires information from the administration concerned about the reasons for the malfunction and makes 'all recommendations which appear likely to solve the problem'. About a third of the cases the Mediator helps to solve concern the payment of pensions.

Thus the Mediator possesses no power of decision, and neither is the goal one of control. The Mediator's role is to identify deficiencies and inadequacies in administrative practice and to propose, on the basis of the particular cases investigated, solutions which will tend to improve relations between ordinary citizens and the administration. The results of the Mediator's activities and the suggestions drawn up for government are the subject of an annual report sent to the president and published. The effectiveness of the Mediator's action concerning the administration is largely dependent on the goodwill of the administration, but the moral 'authority' of the institution gives the recommendations a significant influence, which has been confirmed by the implementation of various measures improving relations between the citizen and the administration. Numerous decisions have been taken in order to increase the information of citizens; the Ministry of Finance is making the most effort in this respect.

Directly inspired by the Mediator's recommendations are two other 'independent administrative authorities' created in 1978; the National Commission on Computerisation and Liberties, and the Commission on Access to Administrative Files. The goal of the first was to see that the creation of computer files by the administration, as well as by private individuals, did not affect individual liberties; the second was responsible for seeing that the administration gave individuals the right of access to administrative files.

These institutions are primarily a response to the need for a less authoritarian conception of how citizens should be treated. Their creation is part of a process of social regulation, enabling the apparent separation of state and civil society to be reduced, and to reconcile citizens with the administration. Even though they hardly have any direct decision-making powers, they present a positive image to the public. Contrary to other 'independent' institutions in the field of television and radio (see Chapter 13), they are not suspected of serving simply partisan or political interests. Without having the task of controlling the administration but being concerned with how it works, these authorities indirectly fulfil a control function, to which their annual reports contribute greatly by the interest they generate. Moreover, their proposals can serve as a point of reference for the implementation of reforms either by the legislator or by government.

In spite of the apparent heterogeneity of the institutions operating within the administration, one characteristic is common to them all. They benefit from legal guarantees of their independence from the administrative authorities, whose actions and decisions they are trying to control. This independence is supposed to guarantee their neutrality in carrying out their tasks, but the power of deciding subsequent action belongs in the end to governments. Control is always likely to produce only limited effects. Leaks, from whichever body they come, shed light on what would remain hidden for reasons of political opportunism, but their function is also to show that control is in effect being implemented, and they aim to emphasise the value of institutions which are often little known to the public.

Conclusions

Can a balance sheet be drawn up of the action undertaken by so many institutions, whose type, functions and targets are so diverse?

The most striking of these changes has been the increased strength of the judicial power of the Constitutional Council. In about fifteen years it has achieved a place of eminence. Its decisions have allowed the rules of the game in the legislative process to be defined in a direction which favours the extension of parliamentary powers. In addition it has contributed to protecting individual liberties against attempts to constrain them.

The growing role of European law which is increasingly taken into account by French courts may be seen as a means of limiting administrative power. But the most remarkable point is that Mitterrand's successful attempt to play a leading political role within Europe has constrained the politicians – particularly the RPR – to change their position regarding the EC. The attention to human rights, illustrated by the acceptance of the full effect of the European Convention on Human Rights, has increased during the last ten years. The difference between Left and Right governments on this issue is quite clear. The repeal in 1989 of the Bill concerning foreigners living in France is a good example: the 1989 Bill inspired by the Socialist President of the Republic gives more guarantees and rights to individuals than the previous one which had been drafted by the RPR.

Recent criticisms of both the Constitutional Council and the Council of State acting in its consultative capacity demonstrate that control exercised in advance, since it can hinder the application of governmental decisions, is resented by governments as an attack on their powers. The decisions of these controlling bodies then appear to reflect political positions which are favourable or unfavourable according to partisan interests. By contrast, controls exerted after the event, whatever the negative consequences for the administration, are rarely exposed to this type of criticism. Because these controls only produce results a long time after the contested facts or decisions have taken place, their authors do not feel responsible for them and may indeed no longer be in office. Only the impersonal administration will suffer the results of the control.

Nevertheless, the controls of the administration described have not resulted in effective ministerial accountability. The ministers, politically responsible as members of the government, are scarcely ever blamed for disorders or irregularities in the services placed under their authority.

It is unlikely that the 1988 reforms, increasing the control which the National Assembly exercises over government action, will bring any change in this regard. As the political control depends only on the desire of the majority to support or criticise the government, Fabius' actions to improve the rights of deputies and senators have, above all, symbolic value.

The multitude of controlling bodies, built up over time, seems at first sight hardly to ensure an efficient system. Such a conclusion would be too hasty. The feeble impact of some controls – of public accounts, for example – is mainly due to the unsuitability of the means for the ends pursued. The complexity of the methods of control corresponds to that of the administrative organisation. Just as political changes of power hardly affect the daily activities of the administration, they hardly affect the forms of control which operate according to apolitical procedural rules.

These remarks do not mean that some types of control examined are wholly ineffective. Their influence varies according to when the controls intervene with respect to the implementation of the decisions and according to the type of actors who are affected by them.

8

Power outside Paris

SONIA MAZEY

Implementation of the 1982 Defferre decentralisation reforms has significantly shifted the territorial distribution of power between Paris and the provinces. A priori administrative and financial control over local government has been abolished; a new tier of regional government has been created; and new policy-making powers and financial resources have been devolved to the departmental and municipal local authorities. In formal terms, the French state is now in several respects less centralised than at any time since the Revolution. However, consideration of these reforms must be placed in the wider context of the theoretical debate surrounding the nature of centre–periphery relations within the French political and administrative systems.

Administrative theories of French local government have traditionally stressed the legal omnipotence of the centralised state bequeathed to the Fifth Republic by the Jacobins and Napoleon; according to this view, local political power prior to 1982 was severely circumscribed. But recent and influential sociological interpretations of the politico-administrative system have confirmed that administrative centralisation is, in practice, a far more complex and flexible phenomenon. These analyses highlight the tight interpenetration of local and national policy-making resulting from the subtle mechanisms of multiple officeholding (*cumul des mandats*) and the local allegiances of state officials. Informal networks between local politicians, administrators and local socioeconomic elites have thus for many years enabled local politicians to influence national policies and circumvent administrative constraints upon local power. These theories have, in turn, been criticised by Marxist analyses which stress the need to consider local economic policy-making within the wider context of the national socioeconomic configuration. More specifically, such studies have sought to demonstrate that local political structures and economic policies generally reflect and sustain the social class relations which characterise capitalist society.

As highlighted below, the Defferre reforms have prompted significant changes within the politico-administrative system, increased the economic importance of local authorities and extended local pluralism. Yet, though far-reaching, these reforms did not mark a dramatic break with the past; in many respects they simply legitimised and extended practices which had, in fact, already emerged by 1982. The impact of the reforms has, in practice, been modified and in some cases tempered by the considerable continuity of local political and administrative personnel. The return to power of a Right-wing government in 1986 further confirmed the incremental nature of decentralisation. The economically liberal government of Jacques Chirac welcomed the development of closer links between local authorities and private capital, but made clear its opposition to any further administrative or political decentralisation.

Administrative and Sociological Theories

The Jacobin Myth

The local government structures affected by the Defferre decentralisation reforms included the 96 *départements* and 36 400 communes which date from the Revolution and the 22 regional public establishments established by the Pompidou Government in 1972. Prior to 1982, each of the 96 *départements* had a directly-elected general council which (like the municipal councils) enjoyed 'general powers' of intervention. The official executive of the council, however, was not the elected council president, but the prefect of the *département*, appointed by and directly accountable to the Minister of the Interior. In theory, the prefect enjoyed extensive local powers. As the representative of the state and the government he or she was formally responsible for coordinating the work of the ministerial field services, ensuring the local implementation of government legislation and maintaining law and order. Second, as the executive of the *département*, the prefect determined the council agenda and prepared the local authority budget. Third, the prefect exercised prior administrative and financial control over all local authority decisions (including those of the municipal councils) which were also subject to prior technical and financial control by the ministerial field services. State administrative control also extended to the 36 400 communes, each of which elected its own municipal council. Once elected, the latter elected its own executive, the mayor, who as state representative and head of the commune was personally accountable to the prefect of the *département*.

The 22 regional public establishments inherited by the Socialist Government in 1981 were created by the 1972 regional reform. Though prompted partly by diverse regionalist pressures, this reform was, in fact, designed primarily to enhance administrative coordination of local authority investment decisions within the framework of regional planning. Juridically inferior to the *départements* and communes, the regions enjoyed only limited powers and meagre resources; in 1975 the budget of a single department, the Nord, slightly exceeded the sum of the 22 regional budgets. Consulted over the regional section of the Plan and informed of state investment decisions, regions were only allowed to contribute financially to investment projects of a regional nature undertaken by the state and/or the constituent local authorities. Widespread demands for directly-elected regional assemblies were rejected by the Gaullist Government. Instead, the region was run by the regional prefect (who acted as the regional executive) and two new indirectly-elected regional assemblies, the Regional Council and the Economic and Social Committee. The former, which exercised deliberative power over the regional budget, comprised all national politicians in the region (who were ex officio members) together with an equal number of local councillors. The Economic and Social Committee, meanwhile, was a corporatist, consultative assembly which brought together representatives of local professional associations, socioeconomic organisations and technical 'experts'.

The *formal* relationship between Paris and the provinces prior to 1982 was thus a straightforward one of administrative control. Local elected councils existed, but their activities were at all times subject to prior administrative and financial control (*tutelle*) by the prefect and technical control by the ministerial field services. The reality of centre–periphery relations was, however, rather different. As highlighted by sociological models of the politico-administrative system, prefects were less pivotal, local political elites were generally more powerful and their relations with state officials considerably more complex than implied by administrative law.

Sociological Bases of Local Power

The Jacobin model of the centralised state outlined above assumes that the central administration constitutes a cohesive entity within which there is effective communication and consensus over objectives. This view has been effectively challenged by organisational analyses of the French Civil Service undertaken by Crozier (1963, 1970), Suleiman (1974, 1978) and Dupuy and Thoenig (1983, 1985), which have revealed the extent to which the administrative Leviathan is, in fact, beset by a series of cross-cutting internal cleavages that serve to fragment and weaken the power of the centre. Horizontal cleavages stem from inter-corps rivalry and ministerial divisions, both of which inhibit effective communication and cooperation between different sections of the administration. Vertical integration of the administrative hierarchy is also weakened by poor communication which means that local officials, in fact, enjoy considerable autonomy over the implementation of central government directives.

Related sociological studies of French local administration by Pierre Grémion (1976) and Jean-Pierre Worms (1966) further confirmed that the relationship between local officials and *notables* (leaders), far from being a straightforward one of administrative supervision prior to 1982, was in fact characterised by 'complementarity and interdependence'. Using the example of the prefect and the president of the departmental council, Jean-Pierre Worms' analysis revealed that, although one represented the state and the other the *département*, a relationship usually developed between the two based upon cooperation, exchange of information and reciprocal influence. Informal alliances of this type were by no means confined to the prefectoral system; members of the specialist field services, for instance, typically helped mayors of rural communes to prepare technical dossiers and obtain ministerial subsidies. Local collaboration between officials and politicians thus served to create an informal (but often effective) source of local power which was able to influence and to some extent counter the power of the centre by 'adapting' the implementation of national policies to suit local conditions.

Sociological models of centre–periphery relations have also highlighted the considerable power wielded by local politicians both nationally and locally. Multiple office-holding is an essential feature of French politics which has traditionally provided local politicians with direct access to Parliament and the means to defend local interests within the context of national policies. At the end of 1984, no less than 212 of the 474 deputies (45 per cent) and

178 of the 296 senators (60 per cent) were general councillors while 383 deputies (81 per cent) and 227 senators (77 per cent) were municipal councillors, 408 of whom were mayors (Rondin, 1986, p. 256). For many years these so-called *grands notables* have enjoyed privileged access to ministerial subsidies (for local sports centres, youth clubs, and so on) and, because of their national standing, have been virtually immune from local administrative control. Mayors of large communes and general council presidents constitute a further category of local politicians who, long before 1982, wielded considerable power within the formally centralised state. Democratically elected, in charge of substantial budgets, backed by powerful party organisations and assisted by competent and independent bureaucracies, these local political leaders were generally acknowledged by all officials (including the prefect) to constitute privileged policy-making partners.

In addition, all local politicians seek to consolidate their position locally by means of political clientelism. The local patron *par excellence*, however, is the mayor, who occupies a pivotal position within the council and local community. It is, for instance, the mayor who determines the municipal budget, regularly visits the prefect and deals with the field services. Such sources of patronage are jealously guarded; few mayors would, for instance, countenance relinquishing personal control over sensitive issues such as the allocation of public housing, supervision of communal welfare agencies or the power to make municipal appointments. In addition, all mayors (and general and regional council presidents) seek to establish close links with the leaders of recognised and respectable interest groups within the locality whose activities and interests are deemed to be consistent with those of the local community. Client groups such as local Chamber of Commerce, large employers (public and private) and professional associations, such as the FNSEA and FEN, also attempt to become the privileged partners of the ministerial field services which directly affect them. Key socioeconomic interests thus become an integral component of local power (P. Grémion, 1976; Dupuy and Thoenig, 1985). The growing politicisation of French local government has neither reduced nor significantly altered the traditional pattern of local clientelism. Though political allegiance plays a role – municipal socialism on the Left is balanced by the politics of the Rotary Club on the Right – it would be electorally suicidal for a mayor to confine patronage to politically sympathetic groups (Dion, 1986).

The centralised state which formed the basis for the Defferre reforms was thus far from monolithic. In practice, centre–periphery relations resembled a 'honeycomb' of cross-cutting linkages between politicians, administrators and socioeconomic groups, all of whom sought to further their own interests within the policy-making process. Within this arrangement local elites were generally able to influence both the formulation and local implementation of national policies and thus undermine the power of the centre to some extent.

The Defferre Reforms

Post-war social, economic and political developments have persuaded all governments of the Fifth Republic of the need to reform centre–periphery relations. The Napoleonic system of local administration based upon *départements* and communes had been designed for a rural society and was no longer able to meet the economic and administrative needs of a modern industrial society. Since 1958 local government reform has rarely been absent from the political agenda as successive governments have sought to reform and rationalise the centralised state. The Defferre reforms should, therefore, be viewed as the culmination of a much longer process of local government modernisation initiated by previous Right-wing governments. During the 1960s and early 1970s Gaullist governments, committed to economic planning and state-led industrialisation, pursued a strategy of 'functional regionalism' which led eventually to the establishment of the regional public establishments (Wright, 1979; Mazey, 1989). Between 1974 and 1981, President Giscard d'Estaing's commitment to economic liberalism was reflected in a series of measures which strengthened local financial autonomy and extended the policy-making powers of the regional public establishments (Mény, 1984).

These earlier developments prepared the way for the Defferre reforms in several respects. Regions had by 1981 acquired an institutional and political identity, while many constraints upon local authority expenditure had already been removed. More generally, these developments served to create widespread support for further decentralisation. Throughout the 1970s, Left-wing demands for greater local participation (*autogestion*) were fuelled by developments within the PS, local electoral success and disillusionment with centralised planning which had, according to Marxist analyses, benefited the interests of private capital at the expense of local communities (Biarez, 1973; Lokjine, 1977; Giard and Scheibling, 1981). Between 1972 and 1981 the PS and PCF, therefore, repeatedly promised that a future Left-wing government would

implement a programme of political and administrative decentralisation as part of its programme of *changement* (reform).

The Defferre Package: Aims and Provisions

The Law on the Rights and Liberties for Communes, Departments
and Regions were presented to the opening session of the new
Parliament in July 1981 by the newly-appointed Minister for the
Interior and Decentralisation, Gaston Defferre, and passed on 2
March 1982. This was essentially an enabling Bill; over the next
four years a further 22 laws and 170 government decrees completed the decentralisation programme. The declared objectives of
the reforms were three-fold: to devolve state responsibilities to
local authorities; to transfer power at each level from the administrative to the locally elected representatives; and to increase opportunities for local participation. The Bill further confirmed that
existing local authority powers and responsibilities would remain
intact and specified that no level of local authority would exercise
formal control over another. As a general principle the *loi Defferre*
(Defferre Law) also promised that any transfer of responsibility
would be accompanied by a financial transfer from the state to
the authority concerned.

In April 1982 executive power at the departmental and regional
levels was transferred from the prefects to the elected presidents
and the state administrative services, and local officials were placed
at the disposal of the latter (which could also appoint additional
independent technical and political advisers). A written agreement
signed by the former prefect and president of the general council
(or regional council) detailed how many officials, cars and offices
were to be transferred from the prefecture to the local authority.
The reforms further specified that those sections of the ministerial
field services responsible for policy areas to be devolved to local
authorities should, by January 1987, also be placed under the
control of the locally elected presidents. To facilitate this process
of administrative decentralisation the Defferre package included a
Civil Service reform designed to boost the hitherto low status of
local officials. This created a new corps of local government
officials and established the principle of parity between local and
state civil servants within a unified administrative system and
career structure.

Meanwhile, prefects – the legendary symbol of state authority
– were replaced by *Commissaires de la République*, who are now
the official representatives of the prime minister, but who need
not be members of the prefectoral corps. While formally they lack

the local executive powers of their predecessors, the *Commissaires* enjoy new powers in relation to economic planning and greater control over the field services. All forms of a priori administrative and financial control over local and regional authority decisions disappeared along with the prefects; local government activity is now subject only to a posteriori legal and financial control by the administrative tribunals of the *Conseil d'Etat* (Council of State) and the newly-created regional *Cours de Comptes* (Court of Accounts). It is the responsibility of the *Commissaires* to refer any illegal acts or irregular budgets to the appropriate regulatory body within two months of receiving notification of the decision.

The 21 metropolitan regional public establishments and the four overseas territories (Guyana, Réunion, Guadaloupe and Martinique) were transformed into fully-fledged regional governments with directly-elected councils. The first regional elections in the overseas territories took place in February 1983, but those in mainland France, initially scheduled for the same year, were repeatedly postponed. They were finally held alongside the legislative elections on 16 March 1986 under the same electoral system: a single ballot in which electors voted for party lists in each *département* with seats being allocated according to the 'highest average' principle. Inevitably the regional contests were somewhat overshadowed by the national election, and unsurprisingly the results closely mirrored those of the legislative ballot. Of the 22 regional councils elected for a six-year period in 1986 all but two (Limousin and Nord-Pas-de-Calais) were controlled by the Right-wing RPR and UDF parties, with the FN holding the balance of power in five regions (Aquitaine, Languedoc-Roussillon, Franche-Comté, Haute-Normandie and Picardie). Significantly, these first regional elections were also dominated by national issues and traditional political elites (Percheron, 1987). In the hope of satisfying regionalist pressures and stemming autonomist violence the Defferre reforms granted a Special Statute to Corsica which set the island apart legally from other regions and provided the territory with additional state subsidies and greater autonomy over educational, social and cultural policies.

All local authorities were given new powers to intervene in the local economy and assist local industries either directly or indirectly by means of loans, grants and tax concessions. In addition, each level of government was granted a specific mission which formed the basis for the devolution of new responsibilities. The *raison d'être* of the region, according to the reforms, remains economic planning and regional economic development. In order to perform this role regions were given specific responsibility for vocational and professional training and accorded a much larger role in the formulation and implementation of the decentralised IX Plan (1984–8). Each regional authority, in consultation with the *Commissaire*, prepared a five-year regional Plan outlining medium-term investment priorities. This document formed the basis of a contractual agreement (*contrat de Plan*) between the state and the region (as well as other interested parties such as other local authorities, nationalised industries, private organisations and public establishments) committing the signatories to the financing of regional programmes for the duration of the IX Plan.

By 1985 all regions, including Corsica, had signed such an agreement and the total amount of money allocated to over 1,000 projects totalled some 63 000 million francs (37 811 million francs on the part of the government and 25 581 million francs on the part of the regions). The dominant themes of the regional planning contracts were vocational training, research and technology, industrial aid, agricultural development and communications (Muret *et al.*, 1986). By the end of 1986 between 46 per cent (Nord-Pas-de-Calais) and 74 per cent (Auvergne) of the investments envisaged in the regional *contrats de Plan* had been realised and in June 1987 the Right-wing Minister for Administration and Planning announced that the decentralised planning exercise was to be repeated for the X Plan (1989–93).

Départements, meanwhile, were given special responsibility from 1984 for the provision and administration of most forms of public health and welfare provision (*solidarité*). While the state retains responsibility for certain forms of health care and the principal social security programmes, the *départements* are now responsible (in conjunction with the communes) for the provision of general medical facilities (including vaccination programmes), maternity care, family welfare and special forms of social assistance for the elderly and physically disabled (such as accommodation). The vocation of communes, according to the Defferre reforms, is town planning and urban development. Since 1983 municipal councils have been responsible for the elaboration of 'Land Use Plans' which outline future construction plans. Once these have been approved by the *Commissaire*, mayors may grant planning permission for specific projects which fall within the parameters of the urban plans without further recourse to the central administration.

Financial compensation for devolved tasks was provided in the form of fiscal transfers and index-linked subsidies. Vehicle registration tax, for instance, has been transferred to the regions to finance the cost of professional and vocational training schemes while road tax (*la vignette automobile*), land registration and property taxes have been transferred to the *départements* towards the cost of providing public welfare services. The reforms also created two new block grants; a Capital Investment Grant (DGE), and a Decentralisation Grant (DGD). The former, which is given to *départements* and communes (but not regions) replaces the previous arrangement whereby local councils received grants from various ministries for specific investment projects. The DGD is used to supplement fiscal transfers to local authorities to finance new responsibilities.

Three further changes – local electoral reform, additional powers for the *conseils d'arrondissement* (electoral constituency councils) of Paris, Lyons and Marseilles and limitation of *cumul des mandats* – were introduced in an attempt to enhance the democratic and representative nature of local politics. The local electoral reform has introduced a degree of proportional representation into municipal elections for communes of more than 3,500 inhabitants. Under the new system, introduced for the 1983 municipal elections, the winning list (which formerly obtained all council seats) is now awarded half the council seats and the remainder are allocated proportionately among all lists (including the winning one). In Paris, Lyons and Marseilles these elections are now combined with those for the electoral constituency councils which are elected from the same party lists as the municipal council. Presided over by the mayor of the *arrondissement*, the electoral constituency councils enjoy only limited powers with regard to the provision of local services such as crèche facilities, cultural associations, sports clubs and parks.

To ignore the practice of *cumul des mandats* would have undermined the whole decentralisation programme, but it was for obvious reasons a sensitive issue. The Debarge report on the subject presented to Parliament in 1982 formed the basis of a government Bill which was finally passed on 30 December 1985. This restricts to two the number of 'significant' offices an individual may hold. Such offices include those of deputy, senator, member of the European Parliament, regional councillor, general councillor, mayor of a commune with more than 20 000 inhabitants or assistant mayor of a commune with a population of more than 100 000. Furthermore, it is no longer possible for an individual to be president of councils in both a *département* and a region. Though this reform will not be fully implemented until after the 1991 cantonal elections (politicians must gradually reduce the number of offices they hold as each election takes place), it has already begun to affect prominent *cumulards* who have, significantly, chosen to give up their regional mandates. *Grands notables* such as Raymond

Marcellin, Michel d'Ornano, Michel Giraud, Bernard Stasi and Jacques Chaban-Delmas, for instance, have all relinquished control of a regional council presidency in order to retain their positions as presidents of *départements*. Although less comprehensive than some would have liked, this reform (combined with the creation of directly-elected regional assemblies) has extended the opportunities for democratic participation.

Decentralisation and Theories of Local Power

Though far-reaching, the Defferre reforms did not constitute a break with the past, but confirmed and accelerated trends which had already emerged. By 1981, mayors of urban communes and presidents of *départements* had become important local policy-makers, and most regional councils had established coherent regional economic investment strategies. The incremental pattern of change in this policy area has been further confirmed by the extent to which the potential impact of the Defferre reforms has, in fact, been limited by the continuing importance of traditional local elites and government resistance after 1986 to any further decentralisation.

Administrative and Political Decentralisation: An Ambiguous Exercise The reforms have without question reinforced the status and power of the presidents of *départements* and regions who now formally enjoy the same executive powers as mayors. The principal beneficiaries in this respect, however, are undoubtedly the presidents of *départements*, whose power is assured by the traditional status of the *départements* and the superior size of their budgets: in 1985, for instance, the regional budget of Basse Normandie was just 300 million francs while that of the principal *département* within the region, Calvados, totalled 1,291 million francs. The transfer of some 12 000 officials from the prefectures to the regional and departmental authorities has further enhanced the importance of local presidents; Michel d'Ornano, president of Calvados general council, for example, heads a departmental administration of 150, of whom 129 are former members of the prefecture.

Most striking, however, has been the proliferation of regional administrations since 1982, which range in size from 30 in Limousin region to 323 in Nord-Pas-de-Calais. Between 1981 and 1985 the total number of regional administrative personnel increased from 413 to 2,713. For the most part, however, these changes have been confined to the politico-administrative system itself. By December 1985, for instance, no fewer than 93 prefects and sub-prefects had taken up posts as directors of regional and local administrations. In one sense, therefore, decentralisation has merely served to reinforce and legitimise the much longer-term trend towards greater interpenetration of the French administrative and political systems documented by de Baecque and Quermonne (1982).

Moreover, in other sectors, administrative decentralisation has been more limited; ministerial opposition, corps resistance and a lack of commitment on the part of the RPR–UDF Government elected in March 1986 has effectively impeded the devolution of most other ministerial services. The one exception has been the field services of the Ministry of Health and Social Security. By January 1987, 99 conventions had been signed by *Commissaires*, local presidents and professional associations which placed 72 per cent of the 53 000 officials working in the DDASS under the personal control of the presidents of *départements*. Powerful opposition to decentralisation has come from more technical departments, such as the ministries of Urban Development, Housing and Transport, which have sought to retain full control over the influential DDE. By January 1987 only 25 conventions had been signed with the above ministries, and just 773 of the 16 419 members of the DDE had been transferred to the general councils (Delcamp, 1987, p. 174). Other ministerial services have simply been placed 'at the disposal' of the local council (as they were prior to the reforms).

'Abolition' of the prefects has also failed to produce the dramatic changes which many people either hoped for or feared. With the exception of three *Commissaires* of *départements* appointed in 1982 and 1983, all state representatives have been members of the prefectoral corps. This particular Socialist experiment was brought to an abrupt end with the election of the Right-wing government in 1986 which made clear its intention of restoring the authority and the tradititional title of the prefects. While they have lost their local executive powers, the *Commissaires* continue to enjoy a close working relationship with local politicians, particularly local presidents. As Terrazoni (1987) and Durantin (1988) point out, the need for negotiation between the state representative and local Executive has in many respects been increased by decentralisation. Several studies have also revealed the extent to which mayors of small communes who lack their own services continue to rely upon the informal advice of the *Commissaire* rather than seek the assistance of the local services of the president of the *département*, not least because they suspect the latter of political bias (Rondin, 1986).

The continuing importance of local collaboration between state representatives and local politicians is perhaps most clearly reflected in the very small numbers of cases involving local authorities referred to the administrative tribunals and regional Courts of Account. Between March 1983 and March 1984, only 809 cases of illegality were referred to the administrative tribunals by *Commissaires* out of more than 2 700 000 local authority decisions (0.04 per cent: Rondin, 1986, p. 242). The number of cases of local authority financial irregularity have also been low. Out of more than 300 000 local authority budgetary acts passed in 1983, only 1,677 cases (0.5 per cent) were submitted to the regional accounts courts by *Commissaires*. In 1984 and 1985 the figures were 1,771 and 1,098 respectively (Varaine and Malingre, 1987, p. 195). As Rondin's study confirmed, local politicians and *Commissaires* have generally sought to avoid legal action by means of prior negotiation (Rondin, 1986). Significantly, the role of the regional Courts of Account was further reduced by government legislation in October 1987, which transferred responsibility for financial control of budgets of small communes (less than 2,000 inhabitants) back to the *Trésorier Payeur Générale* (Treasurer and Paymaster General). The development was a significant victory for rural mayors who have unanimously welcomed the return of the protective umbrella of administrative control.

Decentralisation and Economic Policy-making. Devolution of new tasks and resources has significantly increased the financial importance of the local authorities. Local authority expenditure totalled 499 500 million francs in 1987, nearly 50 per cent of state expenditure compared to 294 500 million francs (36 per cent of state expenditure) in 1982 (see Table 8.1). Local taxation has also become more important as a result of the reforms. Between 1981 and 1984 the fiscal income of the communes increased by 55 per cent (from 63 390 million francs to 98 054 million francs), that of the *départements* by 100 per cent (from 24 974 million francs to 49 961 million francs) and that of the regions by 135 per cent (from 3,662 million francs to 8,590 million francs: Caisse des Dépôts et Consignations, 1986, p. 80). Whereas in 1980, 43 per cent of tax revenue went to the state and 11 per cent to local authorities, by 1987 these figures were 39 per cent and 14 per cent respectively (*Le Monde*, 10 August 1988). Notwithstanding local variations, local authority taxes generally have increased at a faster rate than national ones since 1982, but regional taxes (which still represent only 20 per cent of departmental taxes and 12 per cent of municipal taxes) have risen most sharply following the removal of legal limits upon regional taxation. However, decentralisation has done nothing to reduce the dependence of local authorities upon state subsidies which, in 1988, totalled 141 820 million francs (and which are expected to rise to 163 800 million francs in 1989: *Le Monde*, 6 October 1988).

TABLE 8.1 *Local authority expenditure in millions of francs*

	1981	1987	Increase 1981–7(%)
Communes	190	345	82
Départements	74	126	70
Regions	6.7	28.5	325
Total	270.7	499.5	81

Source: Table compiled from *Caisse des Dépôts et Consignations (1986); Ministère de l'Intérieur, Guide Budgétaire Communal, Départemental et Régional 1988* (Paris: 1988, La Documentation Française).

These developments are, of course, largely due to the transfer of responsibilities and resources from the state to local authorities and most of this revenue – particularly in the case of *départements* and communes – is effectively committed in advance, leaving little room for local economic intervention. Indeed, local politicians from all parties have persistently claimed that annual increases in state subsidies since 1982 have been insufficient to meet the rapidly rising costs of their additional responsibilities. There are some grounds for this complaint. Between 1982 and 1986 local authority finances were affected by the Socialist austerity programmes which resulted in higher interest payments on loans, a freezing of local service charges, and reductions in real terms in the size of state subsidies. During the period of Jacques Chirac's premiership, local subsidies were further reduced and local fiscal moderation encouraged in line with the government's commitment to economic liberalism. As in Britain, local authorities have thus been faced with the choice of reducing local services or raising local taxes. Generally speaking, Left-wing controlled local and regional authorities have been more willing than their Right-wing counterparts to raise taxes to maintain social programmes.

In 1982, decentralised planning and local authority economic intervention was encouraged by the Socialist Government as a means of strengthening local social development and democracy; in 1986 the newly-elected Right-wing government urged local authorities to become more efficient by establishing closer links with private enterprise. Beneath the change in rhetoric, however, there has been considerable continuity in the gradual development of closer links between local authorities and local entrepreneurs. In 1984, local authority intervention to promote industrial, commercial and agricultural development totalled 4 400 million francs of which 2 300 million francs was invested by communes, 1 100 million francs by the departments and 1 000 million francs by the regions. Indirect and direct subsidies, tax concessions and loans have constituted the principal means by which local authorities provided assistance to private firms. These developments have been accompanied by the establishment of closer financial links between local authorities and banks, particularly since the liberalisation of credit facilities for local authorities in 1987. In addition, most regions have established regional development agencies which bring together councillors of both regions and *départements*, representatives of regional banks, chambers of commerce and major employers to advise firms on investment, marketing and export strategies.

Predictably, there is considerable variation regarding the extent and nature of local authority economic intervention. Regions whose primary role since 1972 has been the promotion of regional economic development play the principal part in the coordination of local economic intervention, but large communes also have a significant financial function. Again, Left-wing controlled authorities (notably the Nord-Pas-de-Calais region) have been more interventionist than many Right-wing authorities, which have been more reluctant to subsidise local employment (Muret *et al.*, 1986; Steib, 1987).

Not surprisingly, the above developments have given fresh impetus to Marxist analyses of urban politics and regional planning which have focused upon the economic impact of decentralisation upon working-class communities in an attempt to highlight the limitations of local political autonomy. In particular, these studies have argued that decentralisation has, in fact, been accompanied by financial disengagement on the part of the state, leaving working-class communities to bear the financial and social costs of economic recession. Regional and local councils, it is argued, have to varying degrees defended the interests of capital (for example, by subsidising private investment and financing the cost of vocational training schemes) to the detriment of working-class communities (*Economie et Politique*, 1986; Rosette, 1987).

Conclusion

Judged simply in terms of the amount of legislation involved, the Defferre reforms were without doubt one of the great reforms of the Mitterrand presidency. Moreover, while other Socialist reforms were either reversed or abandoned by the RPR–UDF government elected in 1986, the central provisions of the Defferre programme were left intact. In consequence, the French state is now considerably less centralised than when the Socialists came to power in 1981. Resources and responsibilities have been devolved to local authorities whose activities are no longer subject to prior administrative and financial control and new opportunities for democratic participation have been created by the establishment of a new tier of regional government. Local politics have thus been legitimised and the French state been rendered more democratic. However, these developments have in no sense reduced the relevance of sociological models of local power for, while significant developments have taken place within the politico-administrative system, the system itself has not been transformed. No new forms of citizen participation were created and the decentralised structures remain, for the time being at least, dominated by traditional political and administrative elites who have once again demonstrated their capacity to adapt to changing circumstances. As Yves Mény concluded in 1987, 'far from leading to the dismantling of the state, the reform is rather an element of consensual integration which associates local elites with the administration, while marginalising the most radical nationalist or regionalist dissenters' (Mény, 1987a, p. 261).

PART THREE

Public Policies

9

The State and the Market

PETER A. HALL

In no sphere of French policy have recent developments been more significant than in the area of economic policy. Their thrust has been to reduce the role of the state in the economy and turn the allocation of resources more directly over to market mechanisms. In many respects, this has been a general European trend. After 30 years distinguished by the growing role of the public sector in the economy, many European nations have rediscovered an enthusiasm for the market. The 1980s therefore, mark a watershed in postwar European political economy, and an account of recent developments in the French economy is largely a story of how France, too, came to embrace the market.

French Dirigism

In France, such developments have special significance, because the French state has been one of the most interventionist among the capitalist nations since the war. The French were said to have a *dirigiste* state (one that took an active part in the direction of French industry). Dirigism has had several components.

The first was a system of indicative economic planning. Inspired by a desire to modernise French industry in the wake of the Second World War, French officials established a Planning Commission to present a detailed plan for the allocation of resources among the major sectors of French industry over the following four or five years. They invited industrialists and trade unionists to join a series of modernisation commissions responsible for mobilising support for these plans among the business community.

171

There have been ten such plans since 1946. In the early years, when resources were particularly scarce, the planners played a major role in the allocation of funds among industrial sectors. During the 1960s they no longer had exclusive control over such resources, but instead took on responsibility for predicting the course of the overall economy and identifying the major social as well as economic problems then facing the nation (see Estrin and Holmes, 1983).

French officials also began to operate an active industrial policy, using subsidies and the substantial control they enjoyed over a large, nationalised banking sector to allocate funds to firms engaged in the kind of activities on which it was believed economic growth could be based. During the 1960s, the industrial policy-makers emphasised high-technology projects like the construction of the Concorde supersonic airliner, the development of nuclear power and the abortive *Plan Calcul* designed to create a French computer industry (Zysman, 1977). It became customary for many French firms to look to the state for support. Public officials used loopholes in the taxation system, the extensive network of price controls that prevailed across the economy, the resources of a large sector of nationalised industries and public subsidies to per-suade various firms to invest in particular product lines and merge with one another, where necessary, to create massive conglomer-ates designed to be 'national champions' in international markets. President Charles de Gaulle, in particular, believed that the inter-national stature of France would depend on her economic might and technological prowess. Elite educational institutions like the ENA trained thousands of French officials to think that they could determine the appropriate strategies for French industry and should press those strategies on the private sector.

Even today, a multitude of public organs are involved in the administration of French economic policy. At the top of the hier-archy stands the Ministry of Finance, containing the Treasury, which is ultimately responsible for macroeconomic management, supervision of the banking system in coordination with the Bank of France and National Credit Council, the allocation of industrial subsidies, in concert with the Economic and Social Fund and latterly an inter-ministerial Committee on Industrial Restructuring, as well as its traditional task of preparing the public budget. Despite various changes of name (it is now called the Ministry of Economy, Finance and Budget), the Ministry of Finance has remained the ultimate source of power over the direction of the economy (see Eck, 1986).

Less powerful, but influential on detailed matters, is the Ministry of Industry (now termed the Ministry of Industry, External Commerce and Regional Planning) which supervises the industrial policies of the government and maintains close relations with the major industrial sectors. Of course, policy for some sectors is also supervised by the Ministries of Transport, Defence, Agriculture, Post, Telecommunications and Space, and Public Works and Housing. They, in turn, are surrounded by a variety of public agencies and commissions charged with specific industrial tasks. Overall strategy is supposed to be established by the offices of the president and prime minister and the details of policy are worked out in the many inter-ministerial committees that have lately sprung up.

The Implications of Economic Openness

Since so much has happened in recent years, it is tempting to think that the movement of French economic policy away from state intervention towards greater reliance on market mechanisms is a completely new phenomenon, mainly attributable to the wave of enthusiasm for neo-liberalism that swept across Europe in the 1980s. As we shall see, that wave lent force to some of the more radical measures of recent years, such as the privatisation programme of 1986–8 and the liberalisation of the financial markets. However, the origins of the move from an emphasis on the state to an emphasis on the market lie in a set of longer-term developments that should not be ignored. They have both political and economic dimensions.

The seeds were sown in the 1950s when France joined first the European Coal and Steel Community and then the EC, whose members agreed to open their borders to the free flow of goods among them in a series of stages initially designed to culminate in the late 1960s. Many consequences were to follow from that step. First, as trade increased among the European nations and more generally around the world with the reduction of tariffs negotiated under the General Agreement on Tariffs and Trade, the health of the French economy became increasingly dependent upon foreign trade. Imports and exports accounted for only 13 per cent of France's gross domestic product in 1953; by 1989, they accounted for 26 per cent. Hence, if French industry were to continue to prosper, its firms would have to be competitive with those producing elsewhere in the EC and the world, otherwise no one would buy French exports and even the French would purchase imports rather than domestically produced goods.

At first, French officials did not view this as a problem. After all, they were trying to restructure industry precisely so as to render French firms more competitive. By subsidising coal, steel, ship-building, telecommunications, aerospace, computers and so on, the French state was able to expand production in these sectors. The size of the French economy trebled between 1950 and 1970. While it was relatively easy to churn out higher volumes of steel and cement, however, it was much more difficult for officials to select the products and production processes which would be competitive on world markets. Indeed, precisely because French firms had often been sheltered from foreign competition by subsidies and tariff barriers, they tended to be oriented towards producing more rather than producing more competitively. By the late 1960s, however, when most tariff barriers were finally elimin- ated in the EC, there could be no growth without competitiveness. Many French companies began to lose their share of even the domestic market as foreign products of better price and quality began to cross the borders in larger numbers. West German and Italian products posed a particular threat but products from Japan and the newly-industrialising countries of East Asia also made deep inroads into French markets.

At the same time, the growing interdependence of the world economy began to undercut the leverage that French policy-makers themselves had over industry. In the 1950s and early 1960s, the state controlled a large portion of the funds available for domestic investment. With the growth of international financial markets and freer financial flows in the 1960s and 1970s, however, many firms could turn elsewhere for finance. Hence they no longer needed to follow the suggestions of French officials in order to secure capital. Over time, the EC also began to outlaw the preferential taxation and public procurement policies, non-tariff barriers and industrial subsidies on which French policy-makers had often relied.

As exports and imports began to account for a large proportion of French production, the health of the economy also became increasingly dependent on economic conditions elsewhere. When West Germany faced a recession, many French exporters lost their markets. When the price of oil was raised dramatically in 1974 and 1979, French producers suddenly found their energy costs rocketing, while demand for their products dropped around the world. The French economy became increasingly sensitive to inter- national economic events that policy-makers could neither predict nor control. As a result, the complex macroeconomic forecasts of the Plan became highly inaccurate in the 1970s and many of the state's industrial initiatives were thrown off course by changing international events.

These economic trends, in turn, caused political problems for French policy-makers. During the 'thirty glorious years' that followed the war, when the economy grew strongly, French politicians had become accustomed to claiming credit for economic success. By emphasising the process of economic planning and industrial policy, public officials openly assumed responsibility for the direction of the economy. However, this responsibility became an embarrassment after 1974, when higher oil prices plunged France into an extended economic recession. The state could not stem rising rates of unemployment, and higher levels of inflation necessitated policies of fiscal austerity that were politically unpopular. Someone has to pay the costs of such austerity and many politicians began to seek ways of shifting responsibility for redundancies and bankruptcies away from the state. To claim that it was up to the market, rather than the state, to determine the fate of individual enterprises and their workers seemed to be a way of making such decisions less politically visible (Hall, 1986).

In short, the growing interdependence of the French economy, which the formation of the EC and the growth of international trade set in motion, meant that, if French firms were to survive, they would have to emphasise competitiveness and responsiveness to market conditions in ways that continuing doses of state aid often did not facilitate. These developments eventually undermined the influence of the policy instruments at the disposal of the French state.

The Evolution of Economic Policy

French officials slowly became aware of these problems, and they began to move away from strict dirigism to more market-oriented policies well before the late 1980s. As is often the case, however, this movement took place in halting steps, often taken in response to critical policy experiences.

The first instrument to suffer was the system of indicative economic planning. After the two initial Plans, which had great influence by virtue of the planners' control over scarce financial resources, the impact of planning on the economy as a whole began to wane. During the 1960s it became a largely macroeconomic exercise, designed to pinpoint particular trouble spots in the economy and encourage widespread expansion through optimistic economic forecasts. As early as 1970, some of the planners had developed misgivings about their ability to render industry competitive as opposed to simply larger. However, the critical experience that changed attitudes at both the official and political levels was the recession which followed the 1974 oil price increase. This unexpected event vitiated the rosy forecasts of the VI Plan and persuaded policy-makers to move away from definitive forecasts altogether. Subsequent Plans became pale shadows of their predecessors. They forsook detailed economic forecasts in favor of simply identifying the specific areas to be given priority in public spending (Hall, 1986).

The year 1974 was also a turning point for macroeconomic policy. An initial attempt to deal with the 1974–5 recession through reflationary fiscal policy failed, and policy-makers realised that it would do little good to devalue the exchange rate, as they had done so often in the past to stimulate French exports, because to do so would raise the cost of vital oil imports, denominated in US dollars, to even greater heights. The result was a change in economic strategy between 1976 and 1981, under Raymond Barre, who adopted a fairly austere macroeconomic stance, designed to reduce domestic inflation and spending on imports. To stimulate French industry, he turned to a series of microeconomic measures, including the removal of price controls in some spheres of the economy for the first time in over 100 years, the adoption of tax incentives to stimulate the purchase of shares (which had always been less important than bank loans as a source of funds for French industry), and a system of development contracts for firms that was designed to tie state subsidies more directly to market performance. In addition, Barre took France into the EMS in 1979 in an effort to reduce French inflation by pegging the franc to a basket of currencies based on the Deutschmark, albeit at the cost of limiting France's ability to devalue or adopt an independent monetary policy.

Despite these measures, however, there was still an underlying dirigism to French policy. A collection of new inter-ministerial committees was established between 1974 and 1979 to support industry in the face of continuing recession and stiff regulations limiting lay-offs were passed in 1975. Barre's market rhetoric was still at odds with the thrust of much French policy (Green, 1983). Ironically, the more substantial break with dirigism would have to await the election of the Socialist Government in 1981.

The opening years of François Mitterrand's economic experiment were another of those critical experiences that ultimately pushed France towards a more market-based economic policy. Shortly after its election, the Socialist Government adopted a policy of redistributive Keynesianism, reflating the economy by raising the minimum wage, hiring another 100 000 public employees, reducing the working week from 40 to 39 hours, devoting large sums to manpower training and early retirement programmes designed to reduce rising unemployment, nationalising 49 firms central to French banking and industry, and expanding annual aid to French industry from 35 billion francs in 1981 to 86 billion francs by 1985. These measures were financed by higher social insurance and corporate taxes and a rising budget deficit (Machin and Wright, 1985).

This was a bold stroke, of traditional Socialist provenance, aimed at falling rates of investment and stagnation that had been intensified by a further round of oil price increases in 1979–80. It initially succeeded in raising the rate of growth but failed to increase private investment or employment and soon led to a rapid deterioration in the balance of payments, as consumers bought more imports and global recession hurt French exports. As a result, the exchange rate came under growing pressure in late 1982 and early 1983.

This brought the Mauroy Government to a key turning-point in March 1983. Few moments of decision have been so significant. Faced with growing speculative pressure against the franc, Mitterrand had a choice between two broad strategies. On the one hand, he could have attempted to sustain reflation by devaluing the franc, taking France out of the EMS and putting up protectionist barriers to imports so as to stabilise the trade deficit. To do so would have been to reverse a long-standing movement towards fuller economic integration in the EC. On the other hand, if Mitterrand wanted to maintain France's membership in the EMS and commitment to the EC, he would have to respond to EMS demands to reduce the budget deficit and deflate the economy and find some way, other than macroeconomic stimulation, to improve levels of investment and the performance of French firms. Each strategy had its supporters but Mitterrand chose the latter, perhaps in large measure because the former would have meant a reversal of the trend towards European integration on which French policy had been based for 30 years.

The implications of this choice were profound. Public spending had to be cut back to reduce the budget deficit and restore confidence in the franc. Hence the government could no longer pour funds into the nationalised industries, which had received 62 billion francs between 1982 and 1986. It had to scale down industrial subsidies, letting more firms go bankrupt in the face of recession. Since it was no longer possible to stimulate French industry through the expansion of demand, supply-side measures would have to be used; yet a shortage of funds meant this could no longer be done primarily through subsidies. Moreover, once France's commitment to the EC was confirmed, the emphasis would have to be on measures designed to improve the competitiveness of French firms *vis-à-vis* their European rivals (Fontaneau and Muet, 1985).

Accordingly, it was a Socialist government under a new prime minister, Laurent Fabius, that turned decisively towards the market in 1984–6. Government controls over the nationalised industries were loosened so that they could lay off workers, become more profitable, invest abroad, and even sell off some subsidiaries to raise funds. Corporate taxes were reduced and public sector wages held down so as to enhance corporate profitability. Remaining government subsidies were to be channelled primarily to research and development through a new institution, ANVAR; and the government began to loosen the regulatory framework that French firms faced, particularly to allow further lay-offs (Ross, Hoffmann and Malzacher, 1987).

Less noticeable but even more important in the long run were the measures that Fabius took to deregulate and revive the private capital markets in France. The Socialists expanded the French Stock Exchange through the introduction of new debenture stocks and investment certificates. They established a second market in unlisted securities and a third in financial futures. They authorised many new financial instruments and the creation of quasi-banks specialising in a variety of financial operations. State subsidies on loans were sharply cut back. The idea was to provide firms with new sources of private finance that would reduce their dependence on both the banks and the state. By 1986 bank credits provided only about 40 per cent of the economy's financing needs, compared with 70 per cent in 1982 (Cerny, 1987).

To accompany these measures, the Socialists themselves began to adopt a market rhetoric that made many concessions to the increasing neo-liberalism of the employers' confederation and parties of the Right. When the latter came to power in 1986, they had only to extend and intensify what the Fabius Government had begun.

Economic Policy since 1986

The election of 1986 was significant in this context, not only because it returned a coalition of conservative parties to office in the National Assembly, but because the RPR under the new Prime Minister, Jacques Chirac, emerged with the upper hand over the UDF and Raymond Barre. Like Giscard, Barre advocated an economic strategy that would make use of the market but retain many aspects of the old-style dirigism. By contrast, Chirac and his ministers deliberately set out to dismantle the policy instruments of the *dirigiste* state. Seeking a platform from which to criticise the Socialists, and influenced by the diffusion of ideas from Britain and America, the Right had adopted a strident market rhetoric, which they then put partly into practice.

At the macroeconomic level, the policies of the Chirac Government were designed to give priority to the fight against inflation rather than unemployment. The budget deficit was reduced each year and emphasis was placed on tax cuts rather than public spending increases. For the first time, the government published projections for expected revenue and receipts for three years ahead. Despite pressure from Barre and the CDS in the governing coalition to increase financial aid to corporations, Chirac opted instead to cut corporate taxes by 37 billion francs and taxes on individuals by 31 billion francs over two years.

A number of measures were taken to reduce the network of state-sponsored regulations and subsidies affecting business. The new Minister of Industry himself presided over deep cuts of 500 million francs in the ministry's budget. ANVAR and most of the remaining committees established to channel state aid to the private sector were abolished, with the exception of the inter-ministerial Committee on Industrial Restructuring. The Plan escaped abolition but was left to wither away into little more than an advisory report on economic conditions and an embellished statement of the government's spending priorities. Edouard Balladur, the new Minister of Finance, removed all price controls in 1986 and a variety of regulations limiting lay-offs were repealed. He ended the system of quotas on bank lending that had long been one of the principal means whereby the French state influenced the growth of the money supply and the direction of investment. Instead, high interest rates were used to maintain the exchange rate at relatively elevated levels so as to reduce inflation and put pressure on French firms to compete more effectively on world markets. The idea was to enhance the profitability of French firms in the hope that this would spur them to invest and to remove any limitations on their flexibility to respond to market conditions (Bauchard, 1988).

The most radical of the government's measures, however, was a massive programme to privatise many of the nationalised industries. In August 1986, the government announced a plan to privatise 65 public enterprises. Before the global Stock Exchange crash of October 1987 brought these plans to a halt, it managed to sell off eight major corporate groups (CCF, CGE, Havas, Paribas, Saint-Gobain, Société Générale, Suez and TF1), three smaller banks (BIMP, BTP, Sogenal) and to sell off privately three other firms (CGCT, IDI, MGE) for a price of over 70 billion francs. Two-thirds of the funds raised were devoted to reducing the national debt and another third went to the remaining nationalised industries. The prices at which these firms were offered were very attractive and, in barely two years, the number of shareholders in France rose from about 4 000 000 to over 7 000 000 individuals. However, the government also deliberately sold a 'hard core' of shares, sufficient to confer control over the privatised firm, to a group of firms selected by the Minister of Finance and, in the cases of Matra and Havas, maintained a shareholding of its own for several years so as to prevent messy take-over bids for a few years (Bauer, 1988). This programme was controversial but remarkably successful, given the small size of the French Stock Exchange.

The Chirac Government also pursued and enlarged the programme of financial deregulation begun under the Socialists in 1985. It announced plans to end the monopoly of the traditional brokerage houses in bond and share markets and liberalised the capacity of French banks to offer a wide range of financial services. Even more important, exchange controls on the international flow of funds were also relaxed, and France eliminated them entirely in 1990.

To some degree, these measures resulted from the new-found enthusiasm of the RPR for the market. However, there were deeper trends at work here as well, as indicated by the way in which many of these policies were continued after 1988, when President Mitterrand and another Socialist government (under Michel Rocard) were re-elected. If the turn toward neo-liberalism were simply a passing political fashion associated with the Chirac Government, we would expect it to have been reversed when the Socialists came to power again. On the contrary, the early policies of the Rocard Government display a continued emphasis on the market. Moreover, those policies mark the culmination of a decade of change in the French political economy. Their principal features reflect the changes that have gradually been taking place in French economic policy over several years. Five such features deserve particular mention.

First, French governments seem to have become reconciled to

the fact that they have very limited room to manoeuvre on the macroeconomic front. They discovered in 1981 that a massive reflation simply boosts consumer spending and sucks in imports, given the free trade flows across French borders. They seem to have learned that an economy which is highly dependent on exports and imports cannot rejuvenate itself through domestic reflation alone; its macroeconomic policies must be dictated, in large measure, by the stance of its major trading partners. Accordingly, the initial fiscal stance of the Rocard Government was very cautious. It gave priority to reducing the budget deficit from 3.2 per cent of gross domestic product in 1985 and 2.1 per cent in 1988 to 1.7 per cent in 1989; and, at the end of 1988, Rocard predicted at least fifteen more months of such austerity. As the EC moves toward fuller monetary integration, France's ability to pursue an independent macroeconomic policy will become even more restricted. The emphasis on balanced budgets is likely to continue and reflation will be practicable only in the context of coordinated action among the EC nations.

Second, faced with these limitations on macroeconomic policy, French governments have had to rely more heavily on microeconomic policies, aimed at the supply side of industry, to improve economic performance. Of course, supply side policies are nothing new in France but the nature of those policies has changed dramatically. Whereas the microeconomic policies of the 1960s and 1970s emphasised state direction, present policies are built around the private sector. This is a response to the critical experiences of the 1960s and 1970s, when the poor results that followed from attempts to create national champions and state-directed high-technology projects inclined French policy-makers away from purely *dirigiste* policies towards others that put greater reliance on market competition. During the 1980s, policy-makers discovered that no matter how much they tried to reflate the economy, levels of private investment stagnated because the debt-loads of French firms had become too high and their profit levels too low to accommodate investment. As a result, even the Socialists have begun to focus their attention on ways of improving corporate balance sheets and the profitability of the private sector.

One result has been reform of the financial markets designed to improve the access of French firms to alternative sources of finance. The other has been a continuing effort to reduce the burden of taxes and social insurance on French corporations. Accordingly, like the Chirac Government, the Rocard Government reduced corporate taxes by 10 billion francs in its 1989 budget. It also cut taxes on individuals by 5 billion francs and increased public spending by only 4.5 per cent in line with inflation. Corporate profits, which had fallen to 25 per cent of value-added in 1982, were expected to reach 33 per cent in 1989. In line with this, the major increases in investment were expected to come from the private rather than the public sector.

These developments mark an important shift in French policy. The comparison of 1989 with 1985 is striking. In that year, public investment rose by 8.6 per cent and private investment by 4.1 per cent; while, in 1989, public investment was set to rise by only 3 per cent, whereas private investment was to increase by 7 per cent. The government deliberately shifted the onus for investment and growth from the public to the private sector and attempted to increase profit levels as a necessary step in that direction.

Third, like Chirac and the Socialist Government of 1981–6, Rocard has placed more emphasis on the role of regional and local government in the stimulation of enterprise and employment. Where industrial policy was once directed almost exclusively by the central state, it is now a much more decentralised affair. The ambitious decentralisation measures undertaken in 1982 transferred a good deal of power from Paris and its *préfets* to a new tier of regional governments and they have been particularly active in the economic area. Many local areas negotiated regional development plans with the Plan and the central economic authorities in the 1980s. Both DATAR (the agency responsible for regional development) and the ministries involved in industrial policy have decentralised their operations to work more closely with regional authorities (Schmidt, 1988). The Chirac Government experimented with regional enterprise zones, where new firms were to operate tax-free for ten years; and Rocard has established a Regional Fund for Aid to Local Initiatives and endorsed an approach to economic management that gives the regions a central role in the development of new initiatives.

Fourth, following a trend that has been developing over ten years, the industrial policies of the Rocard Government give special priority to small and medium-sized enterprises. Although French policies in the 1960s and early 1970s concentrated on the construction of giant enterprises in the belief that they would compete best on world markets, policy-makers discovered in the 1970s that small enterprises were much more effective creators of employment and often had a flexibility to weather macroeconomic storms that large firms lacked. As a result, an increasing share of the industrial budget has been earmarked for small enterprise. In 1988, for instance, the Rocard Government diverted 15 billion francs collected from state-sponsored industrial bonds to small and medium-sized businesses and offered 600 million francs to provide subsidised loans to such firms.

Finally, the Rocard Government continued a trend, begun in the early 1980s, towards a more active manpower policy. Until the 1980s, French industrial policy was based primarily on the allocation of capital, which it orchestrated through the large nationalised banks and credit institutions, in contrast to nations like Sweden or West Germany, where industrial policy turned heavily on manpower planning. However, rising levels of unemployment in the late 1970s forced the French to adopt programmes deliberately designed to improve the skills of the workforce and persuade firms to take on new employees. The 1981–6 Socialist Government took many such initiatives; and the Chirac Government implemented a highly successful programme, worth 9 billion francs, that relieved employers of social insurance charges for the new employees that they hired. The Rocard Government has continued in this vein to fund a number of programmes designed to provide training and work experience for young people and has promised to eliminate all social insurance charges for two years for the first new employee that a small firm hires. France now has an extremely active and complex manpower policy.

In other spheres, the Rocard Government has also confirmed recent trends. Sensing the political popularity of privatisation, President Mitterrand promised to accept the privatisations that the Chirac Government had accomplished and to avoid new nationalisations. As befits a former Planning Minister, Rocard has endorsed a 10th Plan to cover the 1989–1993 period but, like its recent predecessors, this Plan is primarily an extended elaboration on the priorities already announced by the government. It emphasises the importance of education and manpower training, competitiveness, social solidarity, the quality of life and improvements in the efficiency of the public sector. With one eye on the need to shift the burden of French taxation from indirect to direct taxes to meet the demands that the EC has associated with the achievement of a unified market in 1992, it also proposes funding a greater proportion of public programmes through income tax. The stamp of the 1980s is apparent in the Plan's declaration that 'the state should decide less, decide better, and decide faster'.

The Outlook for the 1990s

France entered the 1990s in fairly healthy economic condition. After 30 billion francs' worth of corporate tax reductions in the preceding three years, levels of gross investment increased by 7 per cent in 1988 and 6 per cent in 1989, the rate of economic growth reaching 3 per cent for the first time since 1976. Falling commodity prices in 1986–7 reflated the entire European economy, much as they had deflated it a decade before, while the falling US exchange rate inspired some loosening of monetary policy across Europe. All of these factors lent a buoyancy to the French economy that it had long awaited.

However, the economic picture is not entirely rosy. Although exports are increasing again, France has not participated as fully as was hoped in the development of high-technology products fuelling the industrial revolution of the 1970s and 1980s. Her share of world exports of high-technology products is only 6 per cent, as opposed to 22 per cent for Japan, 18 per cent for the USA, 12 per cent for West Germany and 8 per cent for the UK. To cope with this, the government conducted an audit of the export performance of key industrial sectors and proposes increasing expenditure on research and development to 3 per cent of gross domestic product. Long-standing French strengths in armaments, turn-key plants, agriculture, vehicles and luxury goods are balanced by a weakness in the production of capital goods, household appliances and mass-produced consumer goods. Hence French exports are still highly dependent on a few key sectors where state involvement has been high, and her capacity to compete in critical sectors of consumer spending is still somewhat in question (Belassa, 1988).

The advent of 1992 is the decisive challenge currently facing French policy-makers. The decision of the EC to try to create a unified market has been received enthusiastically in France as elsewhere, but it has important economic and political implications. At the economic level, it means that pressure on French industry to become fully competitive will intensify. France has been experiencing those pressures since the 1960s but it will become increasingly difficult to resist them. Anticipation of a more integrated market has already inspired a wave of investment, mergers and industrial restructuring across Europe.

In policy terms, freer trade and financial flows will make it increasingly difficult for French policy-makers to reflate the economy without cooperation from other European governments. If exchange controls are fully eliminated as anticipated in 1990, the French franc will become more vulnerable to speculative pressure and both balanced budgets and high interest rates may have to be used to maintain the position of the exchange rate in the EMS. Hence, if policy-makers want to stimulate industry, they will have to rely to an increasing extent on microeconomic tools. But even this will be difficult since the European Commission itself is assuming increasing responsibility for industrial regulation, and looks with disfavour on policies designed to give special advantages to one nation's industries.

The balance of political forces is also likely to be influenced by a more integrated European market. For instance, it is changing the interests and power of French business. In order to compete on a trans-European market, many French firms are acquiring partners or subsidiaries elsewhere in Europe, Japan and America. As large French firms become more multinational, their policy goals will change as well. They will be less interested in national protection or devaluation and more interested in free trade and financial flows. Moreover, their leverage *vis-à-vis* the French government will increase as they can threaten to move their production to plants in other nations if they do not like the direction of national policy. We are already seeing the emergence of trans-European coalitions among industrialists. Conversely, the more integrated market is likely to weaken the power of the trade unions, at least in the private sector, in the face of threats from employers to close down French plants in favour of foreign ones. Labour has traditionally been less capable of organising European-wide coalitions.

Many of the developments associated with 1992 also pose real headaches for French policy-makers. The most pressing concern taxation. For many years, French governments have depended on indirect taxes to raise the bulk of their revenues, but, to comply with recent EC directives, an increasing share of the tax burden has to be shifted from value-added tax to income taxes. The latter are much more visible politically and we can expect both a political backlash against rising taxes and growing pressure to restrain them.

At the same time, the existing efforts of the government to contain public expenditure so as to restrain tax rates and the deficit are already causing problems. The public spending cuts made over the last five years have meant that the wages of public sector workers are relatively depressed compared to those in the newly profitable private sector. The result has been growing militancy from highly unionised public sector workers seeking to redress the balance. The government faces an unhappy choice. If it grants substantially higher wages, it may have to raise taxes or incur budget deficits that will threaten the stability of the franc in the EMS. If it does not do so it may face a wave of public-sector strikes, of the sort already seen in 1988 and 1989, which would reduce its capacity to govern and alienate the very constituency on which the Socialists most depend for electoral support.

Similarly, the recent moves toward financial deregulation are not without problems. In large measure, they have been a great success. The value of the shares traded on the French Stock Exchange has quadrupled since 1980 and a host of new financial institutions offer innovative services on markets in financial instruments and futures that simply did not exist ten years ago. However, it takes time to learn how to regulate such markets and the burst of speculative activity that has accompanied deregulation is bringing with it a series of financial scandals. One chairman of the Stock Exchange has already been forced to resign in the wake of large losses from its reserve fund, and several close associates of President Mitterrand have been accused of insider trading. Moreover, as the hard core of shares that key French institutions hold in the newly-privatised industries gradually break up in the coming years, there are bound to be highly controversial take-over bids for some of these firms. If these come from foreigners, the government is likely to face pressure from nationalists seeking French control over French industry.

Finally, despite their recent popularity, moves to enlarge the European market and enhance the role of the market in the allocation of resources carry hidden dangers that may yet come to the fore. The market distributes resources quite severely and according to principles of market power rather than economic justice. Accordingly, there are those who will lose out in this system of allocation and some serious economic dislocation can be expected to follow the movement to a unified European market. The potential for a political backlash is great. Even if many large firms become quite Europeanised, many small businesses may feel disadvantaged by greater competition, widening rifts in the business community. Similarly, those regions that are hard hit by European competition may react against the unified market and disaffected groups may rally around the long-standing French theme of economic nationalism.

In such a situation, the French government is likely to come under pressure to move back towards more *dirigiste* economic policies. There are still many on the political scene, from the FN on the Right to the CERES group on the Left, who still favour some return to such policies. The massive apparatus for active industrial policy of the French state has by no means been completely dismantled. Whether we see a movement back toward dirigism in the coming years may well depend on the buoyancy of the French economy and the adeptness of the present government at finding microeconomic tools with which to influence the margins of the market. However, it will be increasingly difficult to move back to the dirigism of the past. Over the course of the past two decades, the nature of the economic playing field has changed. New regional and financial institutions have been created; French business is acquiring an increasingly European outlook. France has a growing range of commitments to its European partners. If the officials of the French state should decide to shift back from the market towards dirigism, they will have to do so with new techniques adapted to the Europe of the 1990s. In the terms of the ancient Chinese curse, these are very interesting times for France.

10

Financial Crisis and Policy Continuity in the Welfare State

GARY P. FREEMAN

Economic dislocation, unfavourable demographic change and a long trajectory of programme expansion have come together in the last fifteen years to push the vast system of social protection into serious financial crisis. Spending for social protection, which had grown at modest but steady rates until the late 1960s, took off in the next decade. Social spending as a proportion of gross domestic product jumped from 20.2 per cent in 1970 to 27.3 per cent in 1980. Social benefits constitute about a third of the average French family's income, and contributions to pay for social programmes weigh heavily on workers' wages and make up as much as 30 per cent of the cost of labour to business.

Expanded in a salubrious economic environment, this elaborate network of programmes was dangerously vulnerable to even small negative changes in economic or demographic aggregates. For every 100 000 workers removed from the social security tax rolls, receipts fall by about 3.5 billion francs. A 1 per cent drop in the rate of growth of gross domestic product reduces receipts by 3 billion francs and a 0.5 per cent decline in the rate of growth of real wages diminishes social security revenues by 700 million francs. Inflation, on the other hand, pushes benefit payments up as they are adjusted to protect their purchasing power.

Recent economic and demographic data are chilling. Gross domestic product grew at a rate higher than 3.5 per cent a year only once between 1975 and 1985. Unemployment, which was below 3 per cent in 1974, climbed to over 6 per cent in 1980 and 10 per cent in 1984. Inflation averaged only 3.9 per cent between 1960 and 1968, but it was 11.1 per cent in 1974, 13.6 per cent in 1980, and 7.6 per cent in 1984. In 1950 there were 4.62 workers paying taxes for every retired person receiving a pension. By 1975 declining fertility rates and lengthening life expectancy had pushed this ratio to 2.66, and it was projected to slip below 2.0 by 2020.

In these straitened circumstances the social policy agenda has been transformed. The traditional concern for eliminating insecurity and poverty has not disappeared, but it is being supplanted by the claims of discrete beneficiary groups protecting their rights and by the pressures of budgetary arithmetic. One may say that social policy is driven by three conflicting rationalities: fiscal rectitude, social justice and responsiveness to consumers. Each of these finds voice in specific state institutions and social and political interests, and pulls policy in different directions. For much of the time since 1945 this triangulated struggle produced a stalemate that avoided structural reforms but was compatible with incremental growth, especially as the fiscal constraints were not severe. The campaign pledges of the Socialists who gained office in 1981 included a number of substantial reforms directed almost exclusively towards achieving a certain conception of social justice. To the extent fiscal problems were admitted, they were to be resolved in ways that seemed to ignore the ability of social security consumers to resist. In the event, the substitution of a government of the Left for one of the Right produced few innovations and no serious attempt at fundamental reform. The lesson of the last decade is that any governing party will have to accommodate the commitment to social equity and the necessity of meeting consumer demands to the unavoidable requirements of fiscal restraint.

Origins and Structure of the Welfare State

The principal social programmes took their present shape after the Second World War. Social policy had developed fitfully during the Third Republic. Major social insurance legislation was passed in 1910 and 1930, but on the eve of the Second World War only a minority of the population was covered against old age, unemployment, sickness or disability, and those who were enjoyed extremely uneven levels of protection and paid grossly unequitable contributions (Hatzfeld, 1971).

After the liberation there was support for a comprehensive and universal system of social protection. This plan was foiled, however, both because the beneficiaries of those programmes already in place were able to guard their advantages and avoid integration in the new scheme and because certain groups – farmers, white-collar workers and the self-employed – managed to secure better benefits than those being offered to ordinary workers (Galant, 1955). The result of these setbacks to universalism is that the French social security system is a strongly particularistic and selective tangle of regulations and administrative units. Although almost the entire population is now covered with respect to basic risks, the benefits to which individuals are entitled and the contributions they must pay vary enormously between workers in industry and agriculture and at different skill levels.

Social institutions are decentralised, autonomous and particularistic. Each of the general, specific, basic and supplementary schemes that make up the social security system is separately administered. The principal unit of administration is the social security fund, which derives from mutual associations that emerged in the nineteenth century before state insurance was introduced (Ashford, 1986, pp. 144–56). They are run by an administrative council representing both the insured and employers. Their primary activity is to collect contributions and pay benefits, but they also engage in a wide range of other social service activities and are major employers in their own right (Beattie, 1972).

The Politics of Social Policy Reform

The process of social policy formulation is statist in style, corporatist in form and pluralist in practice. State officials in Paris tend to act as if social policy is their prerogative and can be formulated in private and announced according to administrative convenience. The formal structures of the social security apparatus, on the other hand, give the system a markedly corporatist flavour which places considerable discretion in the hands of quasi-public regional and local bodies under the control of committees of employers and the unions. It is evident, however, that the actual policy process is a loosely coordinated, highly pluralistic and intensely conflictual struggle among a host of interest groups organised around particular programmes and benefit schemes.

A statist style is consistent with the trend towards executive domination of social policy from the Fourth to the Fifth Republic. Each succeeding incumbent has expanded the presidential sphere so that it now includes social policy. Giscard d'Estaing was the first chief executive to take a personal and public interest in some social issues. François Mitterrand has been more directly involved, but his public role has been limited to those occasions when his ministers could not resolve their own disagreements.

More normally it is the government that takes the lead in fashioning social policy. Within the Cabinet, the social ministers are at the bottom of the pecking order. They routinely lose squabbles with their counterparts at the budget and finance and economy ministries. This is not simply because these departments attract more senior and skilful politicians, but because social policy is typically subordinated to economic and budgetary considerations. The role of Parliament has been sharply diminished. This is most embarrassingly evident when social security legislation is passed through the special powers available under article 38 of the constitution, which permits the Council of Ministers to make policy through ordinances for fixed periods if Parliament consents. Unpopular social reforms were adopted in this way in 1967 and again in 1981 in the first year of the new Socialist Government.

It would be a mistake to assume that social policy is always directed by the central executive, however. Austere, calculated and technocratic in style, social policy is bargained, chaotic and distinctly reactive in substance. While executive officials enjoy the constitutional and statutory prerogative to design and initiate policy, the numerous decentralised social agencies, the professional groups that work within the system (such as doctors, pharmacists and health workers) and the organised beneficiary groups who profit from it resist, reshape and kill government proposals.

It is the decentralised structure of social institutions that gives the system its corporatist form. Social security law grants the insured a direct role in the administration of programmes. Under the 1930 social security act the mutual associations that were incorporated into the state insurance plan were governed exclusively by representatives of the insured. In 1945 these associations were almost entirely replaced by state-created funds. These were headed by administrative councils which were elected by universal suffrage from lists compiled by the trade union federations and employers associations. Three-quarters of the seats were reserved for representatives of the insured (the trade union candidates) and one-quarter for representatives of the employers. Regular social elections were held in 1947, 1950, 1955 and 1962. In 1967, at the behest of the employers federation (CNPF), the government ended social elections and divided seats on the administrative councils equally between the unions and the employers.

Before winning the 1981 elections, the Socialist party was on record in favour of restoring social elections and returning control of the councils to the unions. This plan was more difficult to impose than had been expected. Employers protested so vehemently that they were able to retain a fourth of the seats on the councils and to restrict elections to the funds for sickness, old age and family allowances. Surprisingly, the unions contested the proposals as well. FO, a Left-Centre union federation with close ties to associates of Mitterrand, objected to the election of all union seats and won a concession permitting any officially recognised unions to name at least one member to the councils regardless of the outcome of the voting.

One cannot dismiss the corporatist aspects of French social policy as simply a matter of form. The bitter conflict over the structure and control of the social security funds indicates that they are important to the protagonists. The law gives the unions a legitimate claim to participation in the formulation of policy, and in recent years governments of both the Left and Right have shown an inclination to involve union leaders as well as other non-governmental actors in decision-making.

The statist style and corporatist form are not sufficient to prevent the emergence of a politics of pluralism. This flows almost inevitably from the nature of the groups interested in social policy and the way policy is made. The organised interests may be thought of as the producers and consumers of social protection. The former are most important in the health sector: physicians, nurses, pharmacists and other medical personnel obviously exhibit a keen interest in social policy arrangements and have often demonstrated political clout. When state-run medical insurance was introduced in 1930, doctors managed to preserve free choice of physicians for patients, freedom of prescription for doctors and a fee for service reimbursement system. Over the years the government has chipped away at these practices, but has been unable to end them. The CSMF and other representatives of producers have organised strikes and engaged in direct action to derail reforms that threatened their status. There is a collusive relationship between these producer groups and the consumers of medical and social benefits. The latter are organised around the specific and highly differentiated social security schemes. Any proposed reform of the general system is immediately dissected from the point of view of its relative impact not on the average patient or pensioner, but on the jealously guarded prerogatives of particular beneficiary groups. It is fair to say that while there is strong public support for social security as a general concept, opinion on particular proposals is segmented and divides society into a multiplicity of competing fiefdoms.

The process of social security decision-making also contributes to pluralism. Perhaps the most important feature is that both basic and supplementary schemes are financed on a current-funding or pay as you go basis. This means that each year's receipts from workers' contributions go out immediately in payments to the retired, ill or injured. No effort is made to build up a reserve in anticipation of future obligations. This produces a more or less continuous preoccupation with the quarterly and annual balances in the various funds. Contribution rates are nominally set annually; in fact, they may be adjusted on an *ad hoc* basis at any time during the year. One is tempted to say that social security politics is high drama, but it might be more accurately described as a long-running soap opera. Headlines warn of impending shortfalls in the medical fund; shortly thereafter the government announces that the health portion of the social security tax will be raised by 0.5 per cent, and consternation and bitter accusations follow.

The current funding basis of social security makes it all but impossible to depoliticise policy. Tax and benefit rates cannot be set prospectively over even five to ten years. The constant tinkering with the system contributes to political conflict, but it also makes change routine (Cohen and Goldfinger, 1975). The French attitude towards social security deficits is downright casual compared to the hysteria evoked by similar problems in the USA in the 1970s. Deficits are seen as requiring political rather than technical choices and they are fought over in those terms.

After more than 20 years of governments of the Right, it was only normal to believe that the election of a Socialist Government in May–June 1981 would transform the old politics of social security and break the stalemate supporting rising expenditures and benefits and preventing structural reform. These hopes were unfounded.

Social security In retrospect, it is astonishing how naive and ill-prepared were the PS's attempts to take over social security policy. It had promised to enhance benefit levels, wrest control over the social security funds from employers and broaden participation in policy formulation; all standard fare for the Left. The PS leadership understood, of course, that it would need to deal with the financing crisis but it insisted that previous governments had exaggerated the problem for political purposes. It also assumed · that reforms of the tax mechanisms, especially expanding the base of contributions beyond wages and re-ordering the relationships between the basic plan to which most industrial workers belonged (the general regime) and those of more favoured occupational groups would generate sufficient new revenues. This strategy failed to take into account the power of organised groups to resist egalitarian reforms, missing almost entirely the fact that some of the most entrenched social policy interests were part of the PS's own constituency, and that new taxes would fall heavily on working-class families. Fatally, as it turned out, the PS expected rapid economic growth and full employment to go a long way towards resolving social security's problems. In fact, the recovery did not materialise and the purported negative impact of social charges on international competitiveness proved to be a major obstacle to expansionist reforms (Freeman, 1986).

The governments of Mauroy and Fabius managed to accomplish several of these progressive objectives. They raised minimum pensions by about one-quarter, reduced the retirement age from 65 to 60, restored elections to the administrative councils of the social security funds and increased consultation among interested parties, especially trade unions. However, several of these moves exacerbated the financial difficulties of the system. Reducing the retirement age was politically expedient (it had been promised during the campaign and it was aimed at reducing unemployment), but it was irresponsible from the view of the financial stability of the retirement system and it flew in the face of trends in other industrial countries. Consultation could be defended on many grounds but, at least at the outset, it slowed policy development. The benefits of broadened discussion were, ironically, to await the arrival of the government of the Right in 1986.

When their economic policy failed, the Socialists found themselves desperately trying to manage the cash flow demands of a social insurance system in a stagnating economy. No fundamental reforms of the financial structure were undertaken. After some indecisive discussion of real changes early on, the worsening financial crisis, combined with a strong attack by the ministers of the economy and the budget, led President Mitterrand to replace his idealistic Minister of Solidarity, Questiaux, with his personal adviser, Bérégovoy. The latter announced to the press that 'he knew how to count'. It was a richly symbolic moment in the life of the government. It marked the end of the Socialists' role as insurgent critics and their assumption of full responsibility for managing the welfare state themselves.

Ironically, many of the most significant initiatives by the Socialists came in the absence of campaign pledges or contradicted long records of opposition to precisely such measures. This was especially true in the field of health policy. In the decade from 1971 to 1981 health expenditures had risen on average by 16.6 per cent a year, constituting 8.4 per cent of gross domestic product by 1987. The typical French family was devoting 9.5 per cent of its income to health care in 1971 and 12.5 per cent by the decade's end. Part of this expansion was the result of deliberate policy choice – by 1981 medical insurance had been extended to over 99 per cent of the population – but a large part of the increase was due to inflation and skyrocketing per capitum expenditures. Given the extensiveness of the health care system and the comprehensiveness of medical insurance, there were few equity goals to be advanced by the Socialists. The first Health Minister under Mitterrand, the Communist Jack Ralite, did eliminate the private sector in hospitals, but his efforts were ultimately futile as the Chirac Government reinstituted private beds in 1987. For the most part, attention was focused on controlling costs.

Perhaps the most significant change was the introduction of the comprehensive budget for hospitals in 1983. When fully implemented, various departments within hospitals will have to live within predetermined constraints, rather than pass on the costs of providing services on to the health funds or the state. The Socialists also introduced a modest charge for each day's stay in the hospital which must be paid by the patient and cannot be reimbursed by social security. This was ostensibly meant to shorten stays and avoid unnecessary hospitalisations, but it had even more potent symbolic implications. Both these items had long been on the Right's agenda but had been sharply opposed by the Left.

The Socialists attacked the problem of medical education through a proposal to control the choice of specialists, upgrade medical training by reorganising the work of junior hospital doctors and make the practice of general medicine more attractive. First floated in December 1982, the plan sparked huge protests by medical students. After Ralite left the Health Ministry, and after protracted negotiations with the doctors, the new measures were finally launched in 1984.

Hospital management has also been the subject of intense scrutiny. The general thrust of policy has been to reorganise public hospitals in order to increase consultation between directors and staff, require an annual plan for each functional unit and enhance accountability of staff both to the hospital director and the Ministry of Health in Paris. Two circulars on hospital management issued in 1984–5 foresaw the institution of techniques drawing on ideas associated with management by objectives and diagnostic related groups, both borrowed from the USA. One observer noted that 'the socialist party had proposed nothing of the sort, but one is astonished to see that the American model has been imported into "leftist" France, at the same time that Reagan was generalizing its use in the financing of Medicare' (Delanoe, 1987, p. 79).

Taken together, Socialist policies appear to have brought the health care system close to financial stability by 1986. If we look just at the general regime, which accounts for about 80 per cent of all health spending, one estimate sets its rate of spending growth in current prices at 9.4 per cent annually over 1984–5, about half the rate experienced in 1981. One author refers to a 'veritable rupture in the statistical series' (Delanoe, 1987, p. 73). The sickness insurance fund sported a 6.4 billion franc surplus in 1985 and had a positive balance sheet in 1986–87 as well.

It is not as if the problem of rising medical costs has been permanently solved, however. Indeed, the record of the Chirac Government (1986–8) reads exactly as if the script had been written in the 1970s. M Séguin, the Minister of Social Affairs, was kept busy issuing stopgap measures to close periodic deficits, mostly in the retirement scheme but also in the health system. In other words, had not the government taken swift measures, the recent success in flattening the growth curb of health spending might have been reversed.

The most interesting development on the social protection scene during the period of *cohabitation* under Chirac was the use of new consensus-building consultative mechanisms. The Socialists had started this in 1981, engaging in unprecedented discussions with the unions and other interested parties. But we have already seen that they also resorted to special powers under article 38 to push through controversial policies. The Chirac Government chose not to follow this precedent. Instead, the UDF – RPR coalition reached out beyond its own members for advice. The first instance was the Estates General for Social Protection which was launched in the summer of 1987. A series of regional meetings to sample opinion and develop ideas was followed by a two-day national meeting in Paris in November. Next the government appointed a non-partisan Committee of Wise Men, including a number of distinguished elder statesmen, to make recommendations for the restructuring of the entire system of social protection. The Wise Men reported in October 1987, and their principal recommendation was for a single 'contribution' to be assessed on all incomes, the rate to be voted by Parliament each year. This sensible idea was not politically feasible, but a number of minor recommendations by the Estates General were embodied in law in January 1988.

The official explanation for these unusual procedures was that they were part and parcel of a neo-liberal effort to reduce the meddlesome supervision of the state over social policy and to introduce accountability and control. Behind the scenes, a battle waged between elements within the governing coalition led by Balladur, the Minister of Finance (who favoured radical measures to privatise social security), and a group led by Séguin, the Minister for Social Affairs, which was searching for consensual reforms within the existing system. *Ad hoc* consultative bodies provided the time and cover to develop such proposals. Once these bodies had been convened it was no longer appropriate to employ article 38 to bypass normal parliamentary procedures. In any case, the uncertainties of *cohabitation* may have caused Chirac to hesitate to ask for special powers out of fear that the Socialist president would refuse to sign ordinances drafted in such a fashion.

Family Policy

Family policy posed some troubling issues for the Socialists. France has one of the most generous systems of family allowances in Western Europe. Designed to encourage fertility by subsidising the expenses of large families, it is the special province of a powerful family lobby that is mostly Catholic and conservative. The PS, on the other hand, is strongly secular and committed to numerous feminist policies, including the promotion of women in the workforce and state subsidies for abortions. Moreover, socialists view the family allowance system as an inefficient means of income maintenance and redistribution because its benefits go to rich and poor alike.

The Chirac Government has no such qualms and promptly moved family policy to centre stage. The UDF–RPR election manifesto had promised 'to develop an ambitious family policy; to favour the decision to have a third child.' The premise was that families were confronted with a choice between a third child or a second salary (60 per cent of mothers with two children work; 30 per cent with three do). Two measures addressed this problem: the parent's education grant and the personal retirement pension for mothers of large families. The PS had adopted an education grant in 1984 but it was small (1,500 francs per month) and essentially a maternity grant as it lasted only two years. The new government proposed to raise this to half the minimum wage, give it to all families with three children and remove the requirement of a previous work record.

A significant aspect of the grant, however, was that at least one of the parents had to be a French citizen. This is just one of the ways the Chirac Government sought to link family policy to its immigration policy. In fact they became two sides of the same coin. In part an attempt to outflank the extremist FN, these measures echo traditional themes in French conservatism. Immigration is seen as a threat to national identity and French culture; a reinvigorated family policy designed to increase native French fertility was the response to this crisis. Both immigration and family policy became electoral issues in 1986 and again in 1988. The Right called immigration the 'other cohabitation' and Chirac warned of a coming 'demographic winter' if the birth rate did not rise.

Poverty

There are numerous indicators that poverty is rising in France. The chief culprit is unemployment, in many cases extended unemployment. As of March 1986, 518 000 jobless persons had reached the two-year limit on extended unemployment benefits. A report issued in early 1987 under the auspices of a poverty pressure group, ATP Quart Monde, estimated that 2 500 000 people live in families receiving less than half the minimum wage. One rough indicator of increasing distress is that from 600 000 to 1 000 000 car owners had allowed their insurance to lapse by 1987 (Barthe, 1987, pp. 112–13). As early as 1980 the Oheix Report had established a baseline for discussion of poverty initiatives. A senior civil servant, Oheix had argued that poverty policy must be tied to expanded opportunities for work and that a guaranteed minimum income was impractical and unwise. What was needed, he noted, was an effort to fill in the gaps in the system of social protection and to create better conditions for the insertion of the poor into jobs, housing and educational institutions (Oheix Report, 1981). Much of what Oheix suggested has subsequently been attempted.

In 1982 the Socialist Government launched its first programme against poverty and insecurity. It was a distinctly mixed bag of existing programmes, temporary measures and exhortations. In 1984 new 'emergency' measures were unveiled. Prefects were ordered to assemble all individuals in positions of responsibility in either public or private institutions to develop cooperative strategies to fight poverty in their jurisdictions. By 1986–7, 75 out of 83 *préfectures* had established some general coordination of poverty efforts. One review of these efforts concludes that they had at the very least raised the consciousness of both public and private sectors with respect to poverty and that they had greatly increased the amount of collaboration at the local level between the government and private associations (Mariller and Janvier, 1988, p. 29).

The impulse to deal with poverty through cooperative arrangements between the central and local governments was further developed by the right. The junior minister of social affairs proposed a 300 million franc poverty programme to the Council of Ministers in October 1986. The major proposal was for a minimum income, the local resource supplement, consisting of six monthly payments of 2,000 francs to persons over 25 living in families without income from work. In return, the recipient must agree to work half-time at some public service job supervised by the local authority. By the end of 1987 the government had persuaded 71 departments to set up such programmes but little money has been spent.

The Rocard Government took immediate action to ensure that effective income support should be available in every part of France. In the autumn of 1988 it passed a law to implement Mitterrand's electoral promise of providing a 'minimum income' for everyone without resources who was seeking a job. This 'minimum income' was to be funded by a wealth tax (which was imaginatively titled 'the solidarity tax'). The actual implementation of this was once again a shared centre–local scheme since the prefects and *département* council chairmen were made jointly responsible for its administration in each *département*.

In December 1988 Parliament also passed the so-called Coluche amendment (after the late comedian/activist) which authorised tax exemptions, under certain conditions, for charitable donations; the measure was intended to stimulate private efforts to aid the poor. In the summer of 1989 another measure provided new state resources to support job creation schemes, 'public service employment' (in public service projects) and thus reduced the burden on the welfare system.

Conclusion

When the PS finally arrived in office in 1981 it was already too late to create the kind of welfare state it wanted. The times were not propitious for bold social experiments. Economic stagnation and budgetary constraints overwhelmed the social agenda. Extensive protection schemes were already in place and, imperfect and untidy as they might appear to Socialist eyes, they were deeply entrenched and broadly popular. Any significant steps to make the system more equitable, redistributive and uniform would require the imposition of hardships on sizeable numbers of voters who were part of the Socialist coalition. The tax rates necessary to support the most extensive improvements in benefits would fall heavily on working-class incomes. In other words, Socialist rhetoric was badly out of step with the realities of French social welfare arrangements.

As a consequence the social policy legacy of the PS is not very impressive. If one looks beyond language to actual policies, there are surprisingly few differences in what the governments of the Left and Right did in the 1980s. The Socialists have learned to be accountants when social security is discussed and they have adopted previously dispised American managerial techinques to reorganise the health sector. The Right, heirs to the statist style of General de Gaulle, have become proponents of concertation and have discovered the urgency of poverty. The Right has made the most explicit commitment to a neo-liberal, market-orientated approach to public policy but the PS, especially under Fabius and Rocard, has followed suit. Family policy is the one areas where serious differences emerge, a reflection of the divisiveness of socio-cultural issues and a reminder of the relative consensus that pre-vails over other social policies.

The real question in the future of the French welfare state is not so much which policies to adopt but how to construct a policy-making process that will produce timely and effective choices with-out undue conflict. This requires abandoning the statist policy-making style that has provoked so much discontent over the years, and managing the rampant pluralism that has both stalemated reforms and fed expansion. There are clear signs within govern-ments of both the Left and Right during the 1980s that steps are being taken in this direction: more extensive consultation with the unions and interested parties in the early stages of policy formu-lation than in the past; the use of extra-governmental, non-partisan advisory commissions; and the emphasis on public and private cooperation at the local and regional level in the implementation of social policy.

These structural and procedural changes in the social policy process do not add up to a corporatist system. Given the *ad hoc* and tentative nature of the participation of non-governmental actors, it is probably better to call the new arrangements 'struc-tured pluralism'. They organise and discipline the demands of interest groups while giving them a more regular voice in decisions. They are an attempt to suspend normal partisan conflict over social policy in the search for consensus, but one that will permit painful adjustments rather than protect the status quo.

11

Foreign and Defence Policy: From Independence to Interdependence

JOLYON HOWORTH

The Foreign Policy-Making Process

It has long been a truism, among commentators on French politics, that foreign and defence policy constitute a *domaine réservé* (reserved sector) which effectively offers the president unrivalled powers over policy, patronage and implementation. The truism derives more from practice than from constitutional canon. According to the text of the constitution, although the president is 'the guarantor of national independence, of the integrity of the territory and of respect for Community agreements and treaties' (article 5), and although he or she negotiates international treaties (article 52), Parliament retains the right to authorise any declaration of war (article 35) and to ratify treaties (article 53). Moreover, although the president is supreme head of the armed forces and chairs all the major defence committees (article 15), it is the prime minister who is 'responsible for national defence' (article 21). As in so many other areas of French public policy, the ambiguities of the constitution lie dormant so long as the Elysée, the Hotel Matignon and the Palais Bourbon are in the same political hands.

De facto presidential supremacy is reinforced by a number of indirect factors: the personalisation of both foreign relations (summits and bilateral meetings of heads of state) and defence matters (the president alone has control of the nuclear trigger); the sheer clout of an elective office deriving from universal suffrage for seven years; and the experience in both knowledge and continuity which those attributes confer. Under de Gaulle and Pompidou, as well as under Mitterrand from May 1981 to March 1986, the *domaine réservé* was virtually watertight. Under Giscard d'Estaing, dependent as he was on Gaullist parliamentary support, a number of major compromises had to be struck with the RPR.

Under *cohabitation*, from March 1986 to April 1988, Mitterrand's monopoly of the foreign and defence dossiers was only indirectly (and ineffectively) challenged by his prime minister. Chirac's punches were pulled by his own desire not to weaken the institution of the presidency, by his relative lack of clear direction in these particular areas and by his awareness that the forthcoming presidential contest, on which his eyes were firmly set, would be won or lost on his domestic record. As for the defence and foreign ministers, relations with the Elysée were to some extent predetermined by the fact that Mitterrand was able to exercise maximum influence in these appointments, notably by vetoing a number of Chirac's initial choices.

It is often said that the Quai d'Orsay is a ministry without any real influence, the office-holder acting as a kind of senior civil servant to the president. This is an oversimplification. In the case of Maurice Couve de Murville (1958–68), playing 'second fiddle' to a man like de Gaulle throughout ten momentous years of foreign policy revolution conferred considerable real power and influence. Michel Jobert (1973–4) allegedly took advantage of President Pompidou's rapidly declining health to play a spectacular (albeit brief) role as Henry Kissinger's principal gadfly, but recent scholarship argues that, in effect, Jobert acted as the dying Pompidou's irrascible *alter ego* (Cohen, 1986, p. 105). In the case of Mitterrand's first foreign minister, Claude Cheysson, too much autonomy from the Elysée (the relationship between the two men has been portrayed as that between the fireman and the pyromaniac) led inevitably to the minister's replacement. Under *cohabitation*, the Quai's influence was even further reduced as Chirac siphoned off to Matignon responsibility for *Francophonie* (the French-speaking world) and human rights, and put the South Pacific (Gaston Flosse) and Africa (Michel Aurillac) in the hands of his own personal lieutenants. There was, moreover, no minister for European affairs since this area, along with defence and East – West relations, was unofficially recognised as the president's particular interest.

Although there can be no doubt that the president is pre-eminent in foreign and defence policy, his views are shaped by numerous factors: first, by 'internal' advisers and institutional forces. These range from maverick intellectuals such as Raymond Aron or Régis Debray to vociferous lobbyists for the arms industry (no president can forget that French arms exports per capitum are the highest of any country in the world: three times as high as those for the USA and the USSR (see Kolodziej, 1987, p. 169). They include powerful civil servants whose influence derives as much from the considerable resources available to the Quai d'Orsay as from the inertial conservatism of the Civil Service career structure. They also involve close political allies and influential journalists (although France can boast few leading editors with an impressive command of foreign and defence matters, those she does possess – Jean Daniel, Claude Julien, André Fontaine and Serge July – are among the best in the world). Moreover, the president's views are shaped by intangible factors connected with France's self-perception as a world power, not only militarily and commercially, but also culturally, linguistically and 'intellectually'.

Second, 'external relations' (as 'foreign affairs' came to be known after 1981) also depend on many constraining factors stemming from outside the country. France, for all her international significance, represents less than 1 per cent of the earth's surface and of its population. She has few valuable natural resources and is heavily dependent on trade for energy and raw materials, including strategic ones. The residue of her empire has bestowed upon her 'privileged' contacts with areas which are either diplomatic minefields (South-East Asia), economic deserts (sub-Saharan Africa) or hotly contested strategic outposts (the Pacific), from all of which she derives some diplomatic clout but little material benefit. For all that, the concept and the reality of *Francophonie* play a considerable role in French foreign policy-making. At the same time, despite the sound and fury of Gaullist 'independence', France remains contractually tied to her allies both in Europe (the Brussels Treaty of 1948) and the Western world (the North Atlantic Treaty of 1949). Her margin of manoeuvre in the face of the superpowers is limited, and the originality of her position in Europe severely circumscribed. Despite these constraints, French foreign and defence policy remains endlessly creative, evoking simultaneous reactions of irritation and admiration throughout the world.

In a nutshell, while a vast range of influences, direct or – most often – indirect, are brought to bear on foreign policy-making, the presidency reigns increasingly supreme in this field, unaffected by the significant institutional or procedural checks and balances of either the British or the American systems. For some authoritative analysts, such vast power is counter-productive (the diplomatic structures of the Elysée have not evolved in parallel with the increasing complexities of international politics) and merely underscores the urgent need in France for institutional support systems along the lines of the American National Security Council or for far greater devolution to the Quai d'Orsay (Cohen, 1986, p. 232).

France in Europe between the Superpowers

France's geographical position and historical experience have produced a remarkable oscillation over the past century between 'independence' and 'alliance'. Cavalier and insouciant independence under Napoleon III led, in 1871, to defeat and humiliation at the hands of Prussia. The 'German question' which then arose remains, in slightly different form, to this day. The pursuit of alliances prior to 1914 also led to war and to a bloody stalemate. In 1919, obstinate and independent determination to 'punish' Germany through reparations was followed by a nervous quest for 'collective security' through the League of Nations which, in its turn, was followed by a renewed bout of independence, this time featuring a concrete wall (the Maginot Line) along the German frontier. Further war and humiliation left France, in 1945, desperate to turn once again to alliances, of which she signed four in rapid succession: with the Soviet Union (Moscow, 1944), with the UK (Dunkirk, 1947), with the UK and Benelux (Brussels, 1948) and with the 'victorious' Atlantic nations (Washington, 1949). The first three were primarily conceived as defensive alliances against Germany; the fourth was directed against the Soviet Union.

The 'reversal of alliances' which was consecrated in 1955, when one part of the former adversary, West Germany, became a major ally, has presented French diplomacy with an ongoing conundrum ever since. The previous German problem (a huge and dynamic militaristic power in central Europe) had been 'solved' only by a new and in some ways worse one (a divided Germany underwritten by the occupying armies and the *de facto* economic, cultural and political hegemony of two non-European superpowers). The only conceivable solution to this alternative German problem has appeared to imply the reunification of Germany and the reformulation of the original problem (except that now, the West German challenge is economic and industrial rather than military). But if the German problem continues indirectly to exercise French minds, the primary issue for French diplomacy since 1945 has been one of steering an appropriate national course between the Scylla of sycophancy *vis-à-vis* Washington and the Charybdis of complacency *vis-à-vis* Moscow.

When de Gaulle assumed power in 1958, he immediately reacted against a number of interconnected aspects of the world order: Soviet – American joint global policing; unrestrained and (for de Gaulle) often irresponsible American leadership of the Western Alliance; security dependence on an increasingly questionable American nuclear 'guarantee'; and an American 'open door' economic and trade policy (which was gradually assuming the form of pressure for a supra-national European community to become a dumping ground for surplus American products). De Gaulle's dissidence involved a challenge to all these features, positing as other possible options a multipolar world, with Europe as one centre; a rejection of the blocs in the name of a Europe from the Atlantic to the Urals, a geographical area sufficiently vast and diverse to allow for the containment of German ambitions in central Europe; the extension of the hand of friendship to the East European countries, including the USSR; a refusal to be caught up in every minor quarrel the Americans might choose to pick with the Soviets; an independent French nuclear strike force which would 'sanctuarise' French territory from any potential Soviet threat; and a refusal of supra-national institutions in the name of a 'Europe of nation states'. In a word, a policy of national independence, while respecting the spirit of existing alliances. This policy was most spectacularly illustrated in 1966 by the General's decision to withdraw France from the integrated military command structure of NATO and to expel from France both NATO headquarters and all foreign troops.

De Gaulle's foreign and security policy was given greater credibility by the institutional framework of a strong presidential regime capable of fostering rapid economic growth at home. This has been the lasting legacy of Gaullism, which post-Gaullist presidents have sought to perpetuate to both personal and national advantage. Despite significant prior objections to many aspects of 'Gaullism' both the liberals (under Valéry Giscard d'Estaing) and the Socialists (under François Mitterrand) slipped happily into the General's mantle on entering the Elysée. Thus developed the much-discussed 'consensus' on foreign and defence policy. The consensus, however, is only skin-deep.

The historical circumstances which had allowed Gaullism to exist at all could not last. The supreme irony is that, by the time François Mitterrand succeeded to the presidency (thereby consecrating the 'consensus'), these historical conditions had all virtually disappeared. First, at the level of global strategy, the world had shifted from one in which the USA (in Indo-China and elsewhere) was perceived as the main threat to peace and stability, to one in which the theory and practice of Soviet 'totalitarianism' (Solzhenitsyn, Czechoslovakia, Afghanistan) had subverted all prospect of French impartiality between the superpowers. Moreover the American nuclear guarantee (which, at one level, had acted as a safety net for the Gaullist independent tightrope act) was looking tattier and tattier. Quarrels over 'burden-sharing' and over 'coupling' were exacerbated (among many other factors) by Soviet deployment of SS-20 missiles, the controversy over NATO's Euro-missile response, Reagan's careless talk of 'limited nuclear warfare' in Europe, the growing strength in the USA of both 'isolationism' and the 'Pacific lobby', and the soaring American budget deficit. From outside Europe, all the signs pointed in the same direction: towards a more concerted Europeanisation of Europe's foreign and defence policy.

A second set of historical developments, inside Europe, reflected this global picture. Willy Brandt's *Ostpolitik* produced fresh fears in France of West German 'neutralist drift'. The 'Atlantic commitment' of the FRG had been another necessary prerequisite for the Gaullist dalliance with independence. French concern for the preservation of the 200-mile buffer zone between the Rhine and the Iron Curtain necessitated a new diplomatic approach. Such an approach was also called for as a result of ongoing European integration and attempts on the part of EC countries to arrive at a common foreign policy.

The third set of developments concerned France's own nuclear defences. Here there were three interconnected problems: techno-logical, financial and political. France's original 'triad' of nuclear weapons – air-based (Mirage IV bombers), land-based (S-2 inter-mediate range ballistic missiles) and sea-based – all of them 'second-strike', 'counter-value' systems – were looking increasingly vulnerable to the high precision, 'first-strike' Soviet 'counter-force' weapons, the SS-20s and the SS-18s. France's nuclear weapons were in need of technical modernisation, but modernisation posed a formidable financial problem. Keeping up with the nuclear Joneses, especially after the oil-price crisis of 1974, is an extraordi-narily expensive business, the cost of sophisticated, 'state-of-the-art' weapons of mass destruction rising exponentially far in excess of inflation. A further political dimension has been the worldwide movement of opposition to nuclear weapons, which appeared even to have spread to the White House with the conversion of Ronald Reagan to the anti-nuclear preferences of Mikhail Gorbachev. Under 'Gaullism' France had put most of her resource effort into the nuclear basket, to the considerable neglect of the conventional armed forces. By the late 1980s, she was faced with a painful choice between two equally pressing modernisation programmes: conventional and nuclear. She could probably afford one or the other, but not both. Successive governments have fudged this dilemma by writing into their defence white papers (*lois de programmation militaire*) provision for modernisation in every field, but by neglecting to match those plans with identifiable sources of cash.

The problems in facing up to the basic defence dilemma are exacerbated by the fact that, for 25 years, Gaullism posited a defence strategy diametrically opposed to that of NATO. While France, according to the theory of proportional deterrence (*la dissuasion du faible au fort*), relied on crude strategic nuclear threats and stressed her refusal to contemplate conventional, still less tactical, nuclear war, NATO (through the doctrine of flexible response) has prepared to engage in combat and to contain its impact through 'controlled escalation'. French nuclear weapons are exclusively for the defence of the 'Hexagon' and are underpinned by a declaratory strategy which warns of immediate escalation from tactical to strategic fire. NATO nuclear weapons are at the service of all the nations of the Alliance and so ordered as to make strategic attack an absolute last resort after all other means of 'defence' have failed. While the major Allies made overt their automatic commitment to West Germany by accepting the defence of a specific sector of the central front, France strenuously refused to do so, insisting that she alone would decide when and where her 'vital interests' were threatened and that her conventional armed forces were essentially reserved for the 'Battle of France'.

Since the mid-1970s there have been various attempts to resolve some of these problems. Giscard d'Estaing, an instinctive 'Atlanticist', drove three wedges into the Gaullist edifice as early as 1976. First, he referred to an 'enlarged strategic space' encompassing not just the confines of the Hexagon, but the entire territory of Western Europe. Second, he stated that French tactical nuclear weapons should be considered as battlefield weapons (rather than as precursors of an all-out strategic attack, as in the Gaullist canon). Third, he began to redress the balance of resource allocation away from nuclear programmes (even going so far as to cancel a sixth nuclear submarine which had been ordered under Pompidou) and in favour of halting the decline in French conventional capabilities. All of this was seen as an overt move back towards NATO and brought down upon the young president's head not only the opportunistic wrath of the Socialist and Commu-

nist opposition, but also the genuine fury of the traditional Gaullists. Sheepishly, Giscard was forced to remove his wedges and put
them back in their box.

In transcending Gaullism, François Mitterrand ignored wedges
and adopted the subtler method of discourse deconstruction (and
reconstruction). His achievement has been to appear more Gaullist
than the General through the shrewd use of declarations and
symbols, while quietly discarding a certain amount of actual Gaullist policy. Mitterrand's 'Gaullism' has derived from his ostentatious
reassertion of the primacy of strategic nuclear deterrence, underpinned by the decision to order a seventh nuclear submarine, by
the reiteration of his personal faith in the credibility of deterrence,
best illustrated by his September 1983 statement that the key
element in deterrence was himself, the president. Moreover, unlike
his predecessor, Giscard – who had expressed doubt about his
own ability to trigger France's nuclear firepower – Mitterrand
made it quite clear that he was man enough for the job. The
General's mantle was also donned in a number of dramatic, unilateral gestures such as Mitterrand's controversial speech in the Bun-
destag (West German Parliament) during West Germany's electoral campaign of early 1983, in which he effectively called on
West German voters to return the pro-nuclear Christian Democrats
in preference to the anti-nuclear Social Democrats (Mitterrand,
1986, pp. 183–208). Finally, against increasingly widespread calls
from various areas of the political class for France's short-range
nuclear weapons to be re-assigned to battlefield roles, the president, who is known to have serious doubts about France's very
need for such weapons, has held firmly to the doctrine of the
'ultimate warning shot', according to which the firing of a tactical
nuclear weapon is to be taken by an adversary as the immediate
precursor to a full-blooded strategic nuclear strike.

At the same time, however, Mitterrand has shifted public policy
a considerable distance in the direction of Alliance solidarity. His
staunch advocacy of the deployment of Pershing-II and Cruise
missiles was an important expression of NATO alignment. Mitterrand also broke new ground by hosting and/or attending a variety
of NATO meetings. But his major innovation has been European:
in the area of Franco–German defence cooperation. Taking great
care to situate his initiative under the aegis of the Franco–German
treaty of January 1963, by which de Gaulle had sought to woo
Bonn away from Washington, Mitterrand used the occasions of
the twentieth and twenty-fifth anniversaries of that treaty to reacti-
vate its moribund (or still-born) defence clauses. It is easy to decry
the genuine impact of the many fairly symbolic developments

which have taken place: the establishment of a Franco–German Defence Commission (1982) and Council (1988); the constitution of a French rapid deployment force (*force d'action rapide*) (1983) and the involvement of parts of this unit in joint Franco–German military exercises on the central front in 1987; the creation of a joint Franco–German brigade (1988); and the agreement to consult with Bonn before ordering the firing of short-range nuclear missiles (1986). The list is long and impressive but, for the moment, strong on symbols and weak on substance.

Undoubtedly what the FRG requires of France, first and fore-most, is an unambiguous statement of automatic and instantaneous military support in the event of hostilities on the central front, ideally underpinned by the stationing of French forces on the front line along a specific sector. The UDF explicitly (and Jacques Chirac implicitly) has indicated a willingness to give such a guaran-tee. To date, Mitterrand and his Socialist defence ministers have not been prepared to take that step, even though they have made many statements about the identity of security interests which France shares with West Germany. On the other hand, Mitterrand has also steadfastly resisted pressures from various quarters for France to extend the 'protection' of her nuclear umbrella to the FRG or, indeed, to the whole of Europe.

France's dilemma with regard to West Germany is merely a reflection of the current state of flux in which the overall question of European defences finds itself. NATO is being recast, one way or another, through the gradual construction of an inevitable 'European pillar'. The INF (Intermediate Nuclear Forces) treaty has highlighted uncertainty over the role of nuclear weapons in the future defence of Europe. President Gorbachev's December 1988 speech to the UN, offering significant unilateral Soviet reductions in conventional weapons and troops, posed once again the fundamental question of who and what France and Western Europe are defending themselves against. Mitterrand, having orig-inally argued for an increase in nuclear weapons in order to secure 'balance' is now militating actively in favour of constant, balanced reductions. He appears to be evolving towards a position which sees a minimal sea-based strategic nuclear capacity as the ultimate guarantee of national security, while a modernised conventional multinational or international force would police the Iron Curtain pending its historic demolition as the long-term consequence of a complex policital, economic and cultural process. For this reason, Mitterrand is loath simply to 'swap' an Atlantic bloc for a West European one. He is fully conscious that Europe's security problem is a historico-geographic one which can only be solved by a long-term political process.

This historic vision is very much at odds with that posited by leading Right-wingers such as Giscard, Barre, Giraud and Chirac. For them, some sort of French replacement for the hesitating American force in Europe is both necessary and desirable. This might involve the forward deployment of French tactical nuclear weapons, the development of a new generation of French (or Franco–British) intermediate-range nuclear weapons to 'close the gaps' left by INF, and the extension of French strategic 'cover' to the rest of Europe. The irony of history has willed that the Gaullist vision of a Europe from the Atlantic to the Urals should be sustained by the General's former principal adversary, while the Atlanticist concept of a West European nuclear bloc is now shared both by the UDF and the RPR.

As President Gorbachev continues to whittle away the objects of Western defences, however, and as President Bush contemplates removal of some of their subjects, what the contours of French defence policy will be in 2000 remains ambiguous. The power of the military – industrial complex in France to influence or even subvert government policy was demonstrated in 1987 when, in defiance of both military and political recommendations in favour of French participation in the European fighter aircraft scheme, lobbyists for the industrialists succeeded in ensuring that France would construct her own new fighter, the *Rafale*. If President Mitterrand hopes to push through his aims of developing a minimal French nuclear deterrent and Euro-integrated conventional capacity, his main adversaries will not be in the Kremlin, the White House or Downing Street; they will be in the planning offices of the military – industrial complex and in the defence commissions of the Right-wing opposition parties.

The problems of European armaments cooperation offer a convenient transition to the issue of European integration. While history apparently prepares for a Europe stretching from the Atlantic to the Urals, statesmen have been preparing for another Europe from the Atlantic to the Elbe and from the North Sea to the Aegean. Here, recent developments have broken significantly with Gaullism. Giscard d'Estaing's close personal relationship with Chancellor Schmidt resulted in a number of important steps forward: direct elections to the European Parliament, the creation of the EMS and, above all, a seemingly irreversible reconciliation with the FRG, which has turned the Paris–Bonn axis into the centrepiece of the EC. Mitterrand has played a key (not to say, in many cases, initiatory) role in consolidating this decidedly non-

Gaullist type of Europe. The president gambled on satisfying Margaret Thatcher's demands for financial compensation as the price for having her in rather than out. He was instrumental in facilitating the entry of Spain and Portugal, despite the major threat the new members pose to French agriculture. He has also been a prime mover in decisions about majority voting (thereby reversing one of the General's most negative legacies), about strengthening the EMS (when powerful voices within his own party were clamouring for France to withdraw), about technical and educational cooperation (ERASMUS, EUREKA, COMETT), and about community environmental policies, social policy and a joint space effort. Moreover, he has called repeatedly for greater powers for both the Council and the European Parliament, and has stressed his determination to strengthen the institutions of Europe. Above all, he played a crucial role during the French presidency of the Council in 1984, in pushing forward the Spinelli initiative which eventually led to the decision of 1985 in favour of the Single European Market. Since then, he has emerged as a leading supporter of a common currency and a central bank, despite widespread fears in Establishment financial circles in France that these measures will institutionalise West German domination of the EC's finances.

Mitterrand has coined the expression, 'France is my country [*patrie*] but Europe is my future'. In this he is motivated not only by a nostalgia for a traditional frontierless community of culture, but also by a clear sense that the European nations can only hope to hold their own against the USA and Japan by pooling their resources and expertise. When the history of European integration comes to be written, few individuals will be found to have played a greater role in the process than François Mitterrand. It is perhaps symptomatic of the demise in France of the 'Gaullist' approach to Europe that, during the television debate between the presidential candidates, Mitterrand and Chirac, on 28 April 1988, Chirac (who, in 1979, had said that what divided the Gaullists and the Giscardians on Europe was 'incomparably deeper' than what united them), in his attempt to appear more European than the President, could offer nothing more convincing than that, under his leadership, French industry would be in a stronger position to confront the single market of 1992. Naturally, there are limits to France's 'Europeanness' (the Common Agricultural Policy, standardisation of VAT, accession of non-French citizens to teaching and administrative posts) but, to all intents and purposes, for the French citizens of 2000 Europe seems set to emerge as the genuine future.

France and the World: Creative Diplomacy and Persistent Paradoxes

The contradictions of French foreign policy were best encapsulated (as is so much else of national life) in a cartoon by *Le Monde*'s Plantu in which a PS emissary takes his leave of a Middle-Eastern potentate to whom he has just sold a vast range of military hardware: 'Salut', he is saying, 'je file, j'ai une conférence à faire sur les droits de l'homme!' ('Cheerio, I'm off, I've a speech to deliver on human rights!'). It is this ability to marry the cynicism of fairly indiscriminate arms trading with a 'progressive' universal message on human rights, Third World development and national liberation which fascinates and exasperates France's peers in the world community.

Part of the exasperation stems from the genuine cultural links which continue to ensure close ties between the former colonial power and her ex-colonies, particularly in Africa. After the traumas of decolonisation, all French governments sought to highlight the extent to which France, the nation of the Declaration of the Rights of Man, understood the problems of the Third World. But in considering the balance sheet of French relations with the Third World, one must constantly differentiate between intentions and achievements, between discourse and substance.

There can be no doubt that, from de Gaulle to Mitterrand (but particularly under Pompidou and Mitterrand), France has sought to foster an alternative discourse on most aspects of economic development, aid and cooperation, an approach which has often been in open opposition to positions adopted by the USA and other leading Western nations. Several main features deserve highlighting: first, a commitment to the notion of *development* as a means of permitting Third World countries to become trading partners in their own right. This has mainly taken the form of progress towards the apparently magic sum of 0.7 per cent of gross national product in aid as well as consistent lip-service to the controversial notion of a 'new international economic order'. Second, there is a campaign within the EC to persuade European nations to coordinate their aid and investment programmes, particularly with respect to the former colonial areas now designated ACP (African, Caribbean, Pacific) trading partners under the Lomé Convention. This has been given energy and direction by the appointment to Brussels of committed Third World developers such as Claude Cheysson and Edgard Pisani. Third, there is a demand for the fullest use of UN specialist agencies which, for the most part, Washington has sought either to manipulate or to muzzle. Fourth, support has been given (largely verbal) for Third World countries in their campaign against the monopoly of news and information flows by Western press agencies.

Unfortunately, the record of the first Mitterrand Government hardly matches up to the expectations placed on it, not least by the initial appointment of a convinced *tiersmondiste* (champion of the Third World), Jean-Pierre Cot, as Minister-Delegate of Cooperation and Development. Attempts to create an independent aid agency were frustrated by the civil servants in the various ministries concerned with aid programmes, fearful of their own loss of influence. Hopes of expanding French priority aid programmes beyond the traditional horizons of France's former colonies produced minimal results. Attempts to negotiate long-term aid and development packages with major countries like Algeria, Mexico and India collapsed (in most cases for lack of appropriate structures and funds). Finally, the long overdue replacement of French *coopérants* in Third World countries (where they earn twice their French salaries and live in the lap of luxury) with properly trained nationals from the host countries foundered through lack of resolve in Paris and timidity on the part of the host governments. French aid remained preponderantly tied to promises of preferential trade with Paris and, despite intentions to the contrary, genuine aid has all too often been set aside in favour of off-loading surplus products.

This negative record stresses once again the real limitations of the executive branch in an area where power is alleged to be considerable. It should also include mention of the scandal whereby Cot's replacement, Christian Nucci, was caught siphoning off aid into his own pocket and the PS. But, despite the lack of substance behind the rhetoric, France's 'image' in the Third World remains relatively positive, although there are signs that this is waning. She is still seen as the only credible alternative to Washington and Moscow, a view which is reinforced by her pretensions to minor superpower status. Her military agreements with a dozen or so African nations, her willingness to intervene in trouble spots such as Chad, Zaire and Lebanon, is taken as proof that she is prepared to put her troops where her mouth is (even if this often involves making compromises with regimes with a deplorable record on 'human rights'). This continued aspiration for a genuine world role underlies her recent stormy experiences in the increasingly misnamed Pacific.

New Caledonia, Mururoa and the South Pacific

Three separate areas of the South Pacific are currently classed as French overseas territories: New Caledonia, situated 1,500 kilometres east of Australia and incorporating some 19 000 square kilometres of inhabited territory comprising fewer than 150 000 inhabitants; the Wallis and Futuna Islands, situated 2,000 kilometres north-east of New Caledonia and covering 300 square kilometres inhabited by 10 000 people; and French Polynesia, a further 3,000 kilometres to the east, incorporating 130 islands and 80 000 inhabitants over some 4 000 000 square kilometres of ocean. French Polynesia includes the tourist islands of Tahiti and the nuclear testing atolls of Mururoa and Fangataufa. In recent years, the French presence in the South Pacific has seen diplomatic relations with Australia and New Zealand strained almost to breaking point, mainly as a result of continued French nuclear tests and of the July 1985 sinking in Auckland harbour by French commandos of the Greenpeace vessel, *Rainbow Warrior*. It has seen the development in New Caledonia of a pro-independence movement which has brought the islands to the brink of civil war and, in Tahiti, of increasingly vociferous demands for a review of the century-old links with Paris. It has seen the emergence of the 'South Pacific Forum', a grouping of thirteen independent states of the South Pacific, whose annual agenda is dominated by motions opposing many aspects of French policy in the region.

At the heart of the problem is the French desire to maintain a military presence in a part of the world which is of strategic significance, and which currently contains no American or Soviet military bases. French economic interests in the South Pacific are very limited: her share of the market is 1.75 per cent and her share of investment around 1.5 per cent (both figures being far less than half those for Britain or West Germany). The Defence Ministry offers, as the strategic reason for France's presence, the notion that she contributes to the security of the region by complementing the existing ANZUS forces. Officially, the New Zealand and Australian governments do not demand French withdrawal. What they do demand, however (an end to all nuclear tests in the area – the South Pacific Forum has declared the region a nuclear-free zone – and 'decolonisation' of New Caledonia), runs directly counter to recent French policy.

France has been testing nuclear weapons on the Mururoa atoll since 1966. Since 1975, these tests have been underground. Despite constant protests from Canberra and Wellington, the tests have continued. The French argue that the distance between Mururoa and Auckland (almost 5,000 kilometres) is greater than that between Paris and the main Soviet testing site in Siberia (3,800 kilometres), or between Nevada and New York (3,700 kilometres). The New Zealanders are unimpressed (their main shipping route to the Panama Canal and on to Europe goes right through the area). Several reliable scientific reports claim that extensive damage has been sustained by the atoll and that considerable radioactive leakage has taken place. The controversy rages on, successive French governments refusing to make the slightest concession to popular protest or diplomatic pressure. It is clear that, for the present, France's entire nuclear programme, as well as her global transmissions networks, are dependent on her maintaining the *Centre d'Expérimentation du Pacifique*. But recently, as the protests have spread to France's own territories in Tahiti, there have been signs that Paris is beginning to count the cost of this negative publicity and consider alternative options (such as Nevada). The style of the French presence in the South Pacific may in fact be most substantially affected by the evolution of the situation in New Caledonia.

The advent of the Mitterrand Government in 1981 led to hopes among the Melanesian population of New Caledonia that a new, more liberal statute for the islands could be devised. Social, economic and cultural divisions between the Melanesians (*Canaques*) who represent 43 per cent of the population and the Europeans (*Caldoches*) who make up 37 per cent, had led several times since 1958 – notably under Giscard d'Estaing – to attempts to liberalise the political and administrative framework. A new 1984 statute hammered out by Georges Lemoine, Minister for the Overseas Departments and Territories, and modified by his successor, Edgar Pisani, divided the territory into four regional assemblies, three of which (the predominantly rural ones) came under *Canaque* control in the elections of September 1985. The *Caldoches* held power in the fourth region, which includes the capital, Nouméa, and over 80 per cent of industrial activity. Pisani, who sided openly with the *Canaques*, attempted to provide further compensation for the imbalances on the island in his preparations for a referendum on self-determination which was scheduled to take place before the end of 1987. Sensing the wind of change on their side the more assertive *Canaques*, under the leadership of Jean-Marie Tjibaou, founded the *Front de Libération Nationale Kanak et Socialiste* (Kanak Socialist Independence Front) in September 1984.

The change of government in 1986 was followed by a major shift in policy. The referendum was cancelled, and Pisani's efforts to redress the balance between the populations reversed. Thousands of troops were sent to police the three *Canaque* areas, which considerably exacerbated tensions. A September 1987 referendum on retaining New Caledonia within the French Republic was boycotted by the *Canaques* who felt increasingly compelled to consider armed resistance. When, one month later, six settlers were acquitted by a Nouméa court of the ritual murder of ten *Canaques*, including two of Tjibaou's brothers, tensions rose dramatically and culminated, just prior to the presidential elections in April 1988, in a separate *Front de Libération Nationale Kanak et Socialiste* operation taking 23 French gendarmes hostage. Four other gendarmes were killed. The subsequent storming of the grotto in which the hostages were being held, which ended in the deaths of 21 Melanesians, was one of the more dramatic events of the last days of the presidential campaign and left no doubt as to the South Pacific policy of a future Chirac presidency.

Mitterrand's re-election and the appointment of Michel Rocard as Prime Minister led rapidly to a re-assertion of the principles of the previous Socialist Government. Rocard scored a considerable diplomatic coup by announcing agreement, as early as June 1988, between the leaders of the two main contending parties in New Caledonia on a variety of measures. In an effort to avoid civil war, the French state assumed full administrative responsibility for the territory until 14 July 1989. Meanwhile a referendum was organised, on 6 November 1988, on a new administrative and political structure involving three provinces (two of which are dominated by *Canaques*) and a finely balanced legislature, with executive control resting in the hands of the French High Commissioner. This arrangement is to last ten years, after which, in 1998, a new referendum will be held on independence. The aim is to give both populations the time and the experience necessary to reach a lasting and viable solution. Unfortunately, the RPR called on its voters to abstain and, in the event, only 37 per cent of the French electorate went to the polls (80 per cent of these voting 'yes'). The future of New Caledonia currently lies largely in the hands of the island's political leaders, and especially in their ability to control their own extremist wings.

For the Socialist Government (and in this it has the support of Centrists like Giscard d'Estaing and Barre), long-term French interests in New Caledonia clearly lie in finding a viable political solution, which they recognise must involve greater political responsibility and economic opportunity for the *Canaques*. There is a considerable body of support among the *Canaque* population for maintaining the links with France, but any abrupt changes in the evolving status quo (such as were attempted, in a reactionary sense, by Chirac, or such as might derive from too rapid a declaration of independence) would almost certainly lead to increased polarisation, if not civil war. France's entire presence in the South Pacific hangs on the outcome of the New Caledonian situation. Australia and New Zealand are eager to support the Socialist quest for a political solution and are loud in their condemnation of Chirac's confrontational posture, being conscious of the fact that the outcome of a similar situation in the neighbouring New Hebrides (now Vanuatu) led to the Soviets acquiring a toehold in the region. Recent French governments have pushed their South Pacific presence too far. Currently, Paris is attempting to back-pedal in order to salvage France's long-term interests in the region.

Conclusion

France's pursuit of an independent foreign and defence policy stemmed from four interlocking factors: the example set by de Gaulle, the vestiges of Empire, the refusal to bow to the hegemonic pressures of the superpowers and the acquisition of nuclear weapons. Since the late 1960s, when the General took independence to its extreme limits, global interdependence has flourished and Paris has shown a constant, albeit imperceptible, acceptance of this fact in most areas. Knee-jerk imperialism in the last colonial outpost (the South Pacific) is currently giving way to a subtler, more political effort to retain an influence. A vision of Europe based on the lowest common denominators capable of escaping national vetoes has yielded before a major politico-cultural shift in favour of maximum integration, and the assertion of a historic community of destiny which will eventually reunite the two halves of the continent. A polemical rejection of 'Anglo-Saxon' values has been succeeded by the enthusiastic discovery of a community of culture bridging the two sides of the Atlantic. A sustained attempt to emerge as the natural pole of attraction for the developing Third World has given way to a more realistic acceptance of the role of international agencies (particularly those of the UN) in coordinating this task. A refusal to discuss integrated defence planning has been replaced by a far more accommodating attitude to joint (mainly bilateral) initiatives in Europe and the Middle East. Only in the field of nuclear weapons does France remain intransigently and ostentatiously independent. How long can that attitude be sustained if Gorbachev's dream of a denuclearised and demilitarised Europe comes to fruition?

PART FOUR

Current Controversies

12

Adversary Politics, Civil Liberties and Law and Order

ALAIN GUYOMARCH

During the last decade issues of law and order and civil liberties have often been high on the political agenda. This state of affairs is not new or unique to France. Indeed many of the problems faced by politicians and policy-makers in the 1980s were inherited from earlier decades. Some were closely linked to traditional structures and ethics of the police and judiciary. Others were related to rising crime rates and growing terrorism: international trends since the 1960s from which France has not escaped. How these problems have been treated, however, has depended upon the specific political circumstances and the intense inter-party competition of the 1980s.

After their victory in 1981 the Socialists were keen to demonstrate that a policy different from that of the previous Centre-Right governments (because of its emphasis on crime prevention and civil rights) could be much more effective. They at once initiated a whole programme of reforms. However, even before all their measures had been enacted, the Socialists were losing popularity. It was not surprising that the RPR and UDF, in opposition, should have fanned the flames of discontent by criticising reforms which represented an explicit disavowal of their own policies before 1981. What did cause surprise, however, was the spectacular growth of support for the FN in the municipal elections of 1983 and the European elections of 1984. The FN focused its campaigns not only on the need to limit or reverse immigration, which it argued was a major source of crime and terrorism, but also on the 'urgency' for tougher measures against crime and delinquency in general. Le Pen retained these themes for the 1986 Assembly election and 1988 Presidential and Assembly elections. When the FN appeared to gain popularity whilst the Centre–Right coalition stagnated, several RPR and UDF leaders began to compete with Le Pen on the issue of public security. The media and the opinion pollsters in turn started to ask whether or not there really existed a widespread public feeling of insecurity. When the RPR–UDF coalition returned to power in 1986, with its FN rivals being represented in Parliament for the first time, it adopted a much tougher approach than the Socialists and focused on law and order issues.

The Chirac Government did not, however, undo many major reforms of its predecessors, and neither did its tougher policy stance win it appreciable electoral returns. When in 1988 Mitterrand was re-elected and the Socialists returned to office, crime rates were already falling. The PS leaders claimed that this drop was the result of their reforms between 1981 and 1986. By early 1989 neither Le Pen nor the 'public feeling of insecurity' appeared as serious as before. Nonetheless, whilst the Socialists seemed to have modernised structures, modified ethics and thus shifted the parameters of policy-making on both civil liberties and law and order, some traditional problems still remained unsolved.

Inherited Problems of Policing, Justice and Civil Rights

The 1958 constitution made explicit reference to two great texts, the 1789 Declaration of the Rights of Man and the preamble to the 1946 constitution. It did not, however, change anything in the institutional arrangements which traditionally had made the application of these civil rights texts difficult and created many conflicts. The police forces and the judiciary remained subject to the centralised political control of ministers. Two important ministries, Interior and Defence, controlled the two police forces (the National Police and the Gendarmerie respectively), whilst the Justice Ministry was relatively weak. The politicians of the 1980s thus inherited structures in which conflicts seemed inevitable, but failed to guarantee either effective policing or adequate protection of civil liberties.

One major source of controversy was that senior appointments within the National Police and the judiciary were made directly by the ministers. Hence, senior officers and judges were often criticised for pro-government sympathies. Furthermore, the operational autonomy of police chiefs from ministerial intervention was limited and even judges were subject to pressures from their minister. Prefects, the heads of police forces in every *département*, were still subject to instant dismissal if they acted in a way of which the interior minister disapproved. The justice minister was often able to exert considerable influence through the public prosecutors (*procureurs*) and responsibility for cases was even taken away from troublesome examining magistrates, especially in politically sensitive investigations (F. Nguyen, *RPP*, 1988). Hence in the 1980s, as in previous decades, it was commonplace for critics to assert that the police and judiciary were instruments of government rather than servants of law, order, justice and civil rights (P. Lyon Caen, 1981)

A second traditional problem was the weakness of the justice ministry and the judiciary, both politically and administratively. Before the 1980s the ministry had a poor record in securing increases in spending during budget negotiations, which resulted in shortages of judges and other staff, long delays before cases came to court and decrepit prison conditions. The judicial system not only appeared very slow; it also seemed to have great complexity. All cases relating to state actions within the field of administrative law were judged by the Council of State, whose members were top rank civil servants recruited from ENA. In the civil and criminal courts, however, the judges were recruited from the National School of Magistrates, as were the members of the public prosecution services (*Parquet*). Councillors of State, therefore, were civil servants, whilst prosecutors were magistrates.

The judiciary often appeared weak in its relations with the police. The inquisitorial role of the examining magistrates involved working with the police during investigations to determine whether or not there were sufficient grounds for prosecution. Inevitably many conflicts arose, not least between the examining magistrates and the criminal investigation detectives whose activities they supervised. These conflicts were usually solved in favour of the police, although not always without appeals to ministers. In interministerial clashes the interior minister generally carried greater political weight than his colleague at the Department of Justice.

A third difficulty was the traditional 'police war' between the National Police and the Gendarmerie. The rivalry between these two police forces stemmed from the fact that they were separate services belonging to different ministries with distinct, but sometimes overlapping, responsibilities. The National Police, with 109 992 police personnel in 1987, was responsible for maintaining law and order in towns with over 10 000 inhabitants, for regional crime squads, for border and airport policing and for crowd control by the riot police (CRS). The *Préfecture* of Police in Paris, the biggest single territorial division of the National Police force, had a special status as it had been an autonomous service until 1966. The Gendarmerie, by contrast, with 90 888 officers in 1988, was part of the Ministry of Defence. It was primarily responsible for policing rural areas, traffic policing on motorways and national highways, but its services also included the *Gendarmerie Mobile* which, like the riot squad, was deployed for riot control. Hence in most of the 96 *départements* the National Police and Gendarmerie shared policing responsibilities and the prefects had the thankless task of attempting to coordinate the operations of the two rival services. Given the generous budgetary allocations for the Defence Ministry, the Gendarmerie was much better equipped than its rival. Local conflicts between members of the two police forces also sometimes provoked confrontations at the ministerial level.

In addition to these conflicts between the two police forces, difficulties arose because of the unionisation of the National Police and the magistrates and conflicts between unions of different political tendencies. Police unions in the pro-Socialist FASP clashed with unions in the USCP, more sympathetic to Centre-Right parties. There were also tensions between these bodies and the unions on the extreme Right in the FPIP. In the 1960s and 1970s there were conflicts between unions on the Left and ministers of de Gaulle, Pompidou and Giscard d'Estaing, and especially between the Union of Magistrates (of pronounced Leftist and liberal tendencies) and successive justice ministers.

One other organisational feature of the National Police also provoked frequent problems: the existence of a specialised 'information police', the *Renseignements Généraux*. This service, which has branches in every *département* in France, is responsible for keeping the government of the day informed about all political, economic and social developments in France. Hence, its officers are involved in many different types of information-gathering, from the surveillance of subversive groups to carrying out opinion polls. A frequent criticism of all parties not in power is that the *Renseignements Généraux* are used by the government for its own partisan purposes to spy on its opponents. Civil rights seemed even more endangered when this unit were accused of bugging newspaper offices in the 1970s.

These traditional divisions and organisational problems contributed to keeping the magistrates and police in the forefront of the media and the political debate. Constant public criticism from the Union of Magistrates (before 1981) of the administration of justice encouraged widespread public distrust of the police and judiciary.

Whilst these traditional problems were specifically French, France was not exceptional amongst Western democracies in experiencing a considerable increase in the number of reported crimes and terrorist acts. Table 12.1 presents the crime figures in France during the 1970s. The total number of crimes increased continuously from 1963 to 1985, except in 1976, but the pattern of growth was uneven. Strangely, 1982 was a record year for crime but the following three years had atypically low increases and in 1986 crime rates fell. Between 1972 and 1984 there were increases in almost all types of crime but some were much greater than others: snatch and grab offences increased by 497 per cent and muggings of women by 649 per cent, but muggings of men by 'only' 251 per cent. The total crime statistics in the 1980s show that 'traditional crimes' still far exceeded the 'new' crimes, including both muggings and drug offences. Nonetheless, the accuracy of these statistics is open to question. The real rates of crime have probably not increased nearly as much as have the rates of reported crime.

TABLE 12.1 *Crime increases, 1972–84*

Crime	1984	% change
Murder	2 712	+96
Rape	2 859	+102
All drugs crimes	28 794	+855
Traffic in drugs	3 275	+1 210
All fraud crimes	210 298	+132
Armed robbery (guns)	7 661	+320
Other theft with violence	50 246	+328
Burglary (homes)	236 631	+239
Theft of cars	720 360	+497
Vandalism	206 259	+463
Total reported crimes	3 681 453	+120

Source: *Aspects de la criminalité et de la délinquance en France en 1984*, pp. 13–25.

Terrorist activities have also been taking place on French soil since at least the 1960s. Indeed, recent atrocities pale into insignificance when compared with those of the Algerian War. Nonetheless, the increase of terrorist activities in the 1970s was a worrying phenomenon.

One type of terrorism was related to the presence of foreign groups, particularly from the Middle East, in a country like France with a long tradition of political asylum, with large numbers of immigrant workers, and with long, difficult-to-control frontiers. The settling of scores between pro- and anti-Khomeini Iranians led to embassy occupations in 1979 and 1980, shootings in 1980 and 1981, street brawls in 1981 and 1982 and the hijacking of an Iranian gun-boat in Marseilles. Bombings in Paris involving an Iranian, Gordji, led to his expulsion in 1987, after a major diplomatic incident. The Secret Army for the Liberation of Armenia was responsible for a series of assassination attempts and bomb attacks against Turkish diplomats and airline offices. In 1978 Palestinian groups killed four people at Orly airport; seven PLO representatives in France were killed in 1982; and the 1982 machine-gun attack on a Jewish restaurant in the rue des Rosiers, Paris, was attributed to the PLO.

Distinct from this international and imported terrorism were domestic terrorist activities, both ethnic and political. Ethnic terrorism has been mainly linked to the struggle for regional autonomy or independence. The three main regions involved were New Caledonia (discussed in Chapter 11), Brittany and Corsica. Most violence took place in these regions, although Paris has increasingly become the main target of these regional terrorist groups. Whilst Breton autonomists, who had been very active in the early 1970s, were largely quiescent after the bomb attack at the château de Versailles in 1978, terrorist activities by Corsicans have not died out, although there was a brief truce when the Socialists came to power (Moxon Browne 1984).

Another form of domestic political terrorism, unrelated to regional conflicts, was associated with two groups, the anti-semitic Right and *Action Directe* on the Left. Anti-semitic violence reached a climax in 1980 when, after 30 bomb or machine-gun attacks on Jewish targets, a synagogue in Paris was blown up, killing four and injuring 20. Bomb attacks and the desecretion of Jewish graves continued in 1981. In 1982 gunmen killed six people in a Paris Jewish restaurant (although, as noted above, the PLO was suspected). Since that time, however, Left-wing violence by *Action Directe* has been more frequently in the headlines. Targets have included such symbols of capitalism as banks, computer companies, police stations, job centres and state agencies. In 1986 there was a bomb attack on Interpol headquarters. There have also been attacks on managers of important corporations, including the murder of the managing director of Renault. Inevitably the press and television paid considerable attention to these spectacular outrages. Although the nature and extent of the problems of crime and terrorism did not change when the Socialists were elected to government in 1981, the crime rates and terrorism were to be exploited for electoral ends as the political debates evolved.

The Socialists 1981–6: Policies for Civil Liberties and Policing

After 23 years of Centre–Right governments the election of a Socialist president in 1981 appeared to herald a new era. The protection of civil rights became a high policy priority and the first reforms of the new government included measures to remove repressive laws introduced by their predecessors. Before taking office in 1981, the Socialists had criticised their RPR–UDF opponents for both their partisan choices of judicial and police personnel at top levels and for their restrictions on civil liberties in the name of law and order. They argued that the policies pursued by previous governments were not only wrong but also ineffective. In general, they claimed, repressive and reactive law-and-order policies and policing techniques aroused the hostility of many individuals and groups towards the police and the magistrates. In particular the 'security and liberty' law of the last year of the Giscard d'Estaing presidency appeared markedly to increase the powers of the police and to endanger civil liberties, but the rising crime rates showed that this repressive approach did not work. The PS and PCF advocated the adoption of a preventative approach and stressed the need for the courts and the police to gain broad public respect and support. Once in office their declared goals, therefore, were to protect civil liberties and to establish a more liberal but also a more effective system for maintaining law and order. By 1984 when the Mauroy Government resigned, the most controversial measures to correct the 'errors' of the past had already been taken. Nonetheless, there remained important and complex reforms to be enacted by the Fabius Government (1984–6).

Among the first acts of the new government in 1981 were the abolition of the Court of State Security and the death penalty, and the repeal of two laws: the 'anti-vandal' law of the 1970s and the more recent law on 'security and liberty'. The first institutional change, the abolition of the Court of State Security, was highly divisive. For the Socialists and Communists (and some Centrists), this court had always represented a repressive, biased and undemocratic element in the French judicial system. Its public image of expeditious procedures, harsh sentences and pro-governmental decisions undermined the reputation of French justice among liberal critics at home and abroad.

The abolition of the death penalty brought France into line with all other EC members. For many Socialists this act was a very important symbol but it did not lead to a major political confrontation between the government and the opposition. Indeed there were also many deputies from the Right who had long supported the abolition of the guillotine (not just from the CDS but also from the RPR, including Chirac, its leader). Nonetheless, as the question of the abolition of the death penalty had been kept off the agenda for parliamentary discussion by Giscard d'Estaing, this reform was a direct consequence of the 1981 change of government.

The repeal of the 'anti-vandal' and 'security and liberty' laws provoked much more controversy. The first of these laws had limited the freedom of individuals and organisations to demonstrate by making the organisers legally and financially responsible for any damage which occurred during a demonstration. The second had greatly increased police powers to stop, search and detain suspects. Most controversially, it had sought to give an unlimited right to the police to stop and search any car, though this power had been removed by the Constitutional Council. For the Socialists these laws were infringements of the rights of association and demonstration and an excessve extension of police powers. Their abolition was seen as essential to the restoration of full civil rights.

The Socialists did not only abolish, they also created. Notably, they granted the right of individuals to appeal to the European Commission on Human Rights in June 1982. Giscard d'Estaing had signed the European Convention in 1974 for France but his ratification had specifically precluded the right of individual appeals. The French police and judiciary were henceforth subject to decisions made by the European Court of Human Rights in Strasbourg. This measure provoked the wrath of the anti-European Gaullists.

The Justice Minister, Badinter, initiated several other reforms, largely possible because of his success in obtaining a real increase in the budget for his ministry. To accelerate justice 250 additional judges were recruited in four years. The budget for legal aid was increased markedly and access to these funds was facilitated. Compensation for victims of crimes and violence was increased and speeded up. A programme for improving prison conditions was begun. In 1984 an attempt was made to protect the rights of the accused and to lower the prison population (at that time, almost 40 per cent of the people in jail were awaiting trial) by granting the right of a statement by a defence lawyer to the examining magistrate before preventive detention could be ordered. Journalists even wrote of the 'introduction of Habeas Corpus' (*Le Monde*, 6 March 1984).

The Socialists' initial reforms, however, were not solely concerned with the improvement of civil liberties. A whole series of measures were taken to help institutions adapt to the new problems. One such measure was the appointment in 1982 of a junior minister with special responsibility for public security and, in the same year, Mitterrand created a post on the Elysée Palace staff for a presidential adviser and coordinator for action against terrorism. The preoccupation of the government with improving police structures and adopting preventative approaches was also shown by the appointment of two committees, the Belorgey committee in 1981 and the Bonnemaison committee (composed of mayors) in 1982. The institutional changes which arose from the recommendations of these committees included the creation of a central directorate for police training in the Ministry of the Interior and the establishment of a National Council for the Prevention of Delinquency in 1983. This latter body was intended to bring together experts and the mayors of big towns to identify problems and propose preventative solutions related to delinquency suitable for inner-city areas. Whilst these measures indicated some concern with improving and changing policing methods, they were nonetheless rather limited.

A change in the style of ministerial relations with the police also followed the change of government in 1981. Relations between the police and ministers became extremely tense as ministers sought to reassert citizens' rights by restricting police powers. The Minister of the Interior, Defferre, made no secret of his hostility towards traditional police approaches and his suspicions of the political sentiments of many senior police officers. He ordered an immediate end to unauthorised telephone tapping and to unnecessary identity controls. He also instructed the *Renseignements Généraux* to cease surveillance of non-subversive organisations, such as trade unions. He issued instructions that files held on citizens with no criminal record should be destroyed. He replaced not only the men in traditional spoils posts, including the Prefect of Police and Director-General of the National Police, but also intervened in appointments of the heads of crime squads. Both he and Badinter publicly warned the police that all illegal and unauthorised acts (often referred to as *bavures*) would be punished by stiff penalties. Finally, the National Police was humiliated by

Mitterrand's decision to transfer responsibility for his personal protection to the Gendarmerie.

When in 1984 Joxe replaced Defferre as Minister of the Interior and Decentralisation, there was a clear change of emphasis from the latter to the former part of the title. A plan for substantial reforms in the National Police was on Joxe's initiative adopted by Parliament as the Police Modernisation Act of 1985. The major provisions of this Act included a substantial increase in public spending over four years, 50 per cent more than in previous spending plans. The main spending targets for the additional funds were buildings (100 per cent increase), transport (68 per cent), communications (57 per cent) and computing (40 per cent), whilst 15 per cent of the new resources were devoted to increasing salaries and creating new posts (in 1986). The main aim of the law was to increase effectiveness by improving equipment, techniques, training and public relations. In this respect the law marked a break with previous policies of simply increasing the numbers of police officers to meet rising crime rates.

Alongside this major effort to improve police quality and effectiveness there was also an attempt to reform and simplify judicial structures. The 1985 Badinter Law provided for a 'bench' of three examining magistrates to take charge of an investigation in place of a single individual magistrate. This reform did not lead to much controversy among politicians but was rather reluctantly accepted among the magistrates (*Le Monde*, 15 October 1985).

In his relations with the police the style of Joxe was very different from that of his predecessor. The number of police specialists appointed to Joxe's *cabinet* illustrated the minister's concern. There was no disavowal of Defferre's instructions but the minister made it clear that he wished to work in full cooperation with the whole of the National Police and to enhance the public's respect for its policemen. One important decision he made was to draft a code of police conduct to clarify what was acceptable to police and public alike. In making senior appointments, Joxe attempted to regain the confidence of all sections within the National Police. He even brought back some of those senior officers who had been pushed into sidings by his predecessor. Most symbolic of the new approach and style was the visit by Mitterrand himself to the graduation ceremony of the National School for Police Inspectors in 1985 (*Le Monde*, 16 July 1985).

The approach taken by Joxe did not mean a return to the situation before 1981. On the contrary, the parameters had been shifted by Badinter's judicial reforms, and by Defferre's censure of senior officers whose RPR or UDF sympathies were too public and his rulings about respect for individual rights. Joxe's aim was to create a modernised, well-equipped professional and preventative police, with a less politicised image and greater public respect.

The Right and Insecurity: From Opposition to Power

The early Socialist measures provoked criticisms and opposition from three sources. First, the parties of the former governing coalition, the RPR and UDF, generally opposed this disavowal of their policies as an irresponsible and inexperienced approach to controlling crime and disorder. Elements within the police and judiciary with Right-wing political sympathies comprised the second source. Last was the FN, which used the 'Socialist threat' to law and order as a main mobilising theme, along with immigration (as Schain discusses in Chapter 14). When the elections of 1983 and 1984 showed a dramatic increase in support for the FN, some RPR and UDF leaders sought to compete with Le Pen not only by taking a tougher line on immigration but also by demanding more firmness on law and order. The Chirac Government after 1986 pursued this tougher line but did not succeed in reducing support for the FN; instead, divisions within their coalition and inside its member parties deepened.

In 1981 the Socialists faced vociferous criticisms from the new opposition of the RPR and UDF. The Socialists' appointments of police chiefs and judges were attacked as partisan and their new liberal policies were dismissed as ineffective and irresponsible, more likely to encourage than to check rising crime rates and increasing terrorist activities. The abolition of the Court of State Security was especially disliked by the parties of the Right. This body had been seen by many as an effective and rapid mechanism against terrorisim and political crimes. For the Gaullists it was part of the 'true cross of Lorraine', as de Gaulle himself had pushed for its creation to deal with the OAS (Secret Army Organisation) in 1961. The RPR and UDF also opposed the abrogation of the 'anti-vandal' and 'security and liberty' laws which they themselves had enacted.

Another source of opposition to the Socialist policies concerned the Right-wing unions within the police. They, too, disliked many of Defferre's choices for the top posts. They openly expressed their hostility to abolition of the death penalty. In 1981 and 1982 there were many minor indications of disaffection, but in 1983 hundreds of Right-wing police officers staged mass demonstrations in Paris. Calls by demonstrating policemen for the resignation of the Minister of Justice indicated the strength of feeling against the Socialist Government.

Between 1983 and 1984, however, the whole tenor of the debate was changed by the successes of the FN in the municipal elections and its subsequent high poll in the European elections. The FN not only sought to exploit any populist sentiments against the Left's liberalising measures, it campaigned for the reintroduction of the guillotine and tougher police powers. It also sought to convince the public that immigration and rising crime rates were closely linked. Le Pen repeatedly insisted that there was a growing feeling of insecurity in many sections of the population, which he said was the result of Socialists' laxness and also the consequence of many years of weak government by the Centre–Right coalition.

Several leaders of the RPR and UDF saw that the rise of the FN was as dangerous to their parties as to the Socialists. Their response was to compete with the FN for the support of those voters particularly worried about the issue of law and order. They began to talk of a rising wave of 'public insecurity', although they were no more precise as to what it meant or as to the evidence of its existence than were Le Pen and his friends. There is no doubt, as noted above, that until the mid-1980s crime rates in France continued to rise, that several much reported crimes occurred and that numerous acts of terrorism took place.

Nonetheless, the press, television and the opinion polls, by focusing attention on the competing criticisms from Right-wing politicians, helped to accentuate the feelings of insecurity which they claimed to report. The findings of the polls indicate that after 1984 there was a massive increase in the number of people who were worried about law and order. However, whilst a substantial minority of citizens was anxious about security, this minority was composed of several different groups, each preoccupied by a particular type of crime. The polls showed that the extent of public concern varied considerably according to the question posed. One poll showed that only 20 per cent thought that the problem of insecurity was very worrying in their own home town or district, but 63 per cent thought that this problem was very worrying for France as a whole; 54 per cent of respondents admitted that they never or very rarely worried about their own personal safety. Other polls revealed that people's views about changes in the level of insecurity do not seem to have differed appreciably since the 1970s (SOFRES, 1986).

In 1984–5 the opinion pollsters found a similar complex pattern of views about what should be done and who bore responsibility for the insecurity. There was a strong feeling that something should be done; indeed, 33 per cent of respondents to a 1985 poll selected 'ensure the security of citizens' as one of their top four priorities for the coming years. Only 25 per cent, however, thought that insecurity would diminish if the government paid more attention to the problem, whilst 67 per cent felt this problem was much wider and could be only solved by wide-ranging social reforms. This view, that social reform was needed to solve the problem, was shared by similar proportions of the supporters of all political parties.

In 1986 the polls indicated that large parts of the population felt that both the police and courts were ill-equipped to deal with this problem. They also showed that the police were believed to perform their duties well by far more people (69 per cent) than those (27 per cent) who thought the courts worked well (SOFRES, 1986, p. 126).

When the RPR–UDF coalition returned to power in 1986, the ministerial appointments of Chalandon (Justice), Pasqua (Interior) and Pandraud (Police), all of whom favoured tougher policing and harsher sentencing, illustrated the high priority that the Chirac Government accorded to this apparent feeling of insecurity in the public. Pasqua and Pandraud even attempted to outbid Joxe in their effusions of support for the police and by publicly announcing their intentions to overlook cases of 'excessive zeal' by policemen. They thus clearly indicated that the objective of stopping crime would justify most means. At the same time Chalandon was encouraging the judges to adopt longer sentences, despite over-crowded jails. He used this overcrowding to justify his controversial plans for prison privatisation. In political appointments Pasqua reversed Joxe's moderation and even outdid Defferre: he provoked a very noisy resignation in 1986 by Fougier, the Prefect of Police, and his amendments to the 1986 police promotion list were ruled illegal by the Council of State. Despite Mitterrand's objections, the Director-General of the National Police was replaced after a few months on Pasqua's insistence. There was a significant change of governmental style towards political intervention.

In institutional reforms, however, the 1986–8 Government achieved very little. The RPR and UDF coalition did not reintroduce either the repealed laws or the abolished Court of State Security. This suggests that the Right felt it was possible to combat disorder without them. Pasqua and Pandraud, by presenting themselves as the champions of firmness whilst making no demand for the reintroduction of these measures, provided a tacit retrospective justification of the Socialists' 1981 claims that such illiberal means were unnecessary for the maintenance of law and order.

The main institutional change after 1986 was the introduction of the 'anti-terrorist law', which provided for holding suspects up to four days and moving trials to Paris. This law was backed by the introduction of visas for non-EC citizens. As Schain points out in Chapter 14, circulars from the Interior Ministry imposed a much tighter control of immigration. Pasqua and Pandraud also encouraged their police forces to return to the practice of frequent and systematic identity checks. All these changes represented a reversal of the Socialists' attempts to improve the protection of civil liberties.

This firmer style with tougher policies was not a total success. First, the fall in crime rates in 1986 cannot be proved to have resulted from their measures; indeed, the Socialists claimed that it was the result of Joxe's earlier police modernisation programme. Second, their policies did not produce the expected electoral rewards. Not only did they fail to reduce the vote for the FN but they also provoked doubts amongst their own supporters. They reinforced dissension within the RPR and UDF as well, and especially between the member parties of the UDF, thus weakening Chirac's prospects for the 1988 presidential contest.

The Socialists' Return to Power: 1988 and Beyond

During the period of *cohabitation* Mitterrand did not hesitate to criticise appointments which appeared unduly partisan, or to condemn those policies which he considered divisive, notably those concerning immigrants, the handling of the student demonstration in 1986, the railway strike in 1987 and the New Caledonian crisis in 1988. At the same time, however, he expressed his satisfaction at some policy successes which were popular. One notable example was his congratulation of Pasqua on the arrest of the leading members of *Action Directe* in 1987. Thus the president began to reinforce his own image as an umpire and unifier over and above the parties. Mitterrand's 1988 campaign theme of a 'unified France' and of willingness by the Socialists to make an alliance with Centrists followed the same line.

Mitterrand's re-election and the return of the Socialists to power in 1988, albeit as a minority government, meant that the style of government changed markedly. Joxe returned to the Interior but Justice was given to a widely respected non-Socialist magistrate, Arpaillange, who had even worked on a ministerial staff under

Giscard d'Estaing. The new non-divisive approach was also clear in the appointments made by these ministers to the spoils posts in their ministries, which provoked little comment or criticism except from the FN. Arpaillange quickly identified himself with the civil liberties approach of Badinter. He launched a programme of reforms to improve prison conditions, to recruit and train the magistrates necessary for the implementation of the Badinter Law and to continue the updating of the law codes which Badinter had begun.

At the Interior Joxe re-adopted the firm but fair style of his earlier period. He re-emphasised his goals of improving police professionalism, securing greater public support for the police and encouraging the adoption of preventative measures. He withdrew the circulars of his predecessor on the treatment of immigrants but emphasised the need to control illegal immigration.

Nonetheless, if the new government kept a relatively low profile on civil liberties and law and order issues during the early months, and if its style and policy provoked few attacks except from the apparently declining FN, it still faced several unsolved policy problems.

One of them was the continuing lack of cooperation between the Gendarmerie and the National Police. There has been no significant move towards a unification of police structures or even a clearer definition of the respective powers of each force. Indeed, some argue that tensions have been sharpened by the authorisation (by the Minister of Defence) allowing the Gendarmes, on some occasions, to operate in plain clothes. The 1987 Jobic affair, when officers of the Gendarmerie arrested a senior officer of the National Police, was but a spectacular example of this very long inter-police war.

This situation has been further complicated by the growth of municipal police forces during the last decade. These bodies, often created by Right-wing mayors, have no clear legal status. It has been estimated that the numbers of municipal police had grown from only 4,000 in 1987 to almost 25 000 in 1988. A few notorious examples of their illegal and strong-arm tactics, including a scandal in May 1985 at Fréjus, where Léotard, the UDF leader and the former Culture Minister, was mayor, have contributed to increasing public suspicions of these local policemen.

An additional problem is the continued importance of the most controversial specialist police services, the *Renseignements Généraux*, and the riot police (both the CRS and the *Gendarmerie Mobile*). Caricatures of France as a police state are often based on these services and their extensive networks. There is, however, little evidence to prove that either government or policing is made more effective by the scale and high public profile of such services.

Conclusion

In the 1980s, the political debate over law and order and civil liberties and justice underwent several changes as political parties sought to promote distinctive policies to check crime and terrorism but also to gain electoral advantage over their rivals. Very often electoral imperatives seemed dominant. The Socialists won power in 1981 by insisting on the need to protect civil rights and introduce modern preventative policing techniques. The Centre–Right was soon campaigning against what it saw as a reversal of its own policies. The debate shifted, however, when the FN grew in popularity with slogans of 'insecurity' and overrunning by immigrants. Although some Centre–Right leaders found it easy to compete with Le Pen on this issue whilst in opposition, they soon found it much more difficult once in power to produce better solutions than those of their predecessors. Their policies, however, were sufficiently drastic to incite dissension within their own ranks. By 1988 the Socialists often appeared as the moderates and the Chirac Government as veering dangerously towards extremism.

It is as difficult to measure whether or not the policies pursued or advocated by the different political parties had an influence on electoral behaviour (as opposed to opinion polls) as it is to evaluate the impact of those policies on law and order or civil liberties. Nonetheless, by taking clear positions on civil rights and law and order issues, successive governments have demonstrated their belief in the electoral significance of such issues. However, the Socialists' measures did change the parameters of civil rights protection and law and order maintenance. When the RPR and UDF came back to power in 1986–8 they accepted many of these reforms. On the one hand, this reflected a cross-party consensus that the modernisation of structures and methods of the police represented a positive achievement. On the other hand, it showed that the measures to enlarge civil liberties did not prevent either tough policing or political interventions in police or judicial affairs. The sound and fury of adversary politics did not preclude a wide measure of policy continuity.

13

The Politics of Media Reform

MARTIN HARRISON

Most West European governments have had to pay unprecedented attention to media policy in recent years, but few have found this as contentious, frustrating and intractable as France. There the inherent difficulty of making decisions about complex issues during a period of rapid technical change was compounded by the unaccustomed stresses of *cohabitation* and alternation between governments of differing ideological hues.

The notion of 'media policy' reverberated beyond the media themselves. There were crucial implications for French ambitions to lead in the new technologies of direct satellite broadcasting, fibre optics and informatics: all fields where France might hope to stem the Japanese challenge. Cultural dimensions were no less important: could France preserve her ailing domestic film and television production industries and avoid being submerged by 'Coca-Cola television' (a term reflecting fears about both the quality of programming and the future of the French language)? Sovereignty, cultural autonomy and even national identity were at stake. Media issues were also inseparable from some of the most hotly disputed issues of the day: the level and form of the boundary between the state and private sectors, government regulation, the balance between Paris and the provinces and the extension of public participation.

The result was that in place of a conventional model of ministerial policy formulation followed by Cabinet coordination within a system of presidential leadership, decision-making was uncertain, variable and, at times, incoherent. The ministry with prime

237

responsibility for media matters, Communication, carried little clout in dealings with departments such as Posts and Telecommunications, Culture, Industry, External Affairs and Finance, each of which had its own objectives, traditions and clientele of interest groups. The evangelising technocrats of the Directorate-General of Telecommunications, though nominally subordinate to the Ministry of Posts and Telecommunications, were more than a match for their ministers and at times defied them. Cinema and advertising companies, the space industries, industrial and domestic electronics corporations, national and regional press organisations and the new breed of transnational media conglomerates all pressed their claims.

The rapidity of change, the complexity of the issues and the multiplicity of interests involved meant that interdepartmental committees and prime ministerial 'arbitration', which normally resolved litigious issues, at best worked slowly and at worst were impotent. The president's impact on policy, minimal during the 1986–8 *cohabitation*, at other periods ranged unpredictably between a hands-off approach and intermittently conclusive intervention. Sometimes his forays reflected an urgent need to cut through the deadlock at lower levels. On other occasions he suddenly imposed a change of course after communing with himself or one or two trusted advisers or conducting secret negotiations with results completely at variance with policies his ministers had been pursuing with his apparent blessing. On top of this there were the uncertainties and delays associated with approaching elections and the changes of political direction they brought in their wake. It was scarcely surprising that decisions constantly lagged behind events and the boldest visions were often frustrated or produced only marginal change. Yet, curiously, although the media were the battleground for some of the sharpest adversarial politics of the 1980s, the overall evolution and outcome of policies not only departed from what their progenitors had intended to achieve, they were also markedly more consensual than the clash of ideological confrontation would have led anyone to expect. In some ways that confrontation was triggered by the collapse of an earlier consensus over press and broadcasting dating from the end of the Second World War.

The Press

After Liberation governments tried to create a more pluralistic press, once proprietors whose papers had appeared under German occupation were chased from their presses and a generation drawn from the Resistance had taken their places. Measures were taken to ensure that 'transparency' of newspaper finances, to prevent anyone from controlling more than one title and to create a distribution system ensuring national availability of minority journals. Support for the partisan press also took the form of subsidies such as tax reliefs and subsidised postal and transport charges.

Yet despite (or because of) being cosseted to the tune of over £40 000 000 per year, by 1981 the industry was fragile. Since 1946 the number of papers published in Paris had dropped from 28 to twelve and in the provinces from 175 to 71. Despite rising educational standards the number of copies sold, which had been 244 per 1,000 of the population in 1914 and 370 in 1946, was a mere 195; lower than any other industrialised Western European country except Italy. The most popular paper, the regional *Ouest-France*, sold 700 000 copies; none of the Paris papers exceeded 450 000. Modest circulations do not necessarily spell poverty, but with a lower proportion of gross domestic product spent on advertising than in any other advanced country, the press was suffering acute financial anaemia despite high cover prices. Even *Le Monde*, one of the world's elite journals with the country's second largest sale, came to the brink of bankruptcy in the early 1980s. Many papers lacked the resources to introduce new production methods, especially against union opposition. For years press hostility to developments threatening to reduce revenue closed off options in broadcasting policy whether from genuine concern for the health of the press or fear of its wrath.

Liberation dreams of a pluralist press were disappointed. Apart from a handful of survivors like the Communist *L'Humanité*, the old party press has vanished. Outside Paris few papers have a marked political colouring. Practically every region is dominated by one, or at most two, papers whose dutiful coverage of everyday events in dozens of local editions has built unassailable monopolies. Vitality of political debate and investigative reporting are not their forte. Yet this is the heartland of the daily press: six of the ten best-selling newspapers are regional rather than Paris-based. Moreover, despite the 1944 anti-concentration legislation, the surviving papers have increasingly been incorporated into groups. Although groups had long existed, concentration gathered momentum with the arrival of Robert Hersant, who by 1981 controlled 16.5 per cent of daily sales and numerous weeklies and magazines. He argued with some justification that he had saved papers that would otherwise have gone to the wall. Others saw an ex-collabor-

ator flouting the 1944 ordinances and launching Right-wing diatribes from his Paris flagship, *Le Figaro*.

Concern over declining competition was not confined to the
Left. In 1979 the Economic and Social Council advocated measures
to limit concentration and ensure greater transparency regarding
ownership. The Socialists were slow to grasp the nettle. Their
back-benchers were demanding action against Hersant, but to
enforce the 1944 ordinances would cause a collision with all the
press groups, while major reform was unacceptable to the owners.
Eventually legislation was carried restricting groups to 15 per cent
of provincial circulation, or 10 per cent of provincial circulation
plus three national titles, providing these did not exceed 10 per
cent of national sales. A Commission for Pluralism and Transparency was to check tendencies towards monopoly. Although
inspired by the 1979 report, the legislation was carefully tailored
so as to spare the Communist and Catholic press, while curbing
Hersant (who would have had to shed at least one Paris daily and
limit his ambitions in the provinces); as a result the government
appeared to be conducting a.political vendetta against him. These
measures did nothing to encourage new papers or to ease the
plight of ailing ones, who could no longer look to Hersant for
salvation.

Subsequently the Constitutional Council held that the law could
not have a retrospective effect, which left Hersant unscathed but
prevented anyone else from emulating him. Such a situation could
not endure. However, by the time the Chirac Government
addressed the matter it was no longer appropriate to deal with
the problem of concentration in terms of the press alone. What
emerged (again after intervention by the Constitutional Council,
insisting that pluralism was a 'constitutional value' that must be
effectively protected) was a ceiling of 20 per cent of sales, combined with limits on television, radio and cable. Hersant was left
a little headroom.

The use Hersant might make of his empire – which by 1989
included four 'nationals', eighteen 'regionals', ten weeklies, three
advertising agencies and a score of magazines and numerous print
works, together with radio and television networks – caused appre-
hension even on the Right. Their suspicions deepened when he
brought in a Left-wing editor and toned down *Le Figaro*'s editorial
line within weeks of Mitterrand's victory in 1988. But if his group
was feared politically, financially it was ailing, as were many other
papers despite governmental aid amounting to 13 per cent of
revenue. Broadcasting was absorbing an increasing share of advertising expenditure, while sales were still falling: from over

10 000 000 copies daily in 1980 to 8 600 000 in 1985. Some papers bolstered their position by joining the flourishing free-sheet market, but the only really flourishing sector of the press was magazines, which were now outselling newspapers. Selling around 1 600 000 copies weekly, four mainstream news magazines, *L'Express*, *Le Nouvel Observateur*, *Le Point* and *L'Evénement de Jeudi*, and the irreverently investigative *Le Canard Enchaîné*, thrived on the deficiencies of the daily press. However, concentration has also developed in magazines. In 1988 Hachette claimed to be the biggest magazine publisher in the world but, although other groups were important within France, few had the international standing that was becoming increasingly important for survival.

Broadcasting

For three decades after the Liberation there was consensus among the mainstream parties that broadcasting should be a state monopoly, subject to the dictates of the government of the day. 'Whoever holds RTF' (French Radio and Television), declared the Gaullist Alexandre Sanguenetti, 'decides the country's destiny.' In President Pompidou's classic words broadcasters could never forget that they were 'the voice of France'. The result as the radio networks were joined by three television networks (TF1, A2 and FR3), was a politically domesticated bureaucratic monster. In 1974 President Giscard d'Estaing considered breaking the monopoly, but in the face of Gaullist hostility he settled for dismembering ORTF (The French Radio and Television Corporation) into seven state companies: four concerned with programmes (three television networks and Radio France), one with production (SFP), one with transmission (TDF) and one with archives and education (INA). His vaguely liberal sentiments did not prevent him from using the reorganisation to replace broadcasters whose sympathies were suspect with more pliable appointees. Seven mini-ORTFs, with all the faults of their parent, now competed anarchically.

Mitterrand came to office in 1981 prepared to break the monopoly and proclaiming that broadcasting should be independent of government. The Minister of Communication, an old radio man sacked for his close ties with Mitterrand, resisted pressure from both the Socialist back-benches and the unions to purge the old government's placemen. However, during the year or more it took to produce detailed proposals, a blend of bullying and bribery produced a clean sweep of network heads and new chiefs. Nevertheless, there was now greater emphasis than before on professional competence rather than loyalty.

The Socialists formally ended the state monopoly of programmes and brought the networks under a High Audiovisual Authority charged with guaranteeing the independence of broadcasting, free expression and proper standards of pluralism, fairness and decency. It would appoint the heads of the networks, allocate frequencies and coordinate television programming. However, the government still controlled the broadcasting budget and made decisions on satellite, cable and new channels.

Though hailed by its first president, Michèle Cotta, as marking 'the separation of audiovisual services and State', the Authority remained too 'statist' for the opposition's taste. Its nine members were, on Mitterrand's last-minute insistent intervention in Cabinet, appointed three each by the President of the Republic and the speakers of the National Assembly and the Senate (a mode of selection he had repeatedly denounced for the Constitutional Council). Six of the nine members were Left-wingers, although they had substantial professional experience and Michèle Cotta worked valiantly to make the Authority non-partisan and collegial. Despite occasional lapses it was broadly successful as a buffer between broadcasters, politicians and pressure groups. It stood up to both Socialist prime ministers and sprang to the defence of the state networks when Mitterrand's concessions to new commercial operators threatened their position. Many broadcasters felt they now had greater freedom than ever previously. But with only 36 staff and a budget of £1 000 000 the Authority's resources were hopelessly inadequate. Its brief was too narrow and it was repeatedly by-passed when major decisions were being taken. It was even unable to secure firm action against pirate broadcasters subverting its attempts to bring order to the FM band.

The prospect of a Right-wing government committed to privatisation, deregulation and abolition of the High Audiovisual Authority, produced fresh uncertainty and policy paralysis before the 1986 elections and for some time after. The Chirac Government created the CNCL to oversee broadcasting, cable and some aspects of telecommunications; privatise TF1; award franchises to other private television networks and local radios; and appoint the heads of the remaining public channels (Antenne 2, FR3 and Radio France). It was also to prevent the acquisition of a dominant position by means of combining a mixture of radio and television outlets.

Ostensibly the CNCL was to be free of the political taint of its predecessor. The President of the Republic and the presidents of each of the two Chambers appointed two members each, and three leading judicial institutions and the Académie Française one each. These ten members selected an additional member for each of the fields of 'audiovisual creation', telecommunications and print journalism. However, the CNCL started with an assured Right-wing majority for at least six years. This imbalance might have been overcome had it determinedly attempted to demonstrate its independence. Instead, among its first decisions was to appoint politically acceptable heads for the public networks with a single vote and no discussion in less than an hour. Although many later decisions were unexceptionable it never recovered from this false start, or its failure to enforce fairness in the 1987 New Caledonia referendum and allegations of corruption in assigning radio franchises. Despite a budget ten times that of the High Audiovisual Authority, the CNCL never fully imposed its authority on the private radio stations and cable networks, the telecommunications operations of France-Télécom or the private television channels, which repeatedly flouted the rules on sponsorship, advertising levels and the screening of films.

The Socialist victory in 1988 created another period of uncertainty. Realising that the idea of an independent regulatory authority was in danger of being compromised by repeated changes, the Socialists decided against radical reform. Their new Higher Audiovisual Council (CSA) would have most of the CNCL's powers, but reverted to the method of appointment employed for the High Audiovisual Authority. Mitterrand's declared intention was to enhance the CSA's standing and chances of survival by incorporating it in the constitution. However, the hostility of both the Right and the Communists to the system of appointment showed how hard a task the CSA would have in establishing itself as trusted, authoritative and truly independent.

Radio

During this long search for an acceptable regulatory structure, the 'audiovisual landscape' was constantly changing. The first breaches in the state monopoly came in radio. (Technically it had long been infringed by 'peripheral' commercial stations in Luxembourg, the Saar, Monaco and Andorra, whose programming was more popular and more trusted than that of the state networks, although the sizeable government stake in ownership or management ensured that they never behaved too independently.) The first direct challenge to the conformist, outdated style of the national radios came when the French branch of Friends of the Earth launched Radio

Verte in 1977, exploiting a loophole in the law. However, the Barre Government plugged the gap, introducing severe penalties for breaches of the monopoly. However, despite jamming and prosecutions, the free radio movement grew. The FM band took on the appearance of a late flowering of the spirit of 1968. The transition from cult movement to serious challenge was signalled when Mitterrand used Radio Riposte to protest at the government's abuse of its control of the State networks in 1979.

The movement grew from about 40 stations to several hundred by the time Mitterrand took office, pledged to relax the monopoly for radio. The Socialists envisaged the FM band becoming the haven of pluralism the press had never succeeded in being, with local radio reflecting the views of a wide range of political, social and cultural associations. Generous, unrealistic, inapplicable and unapplied, their 1982 Act was in a sense a victim of its success. The committee charged with considering applications, and later the High Audiovisual Authority, became clogged with 2,650 requests. Although 1,736 were eventually approved, the process took three years. Meanwhile cacophony reigned. Unsuccessful applicants refused to close, while others drove the weaker or more law-abiding to the wall with excessive power. The Cabinet had refused to accept the Minister of Communication's proposal to allow advertising, fearing for the provincial press, so the new stations were starved of revenue. Many defied or evaded the ban and became commercial operations behind the screen of fictitious associations.

In 1984, with unauthorised radio advertising running at around £30 000 000 per year, the government backtracked. Stations could opt for 'associative' status (with modest public subsidies but no advertising), full commercial operation or a mixture. Over 75 per cent opted for full or partial commercial status. Once again, respect for the rules did not pay. Fearing to appear illiberal the Fabius Government was reluctant to allow action against stations running high power, breaking the requirement of 80 per cent local programming or forming unauthorised networks. Even an attempt to stop France-Télécom's satellite being used as a relay for illegal networks collapsed. Changing direction yet again, just before leaving office the government agreed to give the 'peripheral' stations local access to the FM band.

When the CNCL embarked on a fresh reorganisation of the FM band under the Chirac Government it had as much difficulty as the Authority in dealing with excess power, unauthorised networks or the black market in permits. By now most of the pioneers of 'free radio' had disappeared, having failed to win permits, gone bankrupt or sold out to a commercial operator. A decade after the 'free radio' ferment of the 1970s, 'local' radio was dominated by eight thematic networks distributed by satellite from Paris, based on popular music and commercials. Only in a handful of large cities was radio offering a distinctive range of voices. (Paris's mix of entertainment, religious, immigrant and cause group stations was exceptional.) Yet although the outcome would have disheartened the pioneers, many radio stations did offer a local alternative voice to the centralised offerings of the public and private networks, and these new stations were popular. In 1988 they were taking 38 per cent of the audience as against 22 per cent for Radio France and 40 per cent for the 'peripheral' stations, compared with 60 per cent or more a few years earlier.

'Traditional' Television

Television developed within the monopoly, which was more effectively maintained because Télé-Luxembourg, Télé-Monte Carlo and the Swiss and Belgian French-language networks, unlike their radio counterparts, had very limited coverage. The first channel, TF1, was joined in 1963 by Antenne 2, and in 1971 by FR3, the regional network. The main source of finance was the licence fee, although during the 1970s advertising was introduced (severely limited, however, in the interests of the press).

Giscard's 1974 reform was a failure. As the networks competed to raise their audience share – and thus their share of licence revenue – programming became uncoordinated, unadventurous and conformist. Demand for home-based productions dropped, sending the main production company, SFP, into financial crisis. Staff became demoralised and strike-prone. Polls showed most viewers dissatisfied with the service and three in five favoured ending the monopoly. But in 1981 most Socialists still supported the monopoly, seeing it as the means of bringing culture to the masses. However, the high-minded didacticism of their 'new television' (and the insipidity bred by uncertainty over their reform plans) decimated audiences, leaving a record 68 per cent dissatisfied. The public was emphatically signalling its desire for change.

The opportunity came when the 819-line VHF service was withdrawn. Under Giscard these frequencies were to be used for professional and business services during the day and as a paying cinema channel in the evening. However, being antipathetic to pay-television and 'Americanisation', Socialist thoughts initially turned to a cultural channel providing access for minorities and popular associations, and giving programme production a much-needed stimulus. But when the Mauroy Government met economic difficulties, marketing considerations took priority. André Rousselet, head of the Havas advertising agency and a friend of Mitterrand, reported that since the channel would not cover the whole country it could not be financed either by advertising or the licence fee. His solution, reminiscent of the original Giscardian proposal, was a privately-operated film-based subscription service.

In 1983 the government agreed, appointing Rousselet to run it. Canal + had to overcome many difficulties: the hesitancy of the electronics industry to produce decoders for its scrambled transmissions, the reluctance of the cinema industry to release films earlier and the fall in subscriptions when Mitterrand announced two more commercial channels. Rousselet skilfully exploited every crisis to extract more concessions even above the 'most favoured channel' standing it had won initially, including permission to carry advertising. Opening at Christmas 1984 Canal + reached 1 000 000 subscribers in 1986 and 1 800 000 in 1987, bringing it into healthy profit. It proved the one clear success in broadcasting policy, albeit at the cost of a continuing decline in cinema attendances.

When Mitterrand made another of his regal interventions to back private commercial television, the resulting uncertainty stopped negotiations over satellite broadcasting and cable in their tracks as well as bringing Canal + close to bankruptcy. Subsequently an official report suggested that two national channels were feasible technically, but financially there might be room for only one. It also envisaged 60 local stations, using the frequencies assigned to the new channels in the daytime. However, Socialist hopes of locally-based television repeatedly failed to come to fruition in the face of press and cinema opposition and unpromising financial prospects. Mitterrand subsequently intervened again over the heads of his prime minister and ministers of Communication and Culture, conducting secret negotiations leading to one new network being awarded to a Franco–Italian group, the other becoming a music channel.

Expediency had triumphed: difficult elections were approaching; new channels would be popular. The Right was promising privatisation, which might deliver television into the unfriendly hands of Hersant; this might be headed off by a pre-emptive strike. But although the new Italian partner, Silvio Berlusconi, was politically friendly, the rampant commercialism and Americanisation of his operations in Italy had long been denounced by the Left as precisely the evil France must avoid. Now, by presidential fiat, he was granted terms which would have been unthinkable only months earlier, thereby creating fresh problems for the public networks, dismaying many Socialists and undercutting policies that the ministers of Communication and Culture had been pursuing for four years, bringing them to the brink of resignation.

The two channels nevertheless took to the air, albeit with incomplete coverage, just before the election. Channel 5 confirmed the critics' worst fears with its diet of American films and French versions of Italian game-shows, though TV6 won an appreciative young audience for its rock videos. However, the Right's election victory signalled yet another change of direction. TF1 was privatised and the two new channels re-assigned to pro-Chirac men: Channel 5 to Hersant and Channel 6 to a consortium headed by Télé-Luxembourg and the water company Lyonnaise des Eaux headed by ex-RPR Secretary-General, Monod. TF1 was an immediate success, with its star-studded entertainment attracting a 40 per cent or more audience share. Unsure whether it was expected to compete head-on with TF1 or devise a form of public service television France has never known, Antenne 2 plummeted to a 30 per cent share. Shaken by the purges of the Chirac period and successive reorganisations and uncertain of its role, FR3 was still the poor relation and had only 10–12 per cent of the audience. Hersant's '5' was launched ambitiously, failed to win audiences despite breaching the terms of its concession by ploys like screening erotic films in prime time, and made huge losses. The CNCL hesitated to take a firm line lest it collapse completely. M6, with a mere 2 per cent of the audience, also lost money, but hoped to survive by cheaper programming and targeting market niches. When the Socialists returned to power they realised that the system desperately needed a period of stability. However, even if that were granted, it was by no means clear that there was enough advertising support for all these networks to survive.

With its unashamedly 'popular' programming the new system won little critical acclaim. While the SFP remained in financial crisis despite the massive increase in programme output (it had been unable to match Anglo-Saxon imports on price because of its small domestic base and lack of marketing skills), competition and deregulation had resulted in just that 'cocacolonisation' which intellectuals had feared. But viewers were less resentful: indeed, they were spending more time than ever before their sets. And although the state networks remained vulnerable to government interference, news and current affairs programming was often fairer and more balanced than in the past. Coverage of the 1988 presidential and parliamentary elections attracted fewer complaints of bias than any previous campaign during the Fifth Republic, although there was concern at 'Americanised' campaigns tailored for television. If France was truly moving towards greater political pluralism in broadcasting this appeared to owe less to idealism or the new regulatory structure than to entrepreneurs' assessment of their commercial advantage. Whatever the motivation, here at least was welcome progress.

Satellite Broadcasting

One of the most persistent problems of broadcasting policy has been the interaction between the changing pattern of terrestrial broadcasting and the new technologies of satellite and cable. When President Giscard d'Estaing and Chancellor Schmidt agreed in 1979 on a joint programme to introduce direct satellite broadcasting by 1985, they saw this as a means of strengthening Franco–German relationships and gaining a technical lead over the Japanese and Americans based on the successful Ariane rocket, which would bring in lucrative export earnings. Essentially technology-led, the scheme was also a defensive response to the threat of French screens being invaded by American programmes from foreign-based satellites. Little thought was given to programming.

The project was plagued with uncertainty. In 1981 Socialists were not well disposed towards a system which remained so vulnerable to foreign-based competition. In 1984 a report by a former head of the Directorate-General of Telecommunications condemned the satellite, TDF1, as 'unfit for operational service' because it was very expensive, had been overtaken by technological advance and had little commercial future. Supporters, including the two public agencies directly involved with TDF1, *Télédiffusion de France* and the *Centre National des Etudes Spatiales*, and firms with interests in space or electronics, dismissed these criticisms as a ploy by the Directorate-General to protect its interest in cable and its own low-powered satellite. Despite anxiety over rising costs the project was confirmed by the Fabius Government, and protracted negotiations continued over which services should use it, including Byzantine manoeuvres to dissuade Luxembourg from joining an American group to cover France from its own Lux-Sat. However, technical difficulties with TDF1 and Ariane caused delays, and then the announcement of private land-based networks killed any lingering hope of entrepreneurs putting up risk capital.

In 1986 the new Right-wing government again questioned the future of TDF1. The Cabinet was divided, with ministers lining up behind their client bureaucracies and client interest groups. Eventually Chirac ruled, over the public opposition of his Minister of the Budget, that the project should continue. TDF1 was to be

Europe's champion in resisting the Japanese standard for the new generation of high definition television.

TDF1 suffered further delay when its West German sister failed to deploy in November 1987. After the 1988 elections the Rocard Government pondered cancellation yet again, but with some £550 000 000 spent or committed there seemed little point, although all hope of commercial success had vanished. Expenditure had now outrun *Télédiffusion's* resources and the public-sector Directorate-General of Telecommunications (now France-Télécom) was summoned to inject cash and form a joint operating company which would decide whether to proceed with the back-up satellite TDF2: not unlike giving the wolf a casting vote on the fate of Red Riding Hood. TDF1 finally became operational in 1989, at almost the same time as Luxembourg's lighter, cheaper eight-channel Astra. The expected lead had dwindled to nothing.

Characteristic of a project based so heavily on industrial and technological considerations, even as it was launched and after nine years of discussion, the issue of what programmes its five channels would carry (at giveaway rentals) remained unresolved. France now had two incompatible systems delivering satellite broadcasts. It remained to be seen whether either could survive.

Cable

That other 'technology of the future', cable, proved as problematic as satellite broadcasting and as slow to bear fruit. It was neglected until the Socialists came to power in 1981, glimpsing the exciting prospect of covering the country with fibre-optic cable carrying up to 30 television channels, including local productions, videolibrary and videotex services and a wide range of interactive telematic developments. Cable was backed by important industrial interests and the Directorate-General of Telecommunications – its reputation riding high in the wake of its successful modernisation of the telephone network – was pressing to be the agent of French leadership of Europe in information technology. Unlike satellite transmission, cable posed no threat to sovereignty; since content lay entirely within domestic control, some even saw it as a cultural Maginot Line preventing alien invasion of French television screens, and it offered hopes of decentralisation and participation in tune with the new government's aspirations.

In 1982 the Mauroy Government endorsed a Cable Plan for 1 500 000 homes to be cabled over five years at a cost of around £600 000 000. Installation and much of the initial financing would be undertaken by the Directorate-General, which saw the Plan as guaranteeing its landline monopoly into the foreseeable future. The operating companies were to be public–private consortia approved by the High Audiovisual Authority, with local authorities contributing 30 per cent of the initial investments. Adoption of new-technology fibre-optic cable, though costing 50 per cent more than traditional cable, would guarantee the future of the fibre-optic industry. The question of who would bear this additional cost was left unresolved.

In 1983 an Interdepartmental Mission for the Development of Teledistribution Services was created to promote cable and ensure sufficient programmes during the period when subscribers would be too few for production to be economic, with the risk of imports swamping the market. What the government failed to face, despite its ambition to have a coherent communications policy, was whether cable and satellite could be successfully developed simultaneously: whether sufficient homes would be prepared both to subscribe to cable and incur the additional capital costs of satellite reception.

The plan soon ran into difficulties. Local politicians were excited by the electoral attractions of cable but appalled by installation costs three times the initial estimates and by the implications of the introduction of private commercial television. When the government granted them preferential rates the Directorate-General of Telecommunications became alarmed by a programme taking fifteen years to reach 55–60 per cent of the population and incurring astronomical cost, with a rapidly diminishing prospect of profit. Hopes that cable would simultaneously combine the industrial dimension of fibre-optic development, the democratic dimension of decentralisation and the cultural dimension of participation and interactivity faded.

As with satellites the government pressed forward despite mounting doubts. Though still unwilling to let the cable companies take advertising because of press hostility, it conceded lighter 'quality control' of content. Even so, progress was painfully slow. When the Socialists left office in 1986 only one system was fully operational. By this time the Directorate-General had radically changed its line. Abandoning its advocacy of a single network for all landline transmission systems it now favoured splitting television relay from telematics and telecommunications and letting local authorities choose between fibre-optic and copper-coaxial systems. This meant abandoning the earlier vision of France becoming the first comprehensively 'wired society'.

In 1987 the Cable Plan was abandoned. Facing the prospect of deregulation in telecommunications and no longer prepared to cross-subsidise cable from telephone revenues, the Directorate-General of Telecommunications persuaded the Chirac Government that its financial stability and perhaps its very future were at stake. The 52 towns which had signed contracts would get their systems eventually; others would have to wait. Future development would be on a television-only basis with coaxial cable. Even so, installation was slow and consumer response still slower though, with its preference for reliance on market forces, the Chirac Government had relaxed requirements for French and local programming still further. By the end of 1988 cable had swallowed up some £1 200 000 000, with as much again firmly committed, but of the fourteen local systems operating hardly any were reaching even 10 per cent of their market, and none was as yet profitable. Yet it was premature to dismiss cable as a failure. Some towns were installing newer, cheaper systems, and entrepreneurs were coming forward with a variety of 'thematic packages' for them. Cable might have a future after all. However, after years of plans, working parties and debates, and massive inputs of public capital, the outcome would fall far short of the heady social vision with which it began.

Conclusion

That view could well serve as a general verdict on France's handling of media policy. Unlike Britain and the USA, which made no attempt to develop comprehensive policies, France tried to achieve an integrated approach meeting a wide range of policy objectives. The enterprise was difficult, perhaps impossible, when technology was changing so rapidly and the capacity to impose solutions was slipping beyond the reach of any individual state and also when political vicissitudes repeatedly created paralysing uncertainties and delays. Even governments that were firmly in the saddle often failed to follow coherent policies or grasp the implications of their actions for other declared policy objectives. Difficult decisions were evaded, notably the choice between satellite and cable, where failure to choose damaged both and squandered public funds. Deregulation, while sometimes a matter of deliberate choice, was as often the accidental by-product of expedients aimed at compensating one section for the unconsidered consequences of concessions granted to another. Whatever its merits, it conflicted with the declared aims of reviving the production industry and promoting French cultural interests. The outcome of a decade of constant government action was one that virtually nobody had initially sought to contrive. However, the emergence of a system which is more deregulated, more distanced from governmental dictation and has more protection against undue concentration of ownership and control appears to have won something approaching consensus; or perhaps, for the time being at least, the politics of will have simply given way to the politics of exhaustion.

14

Immigration and Politics

MARTIN A. SCHAIN

Since the period of the Third Republic France has welcomed, and at times encouraged, successive waves of immigration. Almost 10 per cent of the French population in 1982 was foreign-born, a percentage considerably higher than that of any other European country and 30 per cent higher than the foreign-born population of the USA. During this long period of immigration, a network of social and political institutions – among which have been the centralised school system, the Catholic church, the army, trade unions and the political parties of the Left – have played an effective role in integrating new immigrants into French social, economic and political life. Although there were numerous instances of anti-immigrant violence, some anti-immigrant movements and high levels of anti-immigrant sentiment in France since the turn of the century, these institutions have been relatively successful in limiting and controlling ethnic-based social violence. They have also managed to keep issues of immigration and ethnic divisions on the periphery of the political process.

In the 1980s, however, this pattern seemed to be changing. Although levels of immigration had been declining sharply since 1974 (when immigration was largely halted) the political importance of immigration seemed to be increasing. It was first raised at national level by the PCF in the presidential campaign of 1981, was an important issue in the local elections of 1983 and became a centrepiece of the election campaigns of 1984, 1986 and 1988.

Immigration as a political issue was clearly magnified when public sentiment was mobilised in the electoral rise of the FN after 1983. Immigration rapidly became an important element of party competition; it forced all other parties to reconsider their own positions on immigration and vastly complicated relations within the Right and the Left. The politicisation of anti-immigrant sentiment has also prompted the organisation of pro-immigrant groups. We shall first examine the change in patterns of immigration in France and then analyse the impact of immigration on the political system.

Changing Patterns of Immigration

The French pattern of high immigration has been unique in Europe and is related to birth rates, which began to decline in France a full century earlier than in the rest of Europe. France is the only European country which has imported manpower since 1850. France recruited many of its engineers, its workers and its soldiers from beyond its frontiers (Long, 1988, vol. 1, p. 23). However, both the level of resident immigrants and the composition of the immigrant population has changed considerably. As the French birth rate declined and as the economy expanded, the proportion of resident immigrants in the population rose steadily from 1 per cent in 1850 to 6.6 per cent at the beginning of the depression in 1931. In the earliest years, the largest number came from Belgium and then, increasingly, from Italy, Poland and Spain. After the Second World War, the percentage of resident immigrants rose once again, from 4.4 per cent in 1946 to 6.8 per cent in the 1980s. During this period, the percentage of European residents (mostly from Italy and Spain until the mid-1960s, and increasingly from Portugal after that) grew a little more than 13 per cent, while Third World residents, mostly from North Africa, increased more than fourteen times. By the 1980s, a majority of the 3.7 million resident immigrants in France were from Third World countries. If we add to these the almost 300 000 migrants from the French overseas territories that have now settled on the mainland, there are now about 2 150 000 Third World immigrants in France.

Immigrant communities increasingly consist of families rather than simply workers. The percentage of immigrants active in the workforce has been declining steadily during the 1980s and is only 42 per cent of the resident immigrant population. Because immigrant families tend to be considerably larger than those of the native French, the proportion of immigrants in schools is greater than their proportion in the general population. By 1981–2 almost 10 per cent of the primary school children were from immigrant families, about half of whom were non-European (mostly from

North Africa). In the Paris region with 24 per cent of immigrant children in schools it was somewhat lower but the proportion of non-European children was higher. By the 1980s, the vast majority of immigrants in France were resident families, mostly from outside Europe, who were not French citizens but who would remain in France.

For the most part, immigrants have come to France for the same reasons for the last hundred years. Many were recruited to work in France. Some were looking for work in an expanding economy (at least until 1973). Others came to join family members already in the country. In 1945, in response to an anticipated need for large numbers of additional workers for post-war reconstruction, France approved new legislation that would facilitate the recruitment of temporary foreign labour. At the heart of the post-war system was the ONI, which established offices in major labour-exporting countries, and recruited labour needed to work in such industries as construction, mining, steel, cars and chemical industries. In principle, all immigrant workers were channelled through ONI. The idea, favoured by the Communist Minister of Labour in the first post-war government, was that temporary immigrant workers would provide a flexible labour force that could be controlled through work permits (Ashford, 1982). According to most accounts this system worked well until the late 1950s, when it began to break down under the pressure of increased demand for labour caused by rapid economic expansion.

Employers began to recruit workers directly, bypassing ONI. They then sometimes arranged to have these workers 'regularised' after they were already in the country. Thus a pattern of illegal immigration emerged during the 1960s, which was initiated by labour-hungry employers and openly tolerated by the state. A Minister of Labour argued that illegal immigration 'was not without usefulness, since if we had stuck to strict application of international regulations and agreements, we would have perhaps lacked manpower' (*Les Echos*, 29 March 1966). By 1968, it was estimated that only a fifth of immigrant workers had entered the country legally. In 1968, a government circular made the 'regularisation' processes official and the state continued subsequently to 'regularise' the status of large numbers of immigrants on the request of employers or on a group basis. Much of the pressure for immigration was therefore based on the anarchic recruitment of workers by employers and on the permissive, even encouraging, attitude of the state.

There was also a pressure which derived from the process of decolonisation. When Algeria achieved independence in 1962, the

French agreed to accept an unlimited number of Algerians in France, although a quarter of the Algerian workforce was already in France. The Algerian Government encouraged these workers to remain there and to continue to send millions of francs back to Algeria. The yearly limits on Algerian immigration were later renegotiated several times and their success or failure became an important factor in Algerian politics. Although the level of immigration from black Africa has been low, limits here were also set through bilateral agreements that were part of French efforts to develop stable relations with former colonies. Immigration limits on Moroccans and Tunisians were negotiated in the same way. Thus, during the 1960s, immigration from former colonies was encouraged and accelerated by foreign policy considerations, as well as labour market needs (Ashford, 1982, pp. 269–74).

Immigration Policy

By the late 1960s pressure was beginning to develop for a new immigration policy. The number of new jobs being added to the French economy was declining each year but the number of foreigners, especially those from North Africa, was still increasing at a rapid rate. What emerged was a series of confused and changing policy initiatives that reflected the conflict between an understanding of immigration as a labour market problem and as a problem of integration and ethnic conflict. On one hand, the French government attempted to curtail immigration; first, through more restrictive bilateral agreements, then through administrative circulars that made regularisation contingent upon labour market conditions, as well as adequate housing (the Marcellin and Fontanet circulars in 1972, both struck down by the Council of State in 1975) and finally by halting regularisation in 1973. In July 1974, at a time of economic crisis, France closed its borders entirely to immigration except for seasonal workers, political refugees and family reunification.

By that time, the problem was being perceived as one of a large resident population that was culturally different from the native French population, rather than simply immigration. In 1975, the Third World population comprised almost 38 per cent of the total immigrant population; by 1982 it was well over half of a larger immigrant population. An official 1978 study concluded that only a third of immigration after 1974 was for work. Most of the remainder was either for family reunification or for political reasons (*Données Sociales*, 1987, p. 28). The vast majority of workers who were legal immigrants after 1974 were either from EC countries or were seasonal workers. The French Ministry of Labour figures indicate a precipitous drop of non-EC workers after 1974 but an undiminished number of family members until 1981 (*Données Sociales*, 1984, p. 34).

By the mid-1970s, more concerted action was taken to curtail the number of immigrants. Detention and expulsions of illegal immigrants (those in the country without proper papers) and sanctions against employers who employed them were increased. In July 1977 family reunification was suspended (although this was reversed by the Council of State in December 1978) and a programme of incentives for workers who returned home was instituted. In the late 1970s, increased efforts were made to halt illegal immigration at the frontiers by turning back large numbers of North Africans, particularly Algerians, at airports. Air police began to demand papers and guarantees that were not required by the bilateral agreements to discourage immigrants. Refusals of entry were stepped up under the Socialist Government between 1981 and 1986, and then further increased by the Chirac Government during 1986–8. Considerable muscle was put behind these efforts by the Pasqua Law and the re-establishment of visas in September 1986, the effects of which were to place much of the burden of entry controls on the consulates in North Africa and to force immigrants to demonstrate their ability to be housed and supported before they were permitted to enter the country.

The state simultaneously increased efforts to police the immigrant communities through increased expulsions, directed against both legal and illegal immigrants who 'constituted a menace to public order'. In 1980, the Bonnet Law widened the criteria for expulsion, although its effects were softened by an amnesty a few months later. Expulsions, even before the Bonnet Law, were high (more than 4,000 a year) but then declined to almost zero when the Socialist Government abandoned the procedures in 1981.

The commitment of the French state to halting immigration was not changed by the Socialist Government. The Mauroy Government did, however, substantially change the means by which this commitment was implemented. Legislation in October 1981 guaranteed due process of law before expulsion could take place and exempted certain categories of immigrants from expulsion – minors, long-term residents, spouses of French citizens and parents of French citizens – even if they were a 'threat to public order'. Other administrative actions such as escorting illegal immigrants back to the border, were also limited. The right of legal immigrants to bring their spouses and minor children to France was officially reaffirmed.

As immigration emerged as a divisive political issue during the 1980s, Socialist governments gave greater priority to halting immigration through control at points of entry to the country and by increasingly severe operations against illegal immigrants. Expulsions of undocumented immigrants began to increase during the Socialist years and then jumped again with the Pasqua Law, which reduced many of the benefits of the 1981 legislation (*Libération*, 28 March 1988, pp. 24–6). Thus the number of immigrants who were refused entry under the Socialists was on average more than 40 000 a year after 1981, roughly twice as high as under the previous governments of the Right. The number of immigrants escorted back to the border also grew impressively during the same period. After the passage of the Pasqua Law in September 1986, refusal of entry immediately increased. In 1987, when refusal of entry should have declined because of visa processing in countries of origin, refusals increased to more than 71 000, which was 50 per cent higher than the year before. Stringent control demonstrated the determination of various French governments since the 1970s to master the immigration problem and they have succeeded in reducing legal immigration to a small stream of workers since 1974. Entries for family reunification were about four times the number of entries for work each year after 1974.

The growing stability of the immigrant population was emphasised in a 1976 report by a Communist senator and future minister. He argued that, in spite of the growing pressure to limit immigration, immigrant workers would be likely to remain an integral part of the French workforce (*Le Monde*, 19–20 June 1977). Thus the 1977 programme of incentives for workers to return home liberated very few jobs for the native French. It cost in excess of 500 million francs (about as much as the French job retraining programme) but only 100 000 people (including families) accepted payment to return home over four years. More than two-thirds of those who left were Spanish or Portuguese and only 3.7 per cent were Algerian. The unintentional effect of this programme has been to reduce the number of European and to increase the proportion of North African immigrants in France. The incentive programme was abandoned by the Socialist Government in 1981 but they re-established it in May 1984 (in a slightly different form) when they were under political pressure to 'do something' about growing unemployment.

One of the limits on halting the expansion of immigrant communities has been the relatively generous procedures through which children born in France of non-French parents can automatically gain French citizenship. The Chirac Government thus proposed several modifications of the existing code that would effectively rescind the automatic granting of French citizenship and make the acquisition of French citizenship more difficult for 'the second generation' of immigrant families. By 1986, however, such changes had become symbolically identified with the positions of the extreme Right (the FN), and were opposed both by the Left opposition (including President Mitterrand), as well as by some members of the Centre–Right majority. General social unrest during the winter of 1986–7 encouraged the Chirac Government temporarily to withdraw the legislation and to set up the *Commission de la nationalité* (Commission on Nationality) to propose long-term policy on naturalisation. Its report, which supported parts of what the government had proposed, was presented on the eve of the presidential campaign but its policy recommendations have not yet been followed up by the Socialist Government (Long, 1988, pp. 214–33).

During the 1988 presidential election campaign both the PS and its candidate, Mitterrand, were unusually evasive on how they would deal with immigration and the initiatives that had been taken by the Chirac Government in this area. In his 1989 New Year speech to the nation, however, Mitterrand formally launched a new effort on behalf of immigrants – the excluded and rejected – which was immediately followed by several circulars from the Ministry of the Interior that would limit the application of the Pasqua Law. The government subsequently abrogated this law, strengthening the judicial role in the expulsion process through new legislation, as well as facilitating the naturalisation process through administrative changes.

A second aspect of immigration policy has been a less publicised effort to integrate immigrant families already settled in the country. This effort also began in the early 1970s, under the governments of the Right, and was continued in the 1980s by the Left. This effort, however, was increasingly influenced by the emerging politics of race in France.

When Giscard d'Estaing took office in 1974, one of his first acts was to create a new Cabinet-level post of Secretary of State for Immigration. Immigrant workers were admitted to be an essential part of the labour force, and a programme to deal with their needs was launched. A series of decrees were issued to alleviate the most pressing problems of immigrant families. An amendment to the 1974 Finance Law set aside a portion of the employers' salary tax for the construction of immigrant housing. A series of decrees in 1975 provided that a third of the instruction in primary schools could be in the language of immigrant children and arrangements were made to recruit teachers from the immigrants' home countries. In addition, the rights of immigrant children to university education were protected. In 1976–7, no fewer than 160 000 scholarships were awarded to young people from immigrant families. By contrast with other European countries, the principle of family reunification was established. In 1975, restrictions on immigrant worker participation in unions were rescinded.

As the government attempted to restrict these rights in the late 1970s, they were opposed by political and legal actions of advocacy groups, particularly the Federation of Associations in Solidarity with Immigrant Workers, the Group for Information and Support of Immigrant Workers and the Movement Against Racism. The formal protection of immigrant families against arbitrary administrative action was further strengthened by the actions of the Socialist Government in October 1981, which also removed the restrictions against the establishment of immigrant associations.

In a number of important ways the new government of the Left expanded its involvement in the process of integrating immigrants at the local level. In education, for example, the government initiated 'zones of educational priority' (defined largely in terms of the percentage of immigrant children in the education district) as a basis for increased funding for special education programmes. The national government also began to take a greater interest in problems of urban decay in cities in which there were large proportions of immigrants, through the establishment of national committees linking mayors directly with administrative authorities.

The removal of restrictions against immigrant organisations in France encouraged a proliferation of new social and political organisations to protect immigrant rights, as well as stimulating activism (particularly among young immigrants). By 1985, there were over 4,000 immigrant associations, about a quarter of them organising North Africans (Wihtol de Wenden, 1986, pp. 740–1). Activism emerged among North African assembly line workers who initiated a series of strikes in the 1980s in which Islam was a major mobilising force. Activism had also been expressed through the march against racism by young immigrants in 1983 and by the organisation of *SOS-racisme* in 1984. By 1988 it was a well-established organisation, which claimed 17 000 members and 35 000 contributors. Its leader, Harlem Désir, had become something of a folk hero of the anti-racist cause.

Thus national policies meant to guarantee protection to immigrants resident in France had become important factors in the process of social and political integration. They were, however, often undermined by conflicting policies and arbitrary administrative actions at both the national and the local levels, which became more pronounced as immigration – associated with unemployment and law and order – became a focus of political competition in the 1980s.

The Politics of Race

The evolution of immigration policy can be understood best if we place policy in the context of the emergence of the politics of race in France. In the 1970s, immigration became identified with North African immigration and the issues have since become defined increasingly as problems of race and ethnicity in France. The political issue of immigration has come to focus, first and foremost, on the meaning of French nationality and citizenship.

The emergence of the politics of race was not provoked by any popular backlash against immigrants. Popular feeling against the presence of foreigners – especially North Africans – in France has been strong for some time but it has not grown by most measures. Since the 1960s, between 60 and 65 per cent of those surveyed have found North African immigrants 'too numerous in France'. On the other hand, surveys also indicate a more complex appreciation of the role that immigrants and immigrant workers have played in France, as well as views that are increasingly more tolerant. Since the economic crisis in 1973, a clear majority of those surveyed have agreed that immigrants were useful for the French economy, despite a growing association of immigrants with increasing unemployment (see below). In 1978, 53 per cent of workers surveyed agreed that immigrants were 'indispensable' (11 per cent) or 'useful' (42 per cent) for the French economy. In the early 1980s a growing majority preferred that immigrants share the same housing as French people, supported the presence of immigrant children in primary schools (at least if their number were kept to less than one-third of the children) and opposed efforts by local governments to impose quotas on the percentage of children in municipal summer camps. Thus, opinion towards immigrants has ranged from hostile to receptive, but it has changed relatively little (and not always in predictable ways) since the 1960s.

What have changed are the ways that political parties have approached immigration issues. While governments were wrestling with how to approach immigration at the national level in the

1970s, local authorities were shaping the issues at the local level. At the same time as the Socialist governments of the 1980s were attempting to develop an approach to immigration that would serve to integrate a resident immigrant population in a flexible way, their options were being limited by increased tendencies within the party system towards the mobilisation of anti-immigrant feeling.

The political issues of immigration were nurtured and defined in an urban context, particularly in cities governed by the Left. By 1977, 55 per cent of towns (over 30 000 population) governed by Communist mayors had immigrant populations greater than 10 per cent, compared with 23 per cent for towns governed by Socialists and 21 per cent of towns governed by the Centre–Right. In 1977, 82 per cent of the larger towns with more than 10 per cent immigrant population were governed by the Left and more than two-thirds of these were governed by the PCF. Although there were cities with high concentrations of immigrants governed by the Centre–Right (including Paris and Lyons), large resident immigrant populations were most characteristic of cities governed by the Left.

For the PCF, the emergence of Third World immigrant communities has been a special problem for more than 20 years, since the pattern of immigration ceased to be predominantly European. In 1969, the Communist mayors of the Paris region protested publicly for the first time against what they termed the inequitable distribution of immigrant workers and their families, although these same families had been welcomed as 'victims of racial discrimination'. Communist mayors reiterated their 1969 declaration in somewhat stronger terms and sent delegations to the *préfectures* to protest against what they contended was the maldistribution of immigrants among cities of different political persuasions. Immigrants 'above all' were citizens of their home countries, the PCF reasoned in 1979; they should seek to work there. They should not be given the right to vote in local elections, 'which would imply those obligations which would push for forced integration of the immigrants, and which, consequently, would infringe their national personality' (Wihtol de Wenden, 1986, pp. 513–5). In contrast to 'the tradition of solidarity' that Communist-governed municipalities had developed towards predominantly European immigrants from the very earliest years of their existence, many of these same local governments began to treat non-European immigrants, as well as non-white French citizens from the overseas departments, as temporary residents who must be encouraged to return home.

More exclusionary policies towards immigrants in Communist-governed municipalities were developed through quiet collaboration with departmental and national administrative officials. For example, the municipal government of Venissieux (outside Lyons) took an initiative to exclude immigrant families from a massive housing development, Les Minguettes, in 1977, with the approval and collaboration of the Lyonnaise regional authorities, state authorities and departmental authorities, as well as the various public and private companies which were among the eleven participants that constructed and administered the complex. This pattern was not, however, unique to Venissieux and towns governed by Communists. Virtually every town in the Lyons region, in collaboration with state authorities and those in the *départements*, made the same kind of decisions during the late 1970s to limit the availability of housing for immigrant families based on the notion of a 'threshold of tolerance'. On the initiative of local governments, the state also collaborated in establishing quotas for immigrant children in primary schools.

The way that Communist local governments dealt with the immigrant problem was not very different from the way that most other local governments, regardless of political persuasion, dealt with the same issue. Local governments, by their actions, defined public policy towards immigrants in essentially exclusionary terms. They all tended to define the immigrant problem as an ethnic problem, of native French against non-Western immigrants and citizens from the overseas territories. Their solutions tended to exclude and limit access for these residents. The role of Communist local governments was important in part because it was *not* different from that of the others but also because so many immigrants were concentrated in Communist-governed towns. This automatically meant that they led policy development. By the time of the presidential campaign of 1980–1, the main lines of local policy had been substantially, if quietly, developed.

Thus, when the politics of race surfaced at the local level during the electoral campaign of 1983, the context had already been set. What provoked the more openly racist campaigns in 1983 was considerable frustration with Socialist austerity and the provocation of the campaign of Le Pen's FN party. The anti-immigrant FN had been in existence since 1972 but it was only in 1983 that the party first began to attract an important electoral following. Le Pen himself ran for the Paris city council and the Front presented lists in numerous other towns, encouraged by the 1983 local election law, which incorporated limited proportional representation.

The general anti-immigrant themes raised by the FN were echoed in the candidates of other parties. In the bitter contest in

Marseille (where in 1984 the FN would outpoll the Communists with 21 per cent of the vote and in 1986 would come in just behind the Socialists with 24 per cent of the vote), the minister of the interior and his UDF opponent clashed on who was and who would be more effective in enforcing security and suppressing immigration (*Le Monde*, 11 and 23 March 1983). The worst confrontation on the immigration issue occured in Dreux, where the Socialist mayor had been particularly outspoken on behalf of immigrants. She won in March by eight votes, but voting irregularities forced a third round and she was forced to cede her leadership to a less controversial man. Nevertheless, the FN list, headed by the party's Secretary-General, won 17 per cent of the vote, a united Right list (including the FN) won in the second round and three FN councillors became assistant mayors.

The politics of race began to emerge at the national level in 1980–1, when the PCF orchestrated a national anti-immigrant campaign that was also directed against French citizens from the overseas territories (Schain, 1985, pp. 185–6). The campaign was widely condemned but the reaction to it demonstrated just how effective the PCF had been in defining the terms of the political debate at the national level. Almost everyone accepted the Communist definition of – if not their solution for – the immigrant problem: that immigration concentration posed problems of ethnic-/racial conflict (Wihtol de Wenden, 1981).

The PCF campaign was not successful in mobilising voters, and was opposed by a majority of Communists. Although the party backed down from its strident campaign, during the local election campaign two years later (in a context of Socialist austerity and growing unemployment) rhetoric similar to that of the PCF was used far more successfully by the FN, as well as by other parties of the Right. The growing tendency by the established opposition parties, as well as by the FN, to link immigrants to problems of law and order and growing unemployment fed into the preconceived notions of a large part of the electorate and put local governments of the Left on the defensive. By the 1984 European election campaign, the FN slogan of 'sending the immigrant home' was the centre of political debate and by the 1986 elections the FN had established its level of support at about 10 per cent.

What most clearly differentiated those who voted for the FN from supporters of *all* other parties is the priority given to law and order and immigrant issues, as was shown in the 1984 European elections. This was decidedly more so in 1986 (see Table 14.1.) and probably increased in 1988.

Table 14.1 *The motivations of voters in 1984, 1986 and 1988*[1]

Percentage of voters who voted for:	Law and Order			Immigrants			Unemployment			The economy			Social inequality		
	1984	1986	1988	1984	1986	1988	1984	1986	1988	1984	1986	1988	1984	1986	1988
PCF	9	13	18	2	7	12	37	59	59	14	14	12	33	30	50
PS	8	10	21	3	8	13	27	40	43	11	10	16	24	25	43
RPR/UDF	17	31	44/31	3	16	21/17	20	50	41/41	11	17	35/35	7	8	17/18
FN	30	50	55	26	60	59	17	35	41	6	7	21	10	10	18
Total	15	24	31	6	17	22	24	46	45	10	13	23	16	17	31

Note:
1. Since several responses were possible, the total across may be more than 100 per cent. For 1988, the results are for supporters of presidential candidates nominated by the parties indicated.
Sources: Exit poll, SOFRES/TFI 17 June 1984; *Le Nouvel Observateur*, 22 June 1984; and SOFRES, *Etat de l'opinion, Cles pour 1987* (Paris: Seuil, 1987), p. 111. Pascal Perrineau, 'Les étapes d'une implantation électoral (1972–1988)', in Nonna Mayer and Pascal Perrineau (eds), *Le Front National a découvert* (Paris: Presses de la FNSP, 1989), p. 62.

The FN's electoral success may not endure but it has succeeded in mobilising a large electorate around the issues of race and immigration. Through the dynamics of party competition, it has forced other political parties, especially those of the Right, to place this issue high on their political agenda.

A great deal has been written about the growing Centrism of the French electorate. What is missing from this analysis, however, is an incorporation of the impact of the rise of the FN on the political agenda, as well as a consideration of the issue of immigration. Most French voters do not give priority to the immigration issue, but a *growing* percentage from *all* political parties do and these are the most likely to vote for the FN (see Table 14.1). Moreover, parties are generally most responsible for setting the political agenda. Evidence that the FN has been attractive to RPR activists is provided by a survey of delegates at the RPR national congress in 1984, which found that they perceived themselves to be considerably further to the Right and closer to the positions of the FN than the party as a whole, and much further to the Right than the delegates at the RPR congress in 1978.

The debates within the RPR–UDF about the proper position to take with regard to the FN (coalition or isolation) that raged in May–June 1987 were comparable to the long debate about alliances and coalitions with the PCF that dominated the Left until the 1980s. If the Left was both challenged and divided about the PCF, the Right has been tempted, challenged and divided by the FN. Thus the division of the UDF (and to some extent the RPR after the June 1988 elections) was related to fears and attractions of the growing influence of the FN.

Within the French political elite, there have been some efforts to reach an understanding about the immigration problem that would reconstruct the implicit understanding of the 1970s. Thus there has been a concerted effort by all of the established parties to lower the tone of anti-immigrant rhetoric during the past few years and to isolate the FN.

The national integration imperative that is implicit in the conclusions of the Long Commission on French Nationality seems to have been generally accepted as a basis for political understanding. Thus in January 1989, the prime minister's office informed the press that 'the only time that the [immigration] problem was treated sanely was during the presidency of M Valéry Giscard d'Estaing'. A month later, the prime minister spoke of immigrants becoming 'Frenchmen of foreign origin', who are beginning to demand 'a right to indifference'. Until recently, Socialists had emphasised the right to be different. On the Right, the RPR and UDF effectively enforced their decision against alliances with the FN in the 1989 local elections.

Nevertheless, divergent political pressures from the FN and from better organised immigrant groups have made an understanding difficult to sustain. The FN has not disappeared and is slowly developing roots at the local level. Although the party did not win sweeping victories in the 1989 local elections, it did achieve considerable presence, with 330 municipal councillors in more than a third of towns with a population of over 20 000. The mere mention of reform of immigration policy by the president evoked sensitive outcries from the opposition, who accused Mitterrand of attempting to divide the Right.

Moreover, it is not at all clear that 'Frenchmen of foreign origin' will be content with 'a right to indifference'. By 1989, many of them seemed determined not to be the objects of politics and were becoming increasingly active in electoral politics. In preparation for the 1989 local elections, *France Plus* organised and bargained for places on the electoral lists of established parties for candidates that they endorsed as representatives of immigrant communities. *France Plus* registered about 450 000 immigrants with citizen rights on electoral lists during 1985–8, and have turned their considerable energy towards directly sponsoring candidates. In 1989 no fewer than 572 candidates ran with their endorsement: 55 per cent on Socialist lists, 2 per cent on Communist lists and the remainder on lists of the parties of the Right. Although there were more

France Plus candidates on the Left, they were better placed on lists of the Right.

Conclusion

The political debate over immigration and integration policy has been shaped by the emerging political forces that have defined the issues and the solutions. As the immigrant population became increasingly non-European, political forces of both the Left and the Right began to see this population as non-assimilable. At the same time an immigrant worker population, with roots in other countries, was transformed into a resident population, 60 per cent of whom were not in the workforce at all. They shopped in the supermarket, lived down the street and their children began to go to school in increasing numbers.

The influx of a large number of resident immigrant families produced social tensions, the reactions to which were defined, shaped and magnified by political forces. In the early 1970s immigration was cut off, except for seasonal workers and family reunifications, but national policy-makers adopted a series of measures to facilitate the integration of immigrant families already in the country. Much of this effort was undermined, however, by locally-elected office holders who collaborated with field officials of the national ministries to exclude non-European residents from housing and schools, regardless of their citizenship status, as well as by national efforts to halt immigration.

In the 1980s, the FN was able to occupy the political space first opened up by the PCF and mobilise anti-immigrant sentiment in racist terms. Although the electoral success of the FN created a clear political dilemma for other parties of the Right, it also moved the definition of the immigrant problem away from the emphasis on integration preferred by the Socialists and many deputies of the Right and the Centre and towards policy choices that would more clearly limit the number of non-Europeans in the country.

Party competition and conflict around the immigrant problem has magnified the importance of the issue for voters of all political persuasions. Although very few voters ranked immigration high as a reason for making their electoral choices in the early 1980s, the percentage had grown impressively by the late 1980s. In addition, mobilisation of partisans for and against immigrant rights had also grown by 1989.

Finally, the debate about immigration and the problem of immigrants has challenged the integrative capacity of the country which has had a legendary capacity to make foreigners into Frenchmen. As the Commission on Nationality argued: 'In the process of integration that we are experiencing today, the population has . . . changed [compared to former times], but perhaps even more, the forms of . . . integration, the nature of the social linkages that unite the whole population in France, national and foreign, [have also changed]' (Long, 1988, p. 27).

15

The Politics of Scandal

STEPHEN E. BORNSTEIN

Introduction

In politics, a scandal may be said to occur when important public figures are widely suspected of contravening prevailing standards of acceptable public or private behaviour and often of attempting to conceal their actions through further illegal or deceitful acts as well (Lowi, 1989, pp. vii–viii). Scandals of this sort have been a very prominent feature of recent French politics. In the 1985 Greenpeace affair, for example, the Minister of Defence, the president's personal military attaché and the director of the Secret Service apparently hatched and implemented a bizarre plan to protect the country's nuclear testing activities in the South Pacific by having military frogmen blow up a boat belonging to the Greenpeace organisation while it was moored in Auckland, New Zealand. The French Government earnestly denied any responsibility for the attack, but persistent efforts by French journalists led to the gradual revelation of the involvement not only of French undercover agents but also of the Minister of Defence, Charles Hernu, and to suspicions that the president himself had personally approved the project. Although the president and the prime minister managed to dodge the bullet, Hernu was forced to resign (Derogy and Pontaut, 1986; Bornstein, 1989).

The Carrefour scandal came to light in 1986 and made the headlines periodically during 1987. It involved a potent blend of money, power, sex and secrecy. Christian Nucci, the Minister of Cooperation (as regards France's relations with her former colonies in Africa), and his chief aide, Yves Chalier, were accused of diverting large sums to fund political campaigns, dubious real

269

estate transactions by a phoney international development agency called 'le Carrefour du développement', and, in Chalier's case, a certain amount of personal self-indulgence involving mistresses, travel, cars and apartments. As if this were not enough, after the 1986 election the new Minister of the Interior, Charles Pasqua, allegedly sought to embarrass the previous Socialist Government by helping Chalier to leave the country with an officially forged passport; he then invoked national security to block the courts from investigating his role (Derogy and Pontaut, 1987).

Another fascinating scandal is the so-called sniffer aeroplane affair. It involves events which took place in the late 1970s but that did not come to light until 1983 when it was alleged that President Giscard d'Estaing and Albin Chalandon, President of the publicly-owned oil firm, ELF, had authorised the illegal transfer of nearly a billion francs to Swiss bank accounts supposedly to pay for the secret development of a revolutionary technology that would make it possible for aircraft to detect (sniff) underground oil and mineral deposits from the air. The technology and the supposed inventors involved were so patently implausible that some observers have suggested that what was involved here was not a misguided venture in secret, state-sponsored industrial innovation but rather a scheme for allowing ELF to transfer huge sums into its own secret foreign accounts to be used for intelligence activities and illegal political contributions (Wolton, 1989, pp. 253–71).

The Luchaire affair resembles the American Iran–Contra scandal, although it lacks some of the latter's more sinister dimensions. A financially troubled, politically well-connected arms producer, the Luchaire company, allegedly received the authorisation of very highly placed officials in the Socialist Government to violate the international embargo on arms sales to Iran. Substantial kickbacks from these illegal sales are said to have made their way into the coffers of the governing party (*Le Point*, 9 November 1987; *Le Monde*, 18 November 1987 and 23 December 1987).

The Société Générale scandal and the Péchiney affair also have a distinctly American ring to them. In both cases, highly placed officials in the Socialist Government are alleged to have allowed their friends, and their party as well, to reap substantial profits by providing them with secret information concerning up-coming financial transactions involving, in the first case, an attempted hostile take-over of the newly 'privatised' banking conglomerate, the Société Générale, and, in the second, the take-over by publicly-owned Péchiney of a major United States firm, American Can. In the Société Générale case, the suspects were in the entourage of the Minister of Finance while, in the Péchiney affair, windfall profits on the purchase of American Can shares were made by, among others, a close personal friend of the president (*Le Monde*, 14, 23 and 26 January 1989 and 3 February 1989; *Manchester Guardian Weekly* 29 January 1989).

The 'affair of the Vincennes Irishmen', finally, bears a certain similarity to Watergate. In the wake of a rash of terrorist bombings and assassination attempts, President Mitterrand appointed Christian Prouteau (a veteran police official) to set up a secret anti-terrorist group directly responsible to him and his staff. Prouteau appears to have engaged in a wide variety of illegal and semi-legal actions of the burglary and wire-tapping variety and to have generated considerable resentment within the regular police and security forces. What got him into trouble, finally, was his attempt to satisfy the President's mania concerning security and terrorism by planting arms and explosives in an apartment in the Paris suburb of Vincennes occupied by a pair of Irishmen connected to the Irish Republican Army (Derogy and Pontaut, 1986, Ch. 1).

It would be amusing to devote the rest of this essay to a fuller discussion of the intricate and titillating details of these and other recent French 'affairs': to indulge, that is, in what one commentator has labelled, 'the pleasure of politics as a spectator sport' (Logue, 1988, p. 254). This chapter will not succumb to that temptation because these scandals can provide the opportunity for an even more interesting intellectual exercise. A major scandal can be to the political scientist what a solar eclipse is to the astronomer: for a few precious moments, the inner workings of an entire political system are suddenly made visible to those outside the tiny circle of privileged insiders. And a *set* of such affairs can be all the more revealing because it allows us to detect important, but otherwise hidden, patterns and peculiarities in a nation's political institutions, processes and culture. The pages that follow attempt to take advantage of the opportunities for comparative political analysis provided by the plethora of recent French scandals. In order to analyse the distinctive features of French politics revealed by such affairs, four questions will be studied: the *nature* of French scandals, their *causation*, their *consequences* and their *developmental tendencies*.

The Nature of French Scandals

The first question that springs to mind when we survey the scandals of the 1980s in France from a comparative perspective concerns their nature, by which I mean the kind of misdeeds that were involved. Anthony King has claimed that political scandals tend to be about one or more of three things: sex, money and power (King, 1986). The French scandals just described display a very striking pattern: money and power are pervasive in them, sometimes singly and sometimes in combination, but sex is almost nowhere to be found. Greenpeace was about the misuse of state power, as was the Vincennes terrorist affair; all the other scandals involved the interaction of power and money. It is only in the Carrefour affair that we get a faint whiff of sexual dalliance, but even here the protagonists' sexual adventures remain of very secondary importance. The absence of sexual scandals in France is not, furthermore, simply a feature of the most recent period. Even if we go back to the Fourth Republic, we find no important scandal in which the sexual misconduct of political leaders was the primary issue (Williams, 1970).

How can we account for this intriguing pattern? Though any answer to this question is bound to remain highly speculative, I suggest that the key can be found in the existence of a consensus shared by both political actors and journalists: namely, that the personal lives and amorous activities of politicians are not an appropriate subject for public discussion. This unspoken convention is, we may surmise, grounded in a broader tolerance of adultery and (probably somewhat less so) of homosexuality than is found among less profoundly bourgeois and sophisticated political elites such as those in North America. This tolerance probably derives in part from the country's religious sociology: until recently, divorce was quite uncommon and marital problems were resolved not by the courts but via extra-marital affairs.

That this unspoken convention is rarely broken is partly attributable to the comparative absence in French popular culture of the sort of prurient, voyeuristic Puritanism that is so prominent in the USA or Britain. It is also due, I think, to the existence in French political culture of a deeply-rooted demarcation between public and private life. France's long experience of monarchy may be credited with establishing the basis for such a separation through its careful differentiation between the monarchy as a historically-rooted political institution and its current incumbent as a mortal and fallible individual. In addition, the profound elitism that has continued to characterise French society despite revolutions and republics has perpetuated a widely held sense that the country's political leaders are, despite all their failings, a sort of natural elite with a variety of justifiable privileges including that of having their private lives protected from the scrutiny of ordinary citizens.

The country's Catholic culture may also be said to have contributed to this separation through its careful differentiation of public figures, both religious and secular, from ordinary men and women and through its emphasis on the external and ceremonial dimensions of religious life rather than on the internal moral and spiritual dispositions that are held to be essential for salvation in most varieties of Protestantism. The same can be said, moreover, of the profoundly bourgeois nature of modern French elite culture with its overriding concern for appearance and for what others will think rather than for the substantive ethical content of one's actions and style of life.

The Causes of Scandal

When we turn our attention from the content of French political scandals to their *causation*, matters become even more interesting. Here, the principal question to resolve is why have recent French politics been so scandal-ridden? The answer lies in a variety of distinctive features that can be found in four areas of French political life: political institutions, political processes and practices, social organisation and political culture.

Institutional Factors

At the institutional level, the most important source of the Fifth Republic's propensity for scandal is the extraordinary concentration of power and initiative in the Executive and especially in the presidency. This hypertrophy of executive authority has affected almost all areas of policy-making but it has been especially pronounced in the areas of defence, foreign and colonial policy, and national security (Cohen, 1986, pp. 9–32). And it has been precisely in these areas that the overweaning power of the French Executive appears to have led it astray in recent years. What made possible the misdeeds and attempted cover-ups in the Greenpeace, Luchaire, sniffer aeroplanes, Prouteau business and the two insider-trading cases were the hegemonic role of the president, the existence of broad areas of policy that had come to be regarded as the 'special preserve' of the presidency, the subordinate role assigned by the constitution and constitutional practice to the prime minister and, finally, the absence in France of any well-established tradition of Cabinet government and collective responsibility. All of these together allowed the president, his top aides and an inner circle of ministers to make dubious decisions in secret and to cut out of the decision loop many members of the government who might have been more squeamish, or more politically circumspect, than they were.

What makes the powers of the French Executive all the more troublesome and scandal-prone is the weakness of the structures that elsewhere serve as effective countervailing forces to Executive abuses. The French legislature, to begin with, is one of the weakest in the Western world as a result not only of the changes in its role introduced by the 1958 constitution but also of three decades of majority control by parties subservient to various presidents. The National Assembly lacks not only effective initiative in legislative matters but also most of the tools required for effectively scrutinising the actions of the Executive: control over its own agenda, an efficient committee system, the capacity to create effective investigatory commissions, the resources and expertise to evaluate the budget and a meaningful question period.

Similarly, the French judicial system lacks the resources and independence required for sanctioning Executive misdeeds. The judiciary is tightly bound to the Executive which controls its courts, judges and prosecutors through the Ministry of Justice, and its investigating magistrates and police officials through the Ministry of the Interior. The autonomy of judges and investigating magistrates is heavily compromised by the fact that their appointments, promotions and assignments are closely controlled by the Executive through the Superior Judicial Council, and neither is there in the Fifth Republic any mechanism for creating the sort of 'special prosecutors' that have played such an important role in recent American scandals or the kinds of prestigious autonomous ('royal') commissions used in Britain and the Commonwealth countries for the same purpose. Similarly, the sort of quasi-judicial regulatory and investigatory bodies that serves, in other countries, to restrict the freedom of manoeuvre of politicians and bureaucrats and to prevent (or at least render more difficult) various forms of misconduct tends in France to be weak, understaffed and legally toothless. Key personnel, moreover, usually consists of civil servants who are merely on temporary leave from their ministries and whose careers continue, therefore, to depend on pleasing their former and future political masters (Coignard and Lacan, 1989, pp. 45–6). It is this lack of real autonomy that helps to explain why, for example, the *Commission des opérations boursières* (Stock Exchange Regulatory Commission) did nothing about the allegations brought to it concerning the Péchiney case until it was dragged into action by the activities of American investigators (Coignard and Lacan, 1989, p. 131).

Several features of French public administration also deserve mention. France stands somewhere between the British (and Commonwealth) tradition of a politically neutral, permanent Civil Service and the 'spoils system' of the United States. In Britain a minister's principal civil servants, with their broad powers and their commitment to an ethos of non-partisan public service, provide a formidable obstacle to corrupt or unfair behaviour (King, 1986, p. 197). In France, and increasingly so since the mid-1970s, the key posts in the staffs of Cabinet ministers tend to be occupied by political appointees attached not to the department but to the minister and/or the minister's party. Sharing as they do their minister's partisan views and depending on their minister for their careers, these people have few incentives to blow the whistle on shady operations and may often be leading actors in them. This increasing politicisation of ministerial staffs goes hand in hand with another notable feature of the French administrative system, *pantouflage*: that is, the widespread migration of top civil servants from government jobs into important positions in the private sector. Often, a civil servant's route to private industry will not be direct but will involve a stop-over in a publicly-owned company in the same industrial sector where the official can solidify the personal and professional ties that will be useful to him or her and potential future private employers. What results is a network of connivance and influence, linking private-sector managers with public officials and offering considerable scope for favouritism and corruption, especially given the comparatively broad role played by the French state not only in regulating economic activity but in funding it, promoting it and engaging in it directly.

Political Factors

French political parties are weak, cadre-dominated, top-down organisations that function less as autonomous political forces than as machines for the support of presidential candidates and presidents. As such, even the largest of them provide very little in the way of countervailing power to check potential abuses of power by their leaders. In addition, with their small memberships and low dues, the parties have very limited internal financial resources. For example, the annual income of the Gaullist RPR from membership dues has been estimated to be a mere 15 million francs (Coignard and Lacan, 1989b, p. 330). These parties are, however, called upon to finance frequent and increasingly expensive election campaigns (Chirac's presidential campaign in 1988 apparently cost over 300 million francs). Since there has been no provision for public funding of election campaigns, party activists are thus under intense pressure to find money. In the absence (until quite recently at least) of any legal restrictions on, or scrutiny of, party finances, the temptation for party fund-raisers to engage in all sorts of chicanery becomes hard to resist.

A final feature of political life that has facilitated widespread corruption is the amazingly loose way in which money appears to be handled within French governmental circles. French elected officials at all levels have developed a broad array of methods for augmenting the incomes of their departments and of their parties. The use of these clandestine funds by the political parties and by individual politicians is subject to surprisingly little public scrutiny: neither political parties nor elected officials are required to open their books. Even officially budgeted monies are quite loosely controlled. Especially noteworthy is the existence in each annual state budget of a 'secret fund' that, in recent years has run to some 400 million francs. The money is allotted to the prime minister's office, ostensibly for funding the undercover operations of the secret services, but at least half of it appears to be distributed every month in cash to the staffs of various ministers to be used, with no accounting required, for a variety of purposes (Giesbert, 1986; Coignard and Lacan, 1989a and 1989b).

The Organisation of Civil Society

In addition to political institutions and to political processes, we must also take into consideration the way in which French society is organised. The conventional wisdom that French civil society is, comparatively speaking, quite poorly organised and thus vulnerable to the arbitrary exercise of state power, is no longer entirely apposite. Organisations representing the country's various *private* economic and professional interests are, with the notable exception of the trade unions, no longer as weak as they once were. What French society lacks are large, prestigious *public*-interest groups. The country's civil rights movement, for example, has always been small, and its effectiveness *vis-à-vis* governments of both the Right and the Left has been undermined by its close identification with the PS. Anti-nuclear movements, peace groups, and ecology organisations have also been comparatively small. The recent emergence of the anti-racist youth movement, *SOS-racisme*, has done something to correct this lacuna but only with regard to a few policy areas. The absence in France of effective, non-partisan, citizens' advocacy groups (such as America's Common Cause or its Public Interest Research Groups) makes the scope for political and bureaucratic excesses considerably broader than it might otherwise be.

A final component of French society deserving of comment is the news media. Independent and effective media not only bring scandals to light but can help to prevent them as well: the successful uncovering of the wrongdoings of major actors will, it is safe to say, make other prospective violators think more carefully before abusing the power of their own offices. The French media, however, are relatively poorly equipped to serve as detectors of, and deterrents to, scandal. The French press lacks a tradition of effective, non-partisan investigative journalism, and the daily press in particular, is heavily dependent both on government grants and on big business interests. Radio and television in France have traditionally been tightly controlled by the state; recent liberalisation measures, such as the ending of the state's monopoly on FM stations, the licensing of several privately owned television networks and the establishment of a non-governmental council to supervise the audiovisual media have not done very much to increase the real independence or investigatory efficacy of radio and television public affairs programming (see Chapter 13).

French Political Culture

The final place to look for answers to our second question is in the attitudes of French elites and of the French citizenry at large. Here, we can find a whole series of widely shared values and attitudes that seem relevant. To begin with, we find among both French political leaders and the French public a rather low level of commitment to what might be called the *procedural* component of democracy as compared with its *substantive* component, in that the French appear to conceive of democracy as concerning equality more than liberty (or at least the liberty of others). Thus, for example, 55 per cent of respondents said they would be made 'unhappy' by the elimination of long-term unemployment benefits and 44 per cent by the abolition of the right to abortion, but only 26 per cent by the suppression of the newspaper *Libération*, 19 per cent by that of the Communist paper, *L'Humanité*, 37 per cent by the suppression of the RPR, and only 28 per cent by the elimination of mosques (SOFRES, 1988, pp. 175–6). French political leaders as well as ordinary citizens seem, similarly, to have a much greater fascination with the state and a much more generous vision of its legitimate requirements than do the politicians and citizens of many other liberal democracies. Thus, when Minister of the Interior Pasqua said – in justification of his refusal to allow investigation of his ministry's role in the Carrefour affair – that 'democracy stops where the interests of the State begin' (*Le Monde*, 28 February 1987), very few protests were to be heard from French politicians, commentators or citizens. This willingness of French elites and mass publics to allow *raison d'Etat* to prevail over civil liberties is especially prevalent in matters of foreign affairs, defence and colonial policy. One of the clearest lessons of the Greenpeace affair is the strength of the consensus that has developed in French elite and mass opinion, not only on nuclear weaponry and on France's colonial possessions (what Mitterrand called 'France's rights in the South Pacific') but also more broadly on a highly chauvinistic vision of France's role in world affairs, and on a defensive – some might say paranoid – view of the pervasive threats to France's international status and also on a highly cynical attitude towards the role of force as compared to that of reason or ethics in international relations (SOFRES, 1988, pp. 181, 208; SOFRES, 1986, p. 211).

A final aspect of French political culture which may be said to contribute to French politicians' propensity for unseemly behaviour is the pervasive cynicism among both elites and masses concerning the nature of political action. For the French, politics is by necessity a dirty business, part of the 'world of the ignoble', in which little in the way of ethical behaviour is to be expected (Grosser, 1982, p. 143). While the French are very impressed by the State, they are much less impressed by politicians, whom they regard as a fundamentally dishonest and self-seeking lot regardless of their political colouration (SOFRES, 1986, p. 241 and 1988, pp. 222–3; Mermet, 1988, p. 224). As such, they do not tend to pay much attention to news of political wrongdoing or to sanction politicians implicated in scandals.

The Limited Impact of French Scandals

Having dealt with our first and second questions we can now turn to the third: why French scandals seem to leave so few lasting marks. French scandals have not brought about the collapse of a government or the resignation of a president or prime minister; none appears to have had much impact on voters' choices, none produced major shifts in policy or legislation. Many of the scandals, moreover, have remained unresolved, with crucial questions of responsibility left hanging and investigative reports swept into drawers. At present, investigations and/or prosecutions remain incomplete in the Luchaire scandal, the Carrefour, the 'sniffer aeroplanes', the Prouteau and the two insider-trading affairs, as well as a number of other less spectacular scandals not discussed here. These buried scandals join a long list of unresolved affairs from earlier years: the Ben Barka kidnapping, the Giscard-Bokassa diamonds scandal, the suicide of Robert Boulin and the murder of the Duc de Broglie, to name but a few. Even when investigations have been completed and responsibility apportioned, morever, very few careers are broken, or made, by French scandals.

How can we explain the seeming immunity of the French body politic to this plague of scandals? To begin with, in virtually all of the scandals under considerations, the opposition parties played a very cautious and moderate role, using hesitantly and ineffectively even the limited resources available to them in Parliament (Bornstein, 1989, pp. 109–11). The major parties appear to be operating under a sort of unspoken consensus that scandals should not be allowed to fester too long nor enquiries to delve too deeply. This consensus derives from a variety of motives. In those scandals involving national defence and foreign relations, the key ingredient is that all the major parties have shared, since the late 1970s at least, the same chauvinistic vision of France's place in the world and the same hard-nosed view of the sort of policies required to cultivate it. In addition, in these scandals (as in those involving domestic activities such as party financing, insider trading, abuse of police powers and so on) what keeps the opposition from an all-out attack would seem to be what one pair of commentators has called 'deterrence': the opposition parties go easy on the current majority because they know that their opponents know that they, too, have closets full of skeletons (Coignard and Lacan, 1989, p. 328). Finally, in some of these scandals – and particularly in those such as Greenpeace, Luchaire, Péchiney and Société Générale and Prouteau, involving allegations of wrongdoing in *very* high places – what seems to restrain the aggressiveness of the opposition parties is a reflex of nervousness about the stability of the Fifth Republic's comparatively young institutions and, in particular, a reluctance on the part of the principal leaders of the opposition to undermine the prerogatives of the presidency, an office they dream of occupying themselves one day and whose powers they would prefer to exercise undiminished.

Even when the opposition, aggressive journalists or determined magistrates do try to penetrate beyond the established limits, French governments are regularly able to thwart their efforts by invoking official secrecy laws and, in particular, the secrecy requirements of national security. The French state has been very successful in protecting its secrets from its own citizens. France was one of the last of the liberal democracies to adopt legislation on 'freedom of information' and the provisions of the law finally introduced in 1978 are extremely weak. In addition, the French courts have been extremely generous in allowing governments to apply the notion of 'military secrecy' to all sorts of government action having very little to do with national security (Péan, 1986; Coignard and Lacan, 1989b, pp. 289–326).

Finally, even when investigators and political opponents have not found their efforts to keep scandals alive stymied by official secrecy, they have often run up against the short attention span, cynicism and moral indifference of French public opinion. French citizens do not seem to revel in scandal the way American or British publics do. They appear much more cynical concerning the likelihood of ever learning the truth about government misdeeds, and thus much less interested in having scandals pursued in the press or in the National Assembly. In the midst of the Greenpeace affair, for instance, a full 61 per cent of a sample of French citizens believed their leaders were lying to them, but only 28 and 24 per cent respectively felt that the prime minister or the president ought, therefore, to resign (*Paris-Match*, 4 September 1985).

Developmental Trends

Let us conclude with a brief consideration of the issue of historical change. How have French scandals been changing in recent years? What is likely to happen to them in the years to come? Perhaps the best place to focus is on a question that has provoked considerable political debate in recent election campaigns: has the level of corruption gone up since the Socialists came to power in 1981?

What is undeniable is that the number of scandals uncovered has gone up significantly. This increase is not the result of any greater proclivity of the Socialists for graft or the abuse of power; instead it should be attributed to four factors. The first is the Socialists' inexperience in the exercise of national political power. What the Greenpeace and Carrefour scandals suggest rather is that having been out of power for a generation, Socialist politicians and their aides were much less skilful than their conservative predecessors at manipulating envelopes full of cash and at controlling aggressive generals and spymasters.

A second factor is the intensification of party competition produced, in the post-1981 period, by three alternations of Left and Right at the helm, and especially by the period of competitive power-sharing between Chirac and Mitterrand from March 1986 to March 1988. It is noteworthy that it was in the 1986–8 period that the number of scandals and controversies escalated dramatically as both Left and Right sought desperately to discredit each other in the run-up to the decisive 1988 presidential elections.

Third, there has been a marked increase in the resources and skills employed by the French press in investigative reporting. Although the French press is still not especially good at such journalism, it improved considerably during the 1980s. Whereas in the 1970s it was only *Le Canard Enchaîné* which devoted substantial resources to unearthing and following up scandals, today many dailies and most weeklies employ several investigative specialists, and even the staid *Le Monde* has developed substantial investigative resources (as evidenced by the pivotal role played by its journalists, Edwy Plenel and Georges Marion, in breaking many of the big post-1981 scandal stories including Greenpeace, the Carrefour and Péchiney).

Finally, it should be noted that political insider-trading affairs were not really likely prior to the mid-1980s when the French stock market first started playing a significant role in industrial financing, and when the 'privatisation' of a slew of nationalised firms provided government officials with a new type of opportunity for doing their friends and their parties large favours.

The experience of the Socialist years suggests that France has clearly remained a 'classic land of the political scandal', and it appears quite likely that it will remain so for the foreseeable future. While French citizens might have ample grounds for finding this a disagreeable fact, this chapter has tried to demonstrate that observers of France and students of comparative politics ought, on the contrary, to be delighted.

16

Conclusion: Political Science, the State and Modernisation

JACK HAYWARD

One reason why it is so difficult to compare political systems is that the subject matter of political activity and the way it is studied by political scientists varies from country to country. Having scrutinised her political and governmental systems, the various public policies pursued and some salient political controversies that have marked recent years, let us consider what is special about the way political activity is studied in France. We shall focus upon three aspects of the role of the state in French political life. First, the pivotal place of the state institutions – government, Civil Service, Parliament, judiciary, police, armed forces – and of law-making has meant that the Anglo–American practice of focusing upon society is a misleading starting point for political science enquiries. Far from it being necessary to reintroduce a neglected state dimension into the study of French politics, it has if anything occupied too much space to the exclusion of the less formal aspects of the political process. Second, what has given French political science its status as a subject of relevance to those exercising power is that it has had a closer relationship to statecraft than in Britain or even the USA. Primary concern with practical problems and public administration have influenced both the methodology used and the subjects that are considered to be most worthy of investigation because they are useful. Instead of a speculative and descriptive emphasis derived from the impact of philosophy and history upon British political science, there has been a stress upon 'applied politics' derived principally from the study of law. Third, when the focus shifts from the administrators to the administered in a context of competitive party politics, French political scientists have devoted a disproportionately large amount of attention to public opinion and to voting behaviour. Here the legacy of political geography, as pioneered in the early twentieth century by André Siegfried, has proved enduring when treated with greater quantitative sophistication. Despite the partial loss of distinctiveness, as France is absorbed into the European and international political system, these features of her national political style still retain their significance for our understanding of her politics.

The process of state-building in France was multi-secular and had apparently achieved great strength in the late seventeenth-century monarchy of Louis XIV. The process of nation-building took longer and the coming of democracy meant that a centralised state found it difficult to legitimise public authority through the development of the accountability of government to Parliament. Both in terms of the allocation of decision-making power within the structures of government and the legal norms that endow the public authorities with legitimate power, the constitution of the sovereign state remained central to the interpretation of French political activity long after it was neglected in the USA and Britain. Like the clock that has stopped but tells the correct time twice daily, the unfashionable French preoccupation with state power is once again intellectually in fashion. Despite the current Anglo–American political vogue for 'rolling back the state', which itself recalls the eighteenth- and nineteenth-century popularity of *laissez-faire* (a French slogan that enjoyed more success as an ideological export than at home), the new academic trend has been to revive concern with the state as a counterweight to the assertiveness of civil society in general and of market forces in particular. In its turn, the dangers of abuse of power by state authorities have revived interest in constitutional constraints upon those who occupy official positions that afford opportunities for the arbitrary exercise of public power.

French political scientists can look on with equanimity as some of their American counterparts preach the need to 'bring the state back in' and the necessity of a 'new institutionalism'. American political scientists had previously expelled the state as too diffuse and value-laden, along with the study of institutions (dismissed as too narrow and legalistic). In their place was enthroned the empirical study of political behaviour. While this would-be scentific dispensation never made the impact upon British political science that it achieved in North America, the academic study of politics increasingly neglected constitutional concerns, an attitude encouraged by its practitioners' divorce both from the study of law and from political and administrative careers. In France, the close connection between public service training and the bureaucratic, business and political elites, represented by the links between the *grandes écoles* and the *grands corps*, has ensured that the interdependence between political education and political action has been jealously preserved and promoted.

Public Power and Pervasive Legalism

The development of French political science as an adjunct of public law has imparted to it an apologetic and propagandistic association with the task of promoting and defending the state-building and state-sustaining authorities. From its origins, it has accorded priority to the practical rather than the academic function of being the advocate of a centralised and concentrated sovereign power located in Paris, capable of giving orders to all and taking orders from none. The fear that the country was perpetually threatened by the danger of relapsing into a lawless disorder meant that the *ancien régime*'s political thinking became concerned with reinforcing public power against the multiple challenges at home and from beyond the state's boundaries. The internal threats came particularly from the Roman Catholic church and later from Protestant churches, from the military nobility, the commercial middle classes, the farmers, and the working classes. Both before and after the advent of political democracy, the state mystique remained the pivotal conception in terms of which the powers that be were organised and legitimised. This central term of French political discourse occupied the summit of a comprehensive, hierarchical structure in which each and all had their designated place.

After the 1789 Revolution, popular sovereignty successfully challenged the earlier monarchical sovereignty as the source of legitimate power but it was accompanied by the appeal to meritocracy as the rival source of authority for those whose specialised skills acquired selectively tested excellence, rather than electively competitive popularity. The initially small numbers of civil servants, judges, police and army officials and officers who provided the public services necessary to an ordered and civilised existence rapidly expanded in the nineteenth and twentieth centuries, as the requirements of internal and external security, welfare and warfare, increased in scale and diversity. The democratic Republic attempted to ensure that these public officials and those elected to political office remained accountable to the people but this has usually been both indirect and ineffective. As French political science in part disengaged from its legalistic matrix, political scientists have divided their time between unceremoniously exposing the popular sovereign's lack of power and showing how the internal checks and balances within the fragmented state apparatus usually ensure that even popularly elected presidents cannot acquire a monopoly of state power. As this book has shown, contemporary France remains a battleground on which an impersonal rule of law struggles to survive in an arena of cooperation and conflict, where many candidates seek to confiscate state power for their own purposes. Hegemony remains elusive as partisan political executives, public and private business executives, senior officials, judges and generals contend for position and policy primacy in this or that sector of public affairs.

It has taken France nearly two centuries of constitutional experiment to achieve a consensus about her state institutions, which have now become an expression of national cohesion as well as one of the instruments by which it is maintained. Instead of legalistically asserting a national unity that was conspicuous by its absence and a façade for a contested authority of government, the Fifth Republic has come to embody a wider measure of agreement about political values as well as political measures than has been possible since the French Revolution. De Gaulle's second great achievement (after his part in the wartime liberation of France) was to reconstitute the notion of a state power of which the supreme expression was the President of the Republic. Although many political scientists and political observers believed in the early years of the Fifth Republic that it would be as ephemeral as most of its predecessors, the more perceptive identified that it provided the longed for basis of a stable and legitimate political authority. The key role of Michel Debré, as the constitution's principal architect and the regime's first prime minister, institutionalised a concept of the nation state that he had acquired as a lawyer in the Council of State and was able, thanks to political circumstances, to implement as a Gaullist politician. The republican monarch at the apex of public power restored the historic link with pre-Revolutionary France and the direct election of the president set the seal of popular legitimacy upon government action. The rejuvenated myth of a unitary republican power 'infused the cold monster of the state authority with the hot blood of democratic nationalism' (Hayward, 1983, p. 2).

However, while democracy imparted legitimacy, effective authority resided above all in the senior public officials – the people's nominal 'servants' – who most intimately and practically embodied the state in its day-to-day administration. This led to an earlier Debré creation, the ENA, which embodied a public administrator's Utopia of a disinterested elite state service which would manage society on the people's behalf and in its interest but was protected from the intrusions and corruptions of sinister sectional interests. In the process a new, modernising political class was trained for the formidable task of restoring France to a position of independent economic, military and political power. Established in 1945, it made its major impact after 1958 but, like the Fifth Republic, it too had pre-Revolutionary roots; after several false starts it became *par excellence* the school of public leadership.

The Political Science of Elite Training

The French state has, from the pre-Revolutionary eighteenth century, been concerned to train its technocratic and bureaucratic officials for public service outside the university system. The universities trained for the liberal professions like law and this has been one important source from which the constitutional and administrative law aspects of political science developed in France. However, a great strength of French political science has been its proximity to the holders of public power, and this meant adopting the technological model of *grandes écoles* training of public sector engineers. Alongside its attempt to develop citizenship education for the newly enfranchised democracy, the French Revolutionary period witnessed endeavours to establish institutions to train its public servants in the new political science of 'ideology'. The leaders required to be trained, at least as much as the led. While the *Ecole Polytechnique*, specialising in mathematics and technology, was successfully launched (and later militarised by Napoleon), no general administration equivalent was established and an 1848 initiative during the Second Republic proved even more ephemeral than that regime. It was left to private initiative to establish in 1871–2, at the dawn of the Third Republic, a School of Political Sciences (renamed in 1945 the Institute of Political Studies, but still known familiarly as *Sciences Po*) to provide 'training for the good of the Nation and the service of the State'. It significantly relied mainly on non-academic teaching by senior public officials in training many of their successors even before the 1945 creation of ENA, which is in many ways a more specialised projection of *Sciences Po*. This close association of political science with training in statecraft rather than detached academic research has encouraged insularity and a neglect of theory except for state-centred legalism or borrowings from a society-centred sociology.

Initially, the prestige of these public sector institutions was such that their trainees occupied not merely the top positions in the Civil Service and public enterprises; they went on to colonise top positions in private banking, commercial and industrial business. In the 1980s, the advent of a market-centred economy and its related values had led to a crisis of self-confidence in the public services, associated with the view that their users would be more efficiently and cheaply served by private-sector methods. American-inspired business schools have begun to challenge the traditional primacy of the publicly-trained administrative and technological elites, suggesting the latter are too bureaucratic in their methods and lack the acquisitive spur of competition for profit. This reflects an important shift in the relative standing of the public and private sectors in favour of the private. It is now the public administration's training methods – which from ENA's inception had included an important element of practical experience as well as academic-style instruction – which must be modelled on the private business sector. After all, the formal split between the two sectors was never operative at the level of the holders of top positions, so the training methods need to be appropriate for private as well as public leadership. When the major firms in the private sector are, furthermore, increasingly international in character, a nation-bound, state-centred form of training is less and less appropriate. If one adds to the pecuniary attractions of private business the power that traditionally was to be found primarily in the public sector, it is not surprising that the disinterested service of the state exercises a diminishing appeal to the ambitious. Because private sector leaders will in the 1990s be decreasingly moulded by statist values, the French state's leading protagonists regard it as a less effective instrument of modernisation than it has been.

Mass Political Culture, Electoral Sociology and Opinion Polling

Can the mass public make up for the loss of self-confidence on the part of the administrative and politial elites? Just as it was hoped that a unified political, administrative and economic elite would be able to overcome the leadership problems of a society wracked by religious, ideological, social, economic and political conflicts, so secular, politically neutral education was considered to be the main instrument of unifying the mass of the people for their role as rational and democratic citizens. This conception too predates the Revolution, an *Essay on National Education* roundly declaring in 1763 that 'the children of the State must be brought up by the members of the State', education being essentially 'of the State, by the State, for the State'. However, the struggle between Church and State came to a head a hundred years ago, with the Third Republic's establishment of a free, secular and compulsory system of public education. It was accompanied by an ambitious attempt at political socialisation to end the Left–Right cultural and political split in French society by enforcing an ideological integration excluding religious teaching and inculcating public values through civic education. The *Ecole Normale Supérieure*, at the apex of a state system of schoolteacher training, was the elite instrument chosen to imbue the mass citizenry with secular and modern values and attitudes.

The failure to achieve this attempt to bridge the cultural divide is clear not merely in the flourishing condition of Church schools, but also by virtue of the fact that religious affiliation still remains the most accurate predictor of the political behaviour of the French electorate (Michelat and Simon, 1979). This fact has been well attested by French electoral sociology, a sphere of political science in which France has played a distinguished role, fostered by the demand for such work by the press and television. If it is generally true that political scientists have the capacity to offer some hindsight, a little insight and almost no foresight, electoral analysis is one of the rare matters where their competence to predict has been recognised by the market demand for their services. Since public opinion polling has been an exceptionally important, even indispensable, technique in providing the data on which political scientists have been able to base their analyses of mass political attitudes and behaviour, its role in linking French politics and political science must be discussed.

Although French sociologists have generally tended to be hypercritical of opinion polling, whereas political scientists have enthusiastically utilised it, it was a sociologist – Jean Stoetzel – who imported this technique from the USA just before the Second World War and popularised it thereafter among specialists. However, it was not until the run up to the 1965 presidential election, in which a 20 per cent fall in de Gaulle's support was detected and the sacrilege of a second ballot predicted, that opinion polls made their public mark. They were not universally welcomed. Those journalists and academics whose qualitative assessments relied upon impressionistic and anecdotal evidence backed by a reputation for sound judgement resented the brash, quantitative competition which threatened to render their expertise suspect, if not superfluous. A pollster recalled the editor of *Le Monde*, France's most authoritative daily, declaring in the early 1970s that he found two contemporary phenomena repugnant: the proliferation of sex shops and of opinion polls (Brulé, 1988, p. 112). However, by the 1980s the popularity of opinion polls had become irresistible, even to *Le Monde*. The 1981 presidential election marked another spectacular surge in French *sondomanie* (opinion poll mania) with the number of published political polls increasing by nearly 50 per cent (from 373 in 1980 to 543 in 1981). There was a further bound of nearly 50 per cent again in 1988, with the number of polls *during the electoral campaign alone* rising from 111 in 1981 to 153 in 1988. *Le Figaro* created a special department of political studies to maintain close contact with academic specialists in psephology (France 'having a tradition in this sphere of political science'), publishing substantial and detailed studies of the 1988 presidential and assembly elections (Habert and Ysmal, 1988, p. 4). Political scientists, who were unable to afford commissioning expensive polls themselves, were only too pleased to be associated with the mass media who could.

The intellectual appeal of opinion polling to political scientists was two-fold. Accustomed to studying elite political life from above, they had, thanks to this new technique, a means of studying mass political attitudes from below. Previously, their view of public opinion was indirect, mediated by the people's parliamentary representatives, who in some cases clearly *misrepresented* public attitudes out of ignorance or partisanship. There was now a wealth of data derived directly from the public, which allowed political scientists not merely to show how public opinion changed before and during electoral campaigns (which was especially valuable at a time when voter volatility was becoming an increasingly important source of electoral unpredictability). Political scientists now, however, were able to disentangle the three distinct components represented by a single electoral verdict: a retrospective assessment of the outgoing government's record, a judgement on the rival teams of leaders, and also on the possible policy priorities (Brulé, 1988, p. 140). Thus, despite the popularity of twelve out of eighteen policies implemented by the Socialist governments from 1981 to 1986, it was possible to show that the Socialists would lose the 1986 general election because they had failed on the one decisive issue: reducing unemployment (Brulé, 1988, pp. 177–9).

The other major advance in explaining mass electoral behaviour achieved thanks to opinion polling was that whereas previously the individual motivation of voters had to be inferred from aggregate geographical data (by region, constituency or even polling station), it could now be studied directly. This meant not only that factors which could be associated with geographical location (such as social class) could be investigated more accurately but other factors (such as sex and age) which were spread evenly could be properly and precisely assessed. As a result it has been possible to identify two surprising and important developments in the 1980s: the swing to the Left of traditionally Right-voting women and, to a lesser extent, the swing to the Right of the traditionally Left-voting young (Brulé, 1988, pp. 34–9, 192–4).

Since the questions that pollsters ask are not necessarily either those the public wish to answer or those the political scientists would like to put, the polling results have their limitations. High 'no responses' to questions are a good indication that on some issues many people simply have no opinion at all. However, the main challenges to the omnipresence and influence of the polls have not been levelled at their technical limitations (the reputable ones have usually been remarkably accurate), but have come from sociological ideologues and resentful politicians. In the years after the events of May 1968 and the resounding electoral success of the Right, the Bourdieu school of sociology hoped to discredit the polls that demonstrated the unrepresentative character of militant Leftist minorities by making unverifiable accusations of mass manipulation. (It is ironic that sociologists have tended to be more politicised than political scientists, and not just in France!) More seriously, despite the evidence to the contrary, politicians persist in fearing that polls influence the electors into voting for the candidate that appears to be winning: the 'bandwagon effect'.

In July 1977, a law was passed banning the *publication* of electoral polls in the last week before the vote (Brulé, 1988, pp. 135–54). This has been doubly futile and undesirable: futile, because the evidence of past elections suggests that the major movements of opinion usually occur either before the campaign or early in the campaign; and undesirable because, as the National Control Commission charged with ensuring the rectitude of electoral campaigns reported after the 1988 elections, 'forbidding publication, which confines knowledge of the opinion poll findings to politicians and the media, is unsatisfactory from a democratic standpoint'. This judgement did not prevent the august Commission from suggesting an *extension* of a ban that, as it had itself acknowledged, denied to the general public what was available to a tiny elite. Efforts by political scientists to reassert and justify the public's right to know have so far been in vain. Opinion polls may not influence the public but they certainly have the power to frighten politicians. However, their frequency, together with the obsessive interest they arouse, suggests that they are the democratic equivalent of the hypochondriac's compulsive seeking for a pulse: it is not so much unhealthy as an indicator of introspective anxiety. The political and administrative elites may be impelled by these indicators of public opinion either to lead from behind whilst expecting defeat or to make them the basis of calculated public relations campaigns in the service of their predetermined strategies.

Modernisation and the Statist Policy Style

The fact that the 1988 elections and referendum in France did not even attempt to melodramatise the voters' selection as choice between a socialist and a liberal system not only reduced turnout. It also signalled a historic retreat from the old-style ideological mobilisation for a heroic battle between the forces of light and darkness and also from the state-led modernisation of society in a socialist or liberal direction. The conspicuous 1980s failures of both Left and Right have induced a greater sense of political modesty, which dispelled the technocratic triumphalism in the service of public or private purposes whose credibility had evaporated, taking with it a naive popular credulity and enthusiasm. Although apocalytic politics had been dying for many years, it required both the educational experience of power by the French Socialists in the early 1980s and the symbolic sharing of power by the protagonists of the two contending cohorts to demystify the public. It was no longer possible to persuade most voters that elections were a life and death matter. Mitterrand's open recognition of this new situation made his low-key presidential campaign credible, whereas Chirac's vociferous attempts to ignore it imparted a pretentious unreality to his exertions. To explain why 1988 was not a temporary aberration but marked the contours of a new pattern we need to go back to the developments that, in retrospect, can be seen to have been creating a new political context.

The Left–Right dichotomy and the traditional faith in state intervention reinforced each other in the nineteenth and early twentieth centuries. Each was the antidote to the other. The Left had emerged to challenge state absolutism, yet the state had to be reinforced to counteract the divisive effects of Left–Right conflict. These mutually-reinforcing tendencies had become mutually demobilising by the late twentieth century: less ideological conflict meant less need for state constraint, which in turn provoked less ideological dispute. This seemingly virtuous circle had side effects however. France's self-image as the country that was at the forefront of intellectual, cultural and political modernity, was closely identified with state leadership, so it is not surprising that when it became conscious that economic decline and military defeat had adversely affected France's status, it was from the state that a solution was expected. By the mid-twentieth century, the consciousness of economic backwardness and the need to modernise the political system to make it capable of steering France in its desperate race to catch up and surpass its rivals was translated into a dramatic demographic, economic and political transformation of the country. A new international political and economic context and an incapacity to prevent this new world was intruding into French life – economically, politically and culturally – the legacy of defeat and decolonisation, which resulted in a major shift in France's dominant meta-political norms. In place of the commitment to stability, modernisation became the general policy reference point of the techno-bureaucratic elite that had its political, business, trade union and farm leader allies. These elites mainly rallied around Mendès-France in the 1950s and de Gaulle in the 1960s, but their initial protagonist was Monnet in the late 1940s.

Monnet was the champion of concerted national economic planning and of the end to economic protectionism through the European Coal and Steel Community, followed by the EC. The Planning 'modernisation commissions' were the initial instruments for socialising French decision-makers into accepting the need for the competitiveness and productivity which was required by the international market, accompanied by public assistance in galvanising and equipping France to face this new world. As the modernising message spread and was accepted in the late 1960s and early 1970s, the Planning Commissariat's activities ceased to be the primary organisational reference point precisely because it had successfully diffused its message. The 'Plan' seemed to become redundant because it had fulfilled its latent function and because modernised French businessmen (many of them former senior techno-bureaucrats who had moved into the private sector) became increasingly confident that they could act in the international market without operating under public auspices.

Both those who take an optimistic and a pessimistic view of France's development in the last 25 years agree that a decisive break occurred in the mid-1960s, (Mendras, 1980, Introduction and 1988, Introduction; Petit, 1988). Even before the 1968 destabilisation of traditional authority in all spheres and the 1973 destabilisation of the expectations of unending economic growth, socioeconomic indicators can in retrospect be seen to have changed direction in 1965. Rapid population growth, the massive transfer of population from agriculture to industry, virtually non-existent unemployment, self-confident national economic planning and the avoidance of dependence upon international trade, among others, changed with a decline in the birth rate, a shift of employment to services, the rise in unemployment, the decline of national economic planning and increased exposure to international economic competition. Largely unnoticed at the time, these changes were to be linked with a devaluation of the authority of the major state institutions – the modernising of a bureaucratic elite, as well as the more traditional military, judicial, cultural and academic elites – and the increased prestige of the wealth-creating enterprise, if not at first of the profit-making entrepreneur, as the main protagonists in the marketplace.

The notion that the assertive will of the modernising public elites could be imposed upon market forces was under pressure on the Right in the 1970s and decisively defeated on the Left in the early 1980s. The emphasis shifted from independence to interdependence and from ambitious state activism into more modest state adaptation to international constraints beyond its control. The mobilising myth of modernisation had undergone a metamorphosis. Modernity was now increasingly identified with adjusting and responding to the 'private' initiatives of others rather than asserting and imposing public preferences, which might be more legitimate but were often no longer capable of effective implementation.

The early 1980s witnessed a spectacularly rapid symmetrical switch by the Socialists from statism to a 'mixed economy' that avoided going the whole hog towards the anti-statism that the Right now cultivated in opposition. The trouble with the Socialist acceptance of the respectabiity and efficiency of private profit as the driving force of an economy governed more by competition than command is that it has been based on an improvised expediency. Consequently, it has led to politically astute but intellectually incoherent policy statements, such as Mitterrand's 1988 presidential election commitment in his *Letter to the French People*, which said that there would be no more nationalisation or privatisation. The 'mixed economy' was presented as a fossilised relationship of the public and private sectors, without any clear conception of whether this would yield the best or worst of both worlds or could even endure for a month or a year. The attempts at surreptitious renationalisation of the Société Générale deposit bank was simply one striking example of the fact that in a dynamic modern economy the truce between nationalisation and privatisation was likely to be shortlived.

While the enthusiasm for market forces, with its tendency to see politics increasingly in terms of market metaphors (parties as political enterprises, politicians as political entrepreneurs and voters as forming a political market) was especially congenial to the liberal parts of the Right, it was by no means confined to it. It corresponds to another version of the attempt to replace politics by economics, in which power struggles are displaced by piecemeal bargaining, with a minimalist state largely confined to routine administration. The political confusion on the Right reflects both the difficulty of securing general acceptance for such a depoliticised conception of politics and the reluctance to adjust to a 'modern' substitution of economic calculation for political constraint and of market power for state power. A more effective compromise between old-style state power and new-style market power than the mixed economy is the recourse to a strengthened rule of law, subjecting the various arms of the monster state to more effective control, as well as changing its modes of operation in order to treat the recipients of public services as consumers rather than as administered subjects.

In discussing France's dual policy at the start of the 1980s, it was argued that even if her normative national 'policy style does not in practice mean integrated or decisive action, it implies a *capacity* for policy initiative, a *potential* for far-sighted planning and *propensity* to impose its will when this is necessary to attain public objectives' (Hayward, 1982, p. 116). While this indicates more a difference of intentions than outcomes, the modernising rhetoric having often been transmitted into incrementalist practice, nevertheless there has been a weakening of the will to impart a state impetus in the context of international economic constraints. It is the general resignation to the reduced capacity to take such initiatives, to formulate and to impose a public will, that has undermined the potential for purposive modernisation. External circumstances and external wills create conditions of such complexity and uncertainty that they usually preclude action in the heroic style of authority that comes naturally to the techno-bureaucratic elites, who often have both objectives and the capacity to achieve them. This new context has undermined the effectiveness of the legal and financial regulatory methods that were used to achieve public objectives with the result that political action falls back upon incremental short-term improvisation and muddling through.

The old-style technocratic French state leadership, which had worked so well in modernising French telecommunications and developing electro-nuclear power in the 1970s, might still be suitable for successfully achieving some major projects such as launching space satellites, the high speed train or the Channel Tunnel, but for most purposes such public enterprises have become inappropriate. They require a less state-centred approach to problem-solving and a new relationship between government and other policy actors which involves mutual accommodation, consultation and compromise rather than an imposed *fait accompli*. As the administrative sociologist Michel Crozier has put it, 'For society to be enlightened, guided and assisted as it changes, politics must become realistic, close to people's everyday needs, the state ceasing to be arrogant and as it so often exhorts us, itself becoming modern by at last becoming *modest*' (Crozier, 1987, p. 44). Michel Rocard's incrementalist government style since 1988, in its more pluralist reliance upon a variety of civil society and business actors to run their own affairs, combined with a lowering of governmental horizons to everyday problems, conforms to this non-*dirigiste*, more tolerant and consensual conception of public authority. The French political class has adjusted with difficulty to this lower profile political style.

Relative Autonomy: France as Fashion Follower

The psychological impact of the 30 post-war years of economic and educational expansion, of rising expectations and incomes, of cultural and technological isolation, coupled with the appreciation of France's modest place in a world of superpowers and international competition, have threatened the view that French practices are self-evidently best. France used to have the best of both worlds. It could believe that it was both distinctive and exemplary, a universal model, to be envied even when it could not be imitated. Now even in cultural matters, where the French intellectual was assumed to reign supreme, foreigners no longer look to Paris for guidance. Increasingly, French natural and social scientists, artists, novelists and philosophers look beyond the Parisian microcosm for intellectual avant-garde fashions. French as the linguistic vehicle of French culture has clearly lost its dominant place, not merely in technological and scientific matters but also in diplomacy and business.

France has been conscious that it has had to catch up with the other advanced industrial societies in economic development as well as in the sociocultural sphere. The more limited and belated development of feminism and environmentalism has meant that France has tended to follow foreign models, American in the case of feminism and West German in the case of the defence of the environment. The 1989 European elections indicated an extension of the Green advance in France, as French voters turned away from the major political parties that had not sufficiently adapted their programmes to take account of newer issues. At the same time French politicians like Jack Lang have built their popularity upon a patriotic cultural populism that seeks to preserve national identity and creativity from the domination of cheap foreign imports. While the Channel Tunnel has more dramatic implications – cultural, economic and political – for Britain than for France, it carries forward the integrative role of transport beyond her most impervious national boundary.

The end of Gaullist dreams of self-assertive, independent national grandeur, at a time when it was accepted by all the French political class in their overt political rhetoric, has meant that the sovereignty of the French state has become ever more circumscribed in practice. Even within the EC, West Germany's relative economic strength has meant that commercial, financial and industrial integration is unlikely to take place under French leadership, which was her consolation for acceptance of the increasingly relative autonomy of national action. The 'special relationship' between France and West Germany had been sold to the French on the implicit assumption that their government would be the senior partner. As it has become increasingly clear that the West German economic giant would not be content with the status of political pygmy, the justification for the pretentious strategy adopted has ceased to be credible, but no substitute for it has been found. The ambitious schemes that French technocrats devise but cannot pursue on their own will become the subject of collective decision-making in which France may not play the dominant role. This is especially true as the EC moves towards a common European currency and a European Central Bank. While the French Chairman of the European Commission, Jacques Delors, has played a crucial part in promoting such developments, West Germany is expected to be the main beneficiary. The lack of a comparably important military counterpart integration, in which France could play a dominant role thanks to her nuclear deterrent, effectively reduces her to the status of junior partner. Europeanism threatens in practice to mean that surreptitious nationalism may have to be incrementally compromised to the point that autonomy has been conceded without being compensated for by French decision-making domination.

French political and administrative elites have not shed their predisposition to sovereign statecraft or enthusiastically embraced the need to defer to heroic entrepreneurs. While they conform to the current fashion which requires them to adopt a more modest posture in dealing with domestic as well as foreign problems, market liberalism is still regarded as an outlandish ideology. What remains distinctive is a proud concern that 'even if France can only occasionally lead, she can at least follow in her own way' (Hayward, 1988, p. 114).

Guide to Further Reading

Introduction

Amongst the English language texts Wright (1989) is comprehensive, up-to-date and readable: Ross, Hoffmann and Malzacher (1987) and Mazey and Newman (1987) examine the 1981–6 period; and Godt (1989) focuses on policy-making. Three journals are especially useful: *Modern and Contemporary France* (Association for the Study of Modern and Contemporary France, UK), *French Politics and Society* (Center for European Studies, Harvard University) and *West European Politics* (Cass, London). A valuable annual book is Howorth and Ross (1987+). In French, *Pouvoirs* (PUF, Paris) consecrates each issue to one topic (except for an up-to-date article on political developments); vol. 49, *La Cinquième République* (1989) is very useful.

Chapter 1   Ideological Change

In matters of ideological change, returning to the French Revolution is unavoidable. For the new orthodoxy, see the persuasive study by Furet (1981). As usual, the Left is better covered than the Right. For a penetrating interpretation of both theory and practice in historical perspective, one should read Judt (1986). For a more institutional perspective, look at Nugent and Lowe (1982). The essays in Duhamel and Weber (1979) still provide a perceptive insight into the process of Communist decline. On the French Right and extreme Right, one can get an up-to-date view of developments from the essays by Habert, Lancelot and Perrineau in Habert and Ysmal (1988) as well as Meyer and Perrineau (1989).

Chapter 2   Changing Patterns of Party Competition

A vast volume of literature exists in English and French on political parties, especially those of the Left; most of it is rather descriptive. On the development of parties and the party system before 1981 see Bartolini (1984), Bell and Shaw (1983) and Wilson (1982). On the 1980s see Levy and Machin (1986), and Wilson's Chapter 5 in Godt (1989). On the

298

developments within the parties see Machin (1989); Chapters 6 and 7 by Lavau and Rémond in Ross, Hoffmann and Malzacher (1987) and Chapters 8, 9 and 10 in Wright (1989). Hanley's contribution in Mazey and Newman (1987) gives a clear picture of the evolution within the French Socialist Party, as does Ladrech (1989).

Chapter 3   Public Opinion and Electoral Change

Recent accounts of electoral behaviour in English include Campbell and Cole (1988) and the regular election articles in *West European Politics*, notably Machin and Wright (1982) and Guyomarch and Machin (1989). Other major studies in French include: Capdevielle (1981), Gaxie (1985) and Lancelot (1983). After each election both *Le Monde* and *Le Figaro* publish special collections of analytical articles as does, since 1988, *Le Journal des Elections*. The polling organisation SOFRES also issues an annual volume of its findings.

Chapter 4   Pluralism and Pressure Politics

The literature in English on organised interests and politics in France is still rather widely scattered. See the early (but magisterial) work of Hoffman *et al.* (1963) and, for more recent overviews, Ashford (1982), which concentrates on policy-making and Wilson (1987), which focuses on organised interests. Keeler (1987) provides an excellent account of pluralist politics in agriculture and Suleiman (1987) covers the illuminating case of the notaries. Suleiman (1978) is a good source on the organisation of elites inside the state itself, and see also Birnbaum (1982). On business interests, see Berger (1981, 1985); on labour under Mitterrand, see Ross and Jenson (1986); on educational policies, Ambler (1985a); on social movements, Jenson (1985), Nelkin and Pollak (1981), and Touraine *et al.* (1983); and on organised interests and the EC, Kirchner and Schwaiger (1981). The basic sources in French include Weber (1986) on the CNPF, Adam (1983) and Reynaud (1978) on the trade unions, as well as Padioleau (1981) and Crozier *et al.* (1974) on state–group relations.

Chapter 5   Political Leadership

The clearest account in English of political leadership is given in the first five chapters of Wright (1989). Also useful are Hayward (1982) on the style of leadership, Hayward (1983), Chapter 4, on the division of decision-making responsibilities and Chapter 8 by Duhamel in Ross, Hoffmann and Malzacher (1987). On the 1970s see Suleiman and Rose (1980) and Frears (1981). In French, Fournier (1987) provides an analysis of decision-making between 1981 and 1986, Frèches (1989) gives a brief insider's account of *cohabitation*, whilst Duverger (1987) provides an over-view. An excellent guide to local leadership is given by Garraud (1989). On the powers of senior civil servants see Suleiman (1974) and Hayward (1986) in English and the classic studies of Bourdieu (1989), Catherine Grémion (1979) and Birnbaum (1977) in French.

Chapter 6   The Administrative Machine

There is no good up-to-date general account of the French administration and its recent changes in English. Many aspects are covered by Suleiman (1974) or Ashford (1982), and an overview is given in Machin (1979). Wright (1989), Chapter 11, covers relationships between the adminis-tration and social groups and in Godt (1989), Chapters 8, 9 and 10 deal with the policy-making operations of some parts of the French state. In French, Dreyfus and d'Arcy (1987) provide a clear and comprehensive account of administrative structures, whilst Thoenig (1987), Bourdieu (1989), Dupuy and Thoenig (1983) and (1985), Pfister (1988) and Lochak and Chevallier (1986) focus on particular problems. Crozier (1987) con-siders the retreat of the state.

Chapter 7   The Control of Governments

Ashford (1982) provides a general overview of the checks and balances which constrain policy-makers. Didier Maus (Chapter 2) in Godt (1989) and Wright (1989), Chapter 7, examine the role of Parliament. On the Constitutional Council, John Keeler and Alec Stone give a very clear picture of the changes in the 1980s in Ross, Hoffmann and Malzacher (1987), complemented by Stone (1988). Stone's chapter in Godt (1989) also considers the Council of State. In French, Dreyfus and d'Arcy (1987) cover all aspects of checks and balances on governments, whilst Colliard and Timsit (1988) focus on regulatory agencies, and Dupuy and Thoenig (1985) concentrate on inter-branch competition.

Chapter 8   Power outside Paris

Keating and Hainsworth (1986) give an outline of the major reforms and some of their effects. Mazey (1989) links the Defferre reforms to earlier attempts at decentralisation. Mény (1987a) provides a well-balanced appreciation and Mazey (1986) an account of the first regional elections and their impact. Wright (1989) Chapter 12, gives a succinct survey of local policy-making. In French see Pierre Grémion (1977) on the period before the Defferre reforms, and Rondin (1986), Dupuy and Thoenig (1985), Percheron (1987) and Terrazoni (1987) on the reforms and their effects. Garraud (1989) is excellent on local politicians.

Chapter 9 The State and the Market

Overviews of economic intervention in France can be found in Kuisel's (1981) historical treatment; Zysman (1977, 1983) emphasises the banking system; Hayward (1986) and Hall (1986) examine the political dimensions of policy-making; and Estrin and Holmes (1983) cover indicative planning. On the economic policies of the Mitterrand Government, see the contributions in Machin and Wright (1985) and Ross, Hoffmann and Malzacher (1987). As yet, there are few good discussions in English of economic policy-making since 1986; however, see Bauer (1988) on financial deregulation. In French, Boyer and Mistral (1983) introduce the important 'regulation' approach to such questions; Fourquet (1980), Bouvier and Bloch-Lainé (1984) and Dumez and Jeunemaître (1989) cover the history of economic intervention from a variety of perspectives; Fontaneau and Muet (1985) provide a well-documented account of policy in the early 1980s, while Jeanneney (1989) and Bauchard (1988) provide journalistic coverage of policy between 1986 and 1988; in addition, Bela Belassa reviews economic policy each year for *Commentaire*.

Chapter 10 The Welfare State

For a general discussion of social policy under the old regime and in the aftermath of the revolution see Rimlinger (1971). The evolution of programmes during the nineteenth and early twentieth centuries is detailed in Ashford (1986). Hayward's (1959) essay is still the best discussion of the important idea of solidarity. A dated but still useful overview of the social security system after the Second World War is Lynes (1967). For more current discussions, Beattie (1972) provides a clear guide through the bewildering maze of social programmes. Godt (1989) Chapter 13, Ashford (1982), Freeman (1986, 1989) and De Ridder (1989) provide commentaries on social policy change, devoting particular attention to the Socialist Government from 1981 to 1986. The classic text on the welfare state is Fournier, Questiaux and Delarue (1989). French social welfare effort is put into a comparative context in *Social Expenditure: 1960–1990* (1985).

Chapter 11 Foreign and Defence Policy

Recent foreign policy developments are surveyed in Aldrich and Connell (1989) and in Chapters 14, 15 and 16 of Godt (1989) by Moïsi (USSR), Moreau Defarges (Europe) and Smouts (Third World). Kolodziej (1987) focuses on the military – industrial complex, whilst Spencer and Connell (1988) cover New Caledonia. Chapters by Levy and Waites in Mazey and Newman (1987) look at the foreign policy and defence changes in the 1981–6 period, as does Section 5 of Ross, Hoffmann and Malzacher (1987).

On earlier policies see Howorth and Chilton (1984). In French, Cohen and Smouts (1985) and Kaiser and Lellouche (1986) are very useful.

Chapter 12   Civil Liberties, Law and Order

A full account in English of police structures (albeit slightly dated) is given by Stead (1983). Also useful in English are Roach (1985) on the police, Moxon Browne (1983) on terrorism, and both Hayward (1983) Chapter 5, and Levy, *et al* (1987) on law and order problems in general. In French, see Gleizal (1974) and (1985) on the police; 'La Justice' in *Pouvoirs* (1988); Imbert (1985) on individual rights; and the annual SOFRES collections (especially 1986, and 1988) on the evolution of public opinion.

Chapter 13   The Politics of Media Reform

The one full account of the problem in English, Thomas (1976), is now sadly dated. The best sources on more recent changes are Kuhn (1985), Dyson (1982) and Dyson and Humphreys (1986a and b) and Chapter 17 by Guehenno in Ross, Hoffmann and Malzacher (1987).

Chapter 14   Immigration and Politics

Ashford (1982) has a chapter which covers immigration politics and policies before 1981, whilst Schain's Chapter 7 in Ambler (1985b) deals with early Socialist policies. Later developments are discussed briefly in Safran's Chapter 12 in Godt (1989). In French, see Wihtol de Wenden (1987) and the report, *Etre Français aujourd'hui* (1988).

Chapter 15   The Politics of Scandal

A fascinating account of scandals during the Fourth Republic and the early years of the Fifth is given by Phillip Williams (1970). On more recent scandals see Markovits and Silverstein (1989) and, in French, Coignard and Lacan (1989) and Derogy and Pontaut (1986). These may be placed in a comparative perspective by reading King (1986).

Chapter 16   Conclusion: The State and Modernisation

For a general view of the conception of the state in France, the best study in English is provided by Dyson (1980). On the particular characteristics of French political science, one should read the article (1982), 'Political Science in France', *Government and Opposition*, vol. 17. For a longer historical perspective see Favre (1989). The French obsession with public opinion polling is trenchantly examined by a pioneering pollster, Brulé (1988). For a general review (with judiciously selected case studies) of contemporary French public policy, one should read Jobert and Muller (1987), while the mobilising theme of modernisation is dealt with best in the first part of Gaffney (1988).

Bibliography

Adam, G. (1983) *Le Pouvoir syndical*, Paris: Dunod.

Aldrich, R. and Connell, J. (eds) (1989) *France in World Politics*, London: Routledge & Kegan Paul.

Ambler, John S. (1985a) 'Neo-corporatism and the politics of French education', *West European Politics*, July.

Ambler, John S. (ed.) (1985b) *The French Socialist Experiment*, Philadelphia: ISHI.

Ashford, D. (1982) *Policy and Politics in France: Living with Uncertainty*, Philadelphia: Temple University Press.

Ashford, D. (1986) *The Emergence of the Welfare State*, Oxford: Basil Blackwell.

Baecque, F. de and Quermonne, J-L. (1982) *Administration et politique sous la Cinquième République*, Paris: FNSP.

Barthe, M-A. (1987) 'Les formes de la pauvreté dans la société française', *Revue française des affaires sociales*, no. 2.

Bartolini, S. (1984) 'The French party system', *West European Politics*, October.

Bauchard, P. (1988) *La Crise sonne toujours deux fois*, Paris: Grasset.

Bauer, M. (1988) 'The politics of state-directed privatization: the case of France 1986–88', *West European Politics*, vol. 11, no. 4 (October).

Beattie, A. (1972) 'France', in Thomas Wilson (ed.), *Pensions, Inflation and Growth*, London: Heinemann.

Belassa, B. (1988) 'L'économie Française à l'aube du nouveau septennat' *Commentaire*, vol. 11, no. 42 (Summer).

Bell, D. and Shaw, E. (eds) (1983) *The Left in France*, Nottingham: Spokesman.

Bercoff, A. (1989) *La France des seigneurs*, Paris: Robert Laffont.

Berger, Suzanne (1981) 'Regime and interest representation: the French traditional middle classes', in Berger, (ed.), *Organizing Interests in Western Europe*, Cambridge University Press, pp. 83–102.

Berger, Suzanne (1985) 'The Socialists and the patronat: the dilemmas of co-existence in a mixed economy', in Machin and Wright (1985).

Biarez, S. (1973) *Institution communale et pouvoir politique*, Paris: La Haye.

Birnbaum, Pierre (1977) *Les Sommets de l'Etat*, Paris: Seuill.

Birnbaum, Pierre (1982) *The Heights of Power*, University of Chicago Press.

Bornstein, S. (1989) 'The Greenpeace Affair and the peculiarities of French politics', in Markovits and Silverstein (1989).

Bourdieu, P. (1989) *La Noblesse d'Etat*, Paris: Editions de Minuit.

Bouvier, J. and Bloch-Lainé, F. (1984) *La France restaurée*, Paris.

Boyer, R. and Mistral, J. (1983) *Accumulation, Inflation, Crises*, Paris: PUF.

Braibant, Guy (1988) *Le Droit administratif français*, Paris: PUF.

Brulé, Michel (1988) *L'Empire des sondages*, Paris: Robert Laffont.

Caisse des Dépôts et Consignations (1986) *Tableau de bord des finances locales, statistiques commentées* 1970–1984, Paris: Moniteur.

Campbell, P. and Cole, A. (1988), *French Electoral Systems and Elections since 1789*, London: Macmillan.

Capdevielle, Jacques *et al* (ed.) (1981) *France de gauche, vote à droite*, Paris: FNSP.

Cerny, P. (1987) 'The Little Big Bang in Paris: financial market deregulation in a dirigiste system', Paper presented to the European Consortium for Political Research, April 1987.

Closets, François de (1985) *Tous Ensemble*, Paris: Seuil.

Cohen, S. (1986) *La Monarchie nucléaire*, Paris: Hachette.

Cohen, S. and Goldfinger, C. (1975) 'From permacrisis to real crisis in French social security: the limits to normal politics', in L. Lindberg *et al* (eds), *Stress and Contradiction in Modern Capitalism*, Lexington, MA: Lexington Books.

Cohen, S. and Smouts, M-C. (eds) (1985) *La Politique extérieure de Valéry Giscard d'Estaing*, Paris.

Coignard, S. and Lacan, J-F. (1989) *La République bananière*, Paris: Pierre Belfond.

Colliard, Claude-Albert and Timsit, Gerard (eds) (1988) *Les Autorités administratives indépendantes*, Paris: PUF.

Conseil National de la Vie Associative (1987) *Bilan de la Vie Associative*, Paris: La Documentation Française.

Cornut-Gentille, François (1986) 'L'insécurité: les enquêtes TFI/SOFRES et Figaro/SOFRES', in SOFRES (1986b), pp. 121–9.

Crozier, M. (1963) *Le Phénomène Bureaucratiques*, Paris: Seuil.

Crozier, M. (1970) *La Société bloquée*, Paris: Seuil.

Crozier, M. (1987) *Etat modeste, Etat moderne*, Paris: Fayard.

Crozier, M. *et al.* (1974) *Où Va l'Administration française*, Paris: Editions d'Organisation.

Daniels, Ione (1987) 'Crime and punishment: the power of the *juge d'instruction* in France', *Contemporary French Civilisation*, vol. 11, no. 2.

Défense, Ministère de la (1988) *La Défense de la France*, Paris: ADDIM.

De Ridder, M. (1989) 'France' in J. DeSario *International Public Policy Sourcebook: Health and Social Welfare*, vol. 1, Westport, CT: Greenwood.

Delanoe, J-Y. (1987) 'Grandes orientations de la politique de santé de 1981 à 1986', *Revue Française des Affaires Sociales*, no. 1.

Delcamp, A. (1987) 'Les Compétences et les services', *L'Actualité Juridique – Droit Administratif*, 20 March.

Derogy, J. and Pontaut, J-M. (1981) *Enquête sur les 'Affaires' d'un Septennat*, Paris: Robert Laffont.

Derogy, J. and Pontaut, J-M. (1986) *Enquête sur trois secrets d'Etat*, Paris: Robert Laffont.

Derogy, J. and Pontaut, J-M. (1987) *Enquête sur un carrefour dangereux*, Paris: Fayard.

Dion, S. (1986) *La politisation des Mairies*, Paris: Economica.

Dreyfus, François G. (1982) 'Political Science in France', *Government and Opposition*, 17, pp. 429–43.

Dreyfus, Françoise and d'Arcy, François (1987) *Les Institutions politiques et administratives de la France*, Paris: Economica.

Duhamel, Olivier and Weber, Henri (eds) (1979) *Changer le PC?*, Paris: PUF.

Dumez, Hervé and Jeunemaitre, Alain (1989) *Diriger l'economie: l'Etat et les prix en France 1936–1986*, Paris: L'Harmattan.

Dupuy, F. and Thoenig, J-C. (1983) *Sociologie de l'administration Française*, Paris: Colin.

Dupuy, F. and Thoenig, J-C. (1985) *L'Administration en miettes*, Paris: Fayard.

Durantin, J-F. (1988) 'L'Avenir du Corps Préfectoral', *L'Actualité Juridique – Droit Administratif*, 20 May.

Duverger, Maurice (1987) *La Cohabitation des Français*, Paris: PUF.

Dyson, K. (1980) *The State Tradition in Western Europe*, Oxford: Martin Robertson.

Dyson, K. (1982) 'West European States and the Communications Revolution', *West European Politics*, vol. 9, no. 4.

Dyson, K. and Humphreys, P. (1986a) 'Policies for New Media in Western Europe', *West European Politics*, vo. 9, no. 4.

Dyson, K. and Humphreys, P. (1986b) 'Satellite Broadcasting Policies and the Question of Sovereignty in Western Europe', *Journal of Public Policy*, vol. 6, no. 1.

Eck, F. (1986) *La Direction du Trésor*, Paris: PUF.

Economie et Politique (1986) Special issue on 'Les Constructions Régionales', no. 116 (December).

Ehrmann, Henry W. (1971) *Politics in France*, 2nd edn, Boston: Little, Brown.

Estrin, S. and Holmes, P. (1983) *French Planning in Theory and Practice*, London: Allen & Unwin.

Etre Français aujourd'hui. Rapport au Premier Ministre (1988) Paris: Documentation Française (2 vols).

Favre, P. (1989) *Naissances de la science politique en France*, Paris: Fayard.

Fontaneau, A. and Muet, P-A. (eds) (1985) *La Gauche Face à la crise*, Paris: FNSP.

Fournier, Jacques (1987) *Le Travail gouvernemental*, Paris: Seuil.

Fournier, J., Questiaux, N. and Delarue, J-M. (1989) *Traité du social – situations, luttes, politiques, institutions*, Paris: Dalloz.

Fourquet, F. (1980) *Les Comptes de la puissance*, Paris: Editions Recherches.

Frears, J.R. (1981) *France and the Giscard Presidency*, London: Allen & Unwin.

Frèches, José (1989) *Voyage au Centre du Pouvoir*, Paris: O. Jacob.

Freeman, G.P. (1986) 'Socialism and Social Security' in Ambler (1985b).

Freeman, G. (1989) 'France', in J. DeSario *International Public Policy Sourcebook: Health and Social Welfare*, vol. 1, Westport, CT: Greenwood.

Furet, F. (1981) *Interpreting the French Revolution*, Cambridge University Press.

Gaffney, John (ed) (1988) *France and Modernisation*, Aldershot: Gower.

Galant, H. (1955), *Histoire politique de la sécurité sociale Française*: 1945–1952, Paris: Colin.

Garraud, Philippe (1989) *Profession: homme politique*, Paris: L'Harmattan.

Gaxie, Daniel (ed.) (1985) *Explication du vote: Un bilan des études électorales en France*, Paris: Hachette.

Giard, J. and Scheibling, J. (1981) *L'Enjeu Régional*, Paris: Messidor Eds Sociales.

Gleizal, J.J. (1974) '*La police nationale: droit et pratique policière en France*', Presses Universitaires de Grenoble.

Gleizal, J.J. (1985) *Le désordre policier*, Paris: PUF.

Godt, P. (ed.) (1989) *Policy-Making in France*, London: Pinter.

Green, D. (1983) 'Strategic Management and the State: France' in K. Dyson and S. Wilks (eds) *Industrial Crisis*, Oxford: Basil Blackwell.

Grémion, Catherine (1979) *Profession: décideurs*, Paris: Seuil.

Grémion, Pierre (1977) *Le Pouvoir Périphérique*, Paris: Seuil.

Grivart de Kerstrat, F. (1985) 'France', in S. Shetreet and J. Deschenes (eds), *Judicial Independence: The Contemporary Debate*, Dordrecht: Nijhoff.

Grosser, A. (1982) 'La Ve République et la société française', *Pouvoirs*, 4.

Guyomarch, A. and Machin, H. (1989) 'François Mitterrand and the election of 1988', *West European Politics*, January.

Habert, P. and Ysmal, C. (eds) (1988) *Elections Législatives 1988*, Paris: Le Figaro.

Hall, P.A. (1986) *Governing the Economy*, New York: Oxford University Press.

Hatzfeld, H. (1971) *De pauperisme à la sécurité sociale: 1850–1940*, Paris: Colin.

Hayward, Jack (1959) 'Solidarity: The Social History of an Idea in Nineteenth-Century France', *International Review of Social History*, vol. 4.

Hayward, Jack (1982) 'Mobilising private interests in the service of public ambitions: the salient element in the dual French policy style', in J. Richardson (ed.) (1982) *Policy Styles in Western Europe*, London: Allen & Unwin.

Hayward, Jack (1983) *Governing France, the One and Indivisible French Republic*, London: Weidenfeld & Nicolson.

Hayward, Jack (1986) *The State and the Market Economy*, Brighton: Wheatsheaf.

Hayward, Jack (1988) 'From fashion-setter to fashion follower in Europe: the demise of French distinctiveness?', *Contemporary France*, vol. 2.

Hoffmann, Stanley, *et al.* (1963) *In Search of France*, New York: Harper & Row.

Hoffmann, Stanley, (1978) *France: Decline or Renewal*, New York: Harper & Row.

Howorth, J. and Chilton, P. (eds) (1984) *Defence and Dissent in Contemporary France*, London: Croom Helm.

Howorth, Jolyon and Ross, George (eds) (1987+) *Contemporary France: A Review of Interdisciplinary Studies*, London: Pinter.

Imbert, Jean (1985) *Les Droits de l'homme en France*, Paris: La Documentation Française.

Jeanneney, Jean-Marcel (ed.) (1989) *L'Economie française depuis 1967*, Paris: Seuil.

Jenson, Jane (1985) 'Struggling for Identity; The Women's Movement and the State in Western Europe', *West European Politics*, vol. 8, no. 4 (October).

Jobert, Bruno and Muller, Pierre (1987) *L'Etat en action*, Paris: PUF.

Judt, Tony (1986) *Marxism and the French Left*, Oxford University Press.

'La Justice' (1988), *Pouvoirs*, no. 16.

Kaiser, K. and Lellouche, P. (eds) (1986) *Le Couple franco–allemand et la défense de l'Europe*, Paris: IFRI.

Keating, M. and Hainsworth, P. (1986) *Decentralisation and Change in Contemporary France*, Aldershot: Gower.

Keeler, John T.S. (1987) *The Politics of Neo-Corporatism in France*, New York: Oxford University Press.

King, A. (1986) 'Sex, Money and Power', in R. Hodder-Williams and J. Ceaser (eds) *Politics in Britain and the United States, Comparative Perspectives*, Durham, NC: Duke University Press.

Kirchner, Emil and Schwaiger, K. (1981) *The Role of Interest Groups in the European Community*, Aldershot: Gower.

Kolodziej, E.A. (1987) *Making and Marketing Arms: The French Experience and its Implications for the International System*, Princeton University Press.

Kuhn, R. (1985) 'France and the "New Media"', *West European Politics*, vol. 8, no. 20.

Kuisel, R. (1981) *Capitalism and the State in Modern France*, New York: Cambridge University Press.

Ladrech, R. (1989) 'Social movements and party systems', *West European Politics*, July.

Laird, R.F. (ed.) (1986) *French Security Policy: From Independence to Interdependence*, Boulder, CO and London: Westview Press.

Lancelot, Alain (1983) *Les élections sous la Cinquième République*, Paris: FNSP.

Levy, D. and Machin, H. (1986) How Fabius Lost: the French elections of 1986', *Government and Opposition*, vol. 21, no. 3.

Levy, Reine *et al* (1987) 'Police performance and fear of crime: the experience of the Left in France between 1981 and 1986', *International Journal of Sociology of Law*, vol. 15, no. 3.

Lochak, D. and Chevallier, J. (eds) (1986) *La haute administration et la politique*, Paris: PUF.

Logue, J. (1989) 'Conclusion', in Markovits and Silverstein (1989).

Lojkine, J (1977), *Le Marxisme, l'Etat et la question urbaine*, Paris: PUF.

Lowi, T. (1989) 'Foreword' in Markovits and Silverstein (1989).

Lynes, T. (1967) *French Pensions*, London: Bell.

Machin, Howard (1977) *The Prefect in French Public Administration*, London: Croom Helm.

Machin, Howard (1979) 'France', in F.F. Ridley (ed.), *Government and Administration in Western Europe*, Oxford: Martin Robertson.

Machin, H. (1989) 'The Evolution of the French parties and party system', *West European Politics*, (October).

Machin, H. and Wright, V. (1982) 'Why Mitterrand Won', *West European Politics*, (January).

Machin, H. and Wright, V. (eds) (1985) *Economic Policy and Policy-Making under the Mitterrand Presidency*, London: Pinter.

Magistrats et Avocats: Formation, Carrière, Activité Professionelles (1987) Groupe de travail présidé par François Terre, Paris: La Documentation Française.

Mariller, N. and Janvier, G. (1988) 'Les programmes gouvernementaux de lutte contre la pauvreté et la précarité', in *Revue française des affaires sociales*, no. 2.

Markovits, A. and Silverstein, M. (eds) (1989) *The Politics of Scandal*, New York: Holmes & Meier.

Martinet, G. (1973) *Le Système Pompidou*, Paris: Seuil.

Mazey, S. (1986) 'The French regional election of 16 March 1986', *Electoral Studies*, vol. 5.

Mazey, S. (1989) 'Centre–Periphery Relations in the Fifth Republic', in P. Godt (ed.) *Policy-Making in France from De Gaulle to Mitterrand*, London: Pinter.

Mazey, S. and Newman, M. (eds) (1987) *Mitterrand's France*, London: Croom Helm.

Mendras, Henri (ed.) (1980) *La Sagesse et le désordre, France 1980*, Paris: Gallimard.

Mendras, Henri (1988) *La seconde révolution française, 1965–1984*, Paris: Gallimard.

Mény, Y. (1984) 'Central control and local resistance', in V. Wright (ed.) *Continuity and Change in France*, London: Allen & Unwin.

Mény, Y. (1987a) 'The Socialist Decentralisation' in G. Ross, S. Hoffmann and S. Malzacher (eds), *The Mitterrand Experiment*, Oxford: Polity Press.

Mény, Y. (1987b) in E. Page and M. Goldsmith (eds) *Central–Local Government Relations: A Comparative Analysis of West European Unitary State*, London: Sage.

Mermet, G. (1988) *Francoscopie: Les Français Qui sont-ils? Où vont-ils?*, Paris: Larousse.

Meyer, N. and Perrineau, P. (eds) (1989) *Le Front National à découvert*, Paris: FNSP.

Michelat, G. and Simon, M. (1977) *Classe, religion et comportement politique*, Paris: FNSP.

Mitterrand, F. (1986) *Réflexions sur la politique extérieure de la France*, Paris: Fayard.

Moxon Browne, Edward (1984) 'Terrorism in France', *Conflict Studies*, no. 144.

Muret, J.P., Fournier, D. Peyré, S. and Pian, F. (1985) *Le Conseil Régional*, Paris: Syros.

Nelkin, D. and Pollak, M. (1981) *The Atom Besieged*, Cambridge, MA: MIT Press.

Nugent, N. and Lowe, D. (1982) *The Left in France*, London: Macmillan.

Oheix Report (1981) *Contre la précarité et la pauvreté*, Paris: Documentation Française.

Padioleau, Jean (1981) *Quand la France s'enferre*, Paris: PUF.

Pean, P. (1986) *Secret d'Etat*, Paris: Fayard.

Percheron, A. (ed.) (1987) *La Région An I; Etat des Regions Françaises un An après les Elections de 1986*, Paris: PUF.

Petit, P. (1988) 'The economy and modernisation', in Gaffney (1988).

Pfister, Thierry (1988) *La République des fonctionnaires*, Paris: Fayard.

Politique Etrangère, (1987), quarterly review of *Institut Français des Relations Internationales*, Paris special issue on 'La France et le Pacifique Sud', vol. 1.

Revue Politique et Parlementaire (1988) 'La justice, rempart de la démocratie', no. 937.

Reynaud, Jean-Daniel (1978) *Les Syndicats, les patrons, L'Etat*, Paris: Editions d'Organisation.

Rimlinger, Gaston V. (1971) *Welfare Policy and Industralization in Europe, America, and Russia*, New York: Wiley.

Roach, John (1985) 'The French Police', in J. Roach and J. Thomaneck (eds), *Police and Public Order in Europe*, London: Croom Helm, pp. 107–42.

Rondin, J. (1986) *Le Sacre des Notables; la France en décentralisation*, Paris: Fayard.

Rosette, M. (1987) 'La gestion des collectivités territoriales: une question politique', *Cahiers du Communisme*, vol. 63.

Ross, G. Hoffmann, S. and Malzacher, S. (eds) (1987) *The Mitterrand Experiment*, New York: Oxford University Press.

Ross, George and Jenson, Jane (1986) 'Pluralism and the decline of Left hegemony: the French Left in power', *Politics and Society*.

Schmidt, V. (1988) 'Industrial management under the Socialists in France: decentralised dirigisme at the national and local levels', *Comparative Politics*, vol. 21, no. 1 (October).

Social Expenditure: 1960–1990 (1985), Paris: OECD.

SOFRES (1986) *Opinion Publique 1986*, Paris: Gallimard.

SOFRES (1988) *L'Etat de l'Opinion: Clés pour 1988*, Paris: Seuil.

Spencer, M. and Connell, A.W.J. (1988) *New Caledonia*, University of Queensland Press.

Stead, Philip, J. (1983) *The Police of France*, New York: Macmillan.

Steib, J. (1987) 'Un bilan des interventions économiques des collectivités locales depuis 1982', *Problèmes Economiques*, no. 2040.

Stone, A. (1988) 'In the shadow of the Constitutional Council', *West European Politics*, vol. 12, no. 2 (April).

Suleiman, Ezra (1974) *Politics, Power and Bureaucracy in France*, Princeton University Press.

Suleiman, Ezra (1978) *Elites in French Society*, Princeton University Press.

Suleiman, Ezra (1987) *Private Power and Centralization in France: The Notaires and the State*, Princeton University Press.

Suleiman, Ezra and Rose, Richard (eds) (1980) *Presidents and Prime Ministers*, Washington DC, American Enterprise Institute.

Terrazoni, A. (1987) *La Décentralisation à l'épreuve des faits*, Paris: LGDJ.

Thomas, R. (1976) *Broadcasting and Democracy in France*, London: Bradford University Press and Crosby Lockwood Staples.

Thoenig, Jean-Claude (1987) *L'Ere des Technocrates*, Paris: L'Harmattan.

Touraine, A. *et al* (1983) *Anti-Nuclear Protest*, Cambridge University Press.

Varaine, P. and Malingre, D. (1987) 'L'action des chambres régionales des comptes', *L'Actualité Juridique – droit administratif*, 20 March.

Weber, Henri (1986) *Le Parti des patrons*, Paris: Seuil.

Wihtol de Wenden, Catherine (1987) *Citoyenneté, nationalité et immigration*, Paris: Arcantère.

Williams, P. (1970) *Wars, Plots and Scandals in Post-War France*, Cambridge University Press.

Williams, P.M. (1964) Crisis and Compromise, London, Longmans.

Wilson, F. (1982) *Parties under the Fifth Republic*, New York: Praeger.

Wilson, Frank (1987) *Interest Group Politics in France*, Cambridge University Press.

Wolff, G. (1988), *Le Contrôle des dépenses de l'Etat par la Cour des Comptes*, Paris: PUF.

Wolton, T. (1989) *Les Ecuries de la Ve*, Paris: Grasset.

Worms, J-P. (1966) 'Le préfet et ses notables', *Sociologie du Travail*, vol. 8, pp. 249–75.

Wright, V. (1979) 'Regionalisation under the French Fifth Republic; the triumph of the functional approach', in L.J. Sharpe (ed.) *Decentralist Trends in Western Democracies*, London: Sage.

Wright, V. (1989) *The Government and Politics of France*, 3rd edn, London: Unwin Hyman.

Zysman, J. (1977) *Political Strategies for Industrial Order*, Berkeley, CA: University of California Press.

Zysman, J. (1983) *Governments, Markets and Growth*, Ithaca, NY: Cornell University Press.

Index